MW01716422

Teacher's Resource Book

HARCOURT BRACE SPELLING

LEVEL 2

HARCOURT BRACE & COMPANY

Orlando Atlanta Austin Boston San Francisco Chicago Dallas New York Toronto London

http://www.hbschool.com

ACKNOWLEDGMENT

Composition Evaluation Forms A and B are from the Teacher's Resource Book which accompanies *LANGUAGE FOR DAILY USE*, Voyager Edition, Level 2. Copyright © 1986 by Harcourt Brace & Company. Reprinted by permission of Harcourt Brace & Company.

Printed in the United States of America

ISBN 0-15-313666-9

This Teacher's Resource Book, when used with the student textbook and the Teacher's Edition, provides a complete elementary spelling program and classroom management system.

A Teacher's Resource Book is not automatically included with each shipment of a classroom set of textbooks. However, a Teacher's Resource Book will be forwarded when requested by a teacher, an administrator, or a representative of Harcourt Brace & Company.

Reproduction of Copying Masters

The copying masters in this Teacher's Resource Book are intended primarily for use with photocopiers and may not reproduce clearly with heat-sensitive copiers.

Contents

Extra Practice Masters and Answer Key

The following section provides black-line copying masters for reinforcement and extended practice of spelling words and skills.

For each instructional unit, you will find four masters: (1) **Extra Practice Master: This Week's Words,** (2) **Extra Practice Master: Mastery Words,** (3) **Extra Practice Master: Bonus Words,** and (4) **Spelling and Language Master.**

For each review unit, you will find six masters: (1) **Review Master A,** (2) **Review Master B,** (3) **Review Master C,** (4) **Language Study Master,** (5) **Mastery Words Review,** and (6) **Bonus Words Review.**

Each copying master also appears in reduced form within the teaching plan it accompanies.

The **Answer Key** for the activities follows these copying masters in this Teacher's Resource Book. Note that for activities with unnumbered items, the order of items is generally determined by reading across the page. Also note that for some activities the order of answers may vary.

Contents

Name

Extra Practice

This Week's Words

UNIT 1

Draw a line from dot **A** to all the words that begin with a consonant letter. End at dot **B.** Connect the words in the right number order.

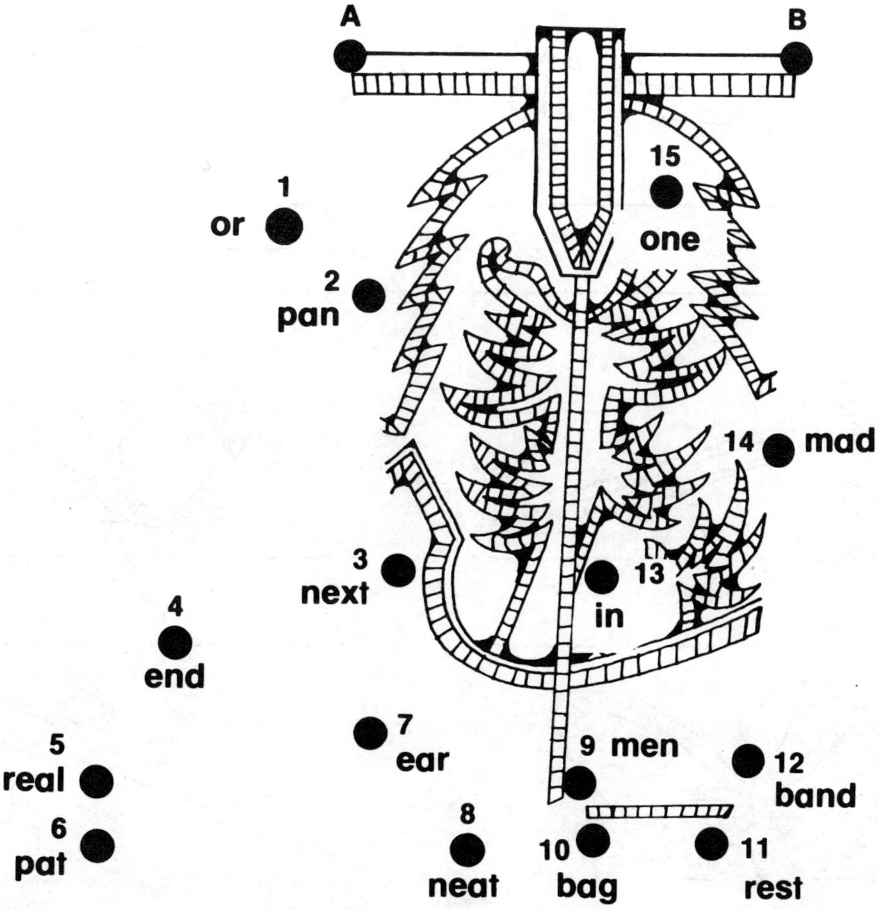

Write the words you drew the line to in the puzzle.

Name

Extra Practice

Mastery Words

UNIT 1

Write the Mastery word that begins with the same sound as each picture name. Use each Mastery word twice.

1. ______

2. ______

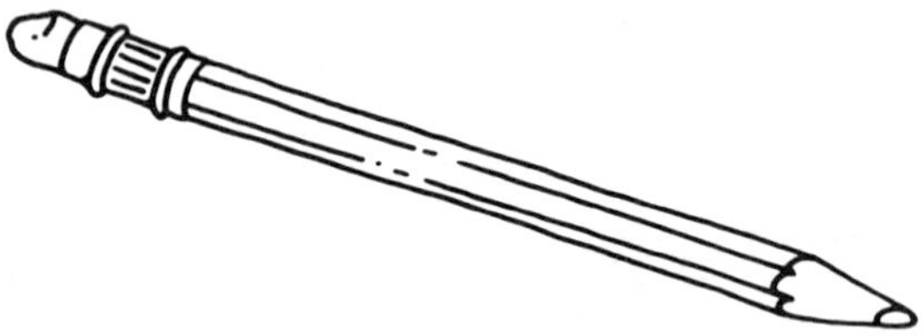

3. ______

4. ______

5. ______

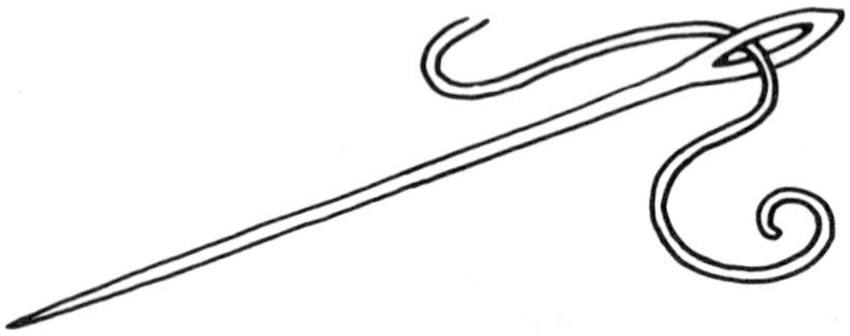

6. ______

7. ______

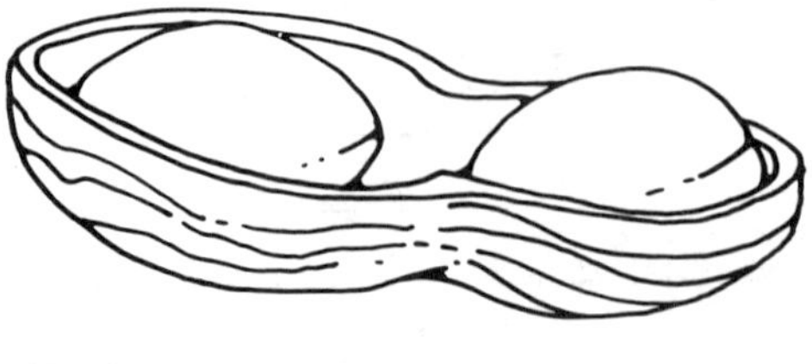

8. ______

pig ran be no

Name

Extra Practice

Bonus Words

UNIT 1

A. Follow the directions. Use the Bonus words.

1. Write the word that names a bird.
2. Write the word that begins with the same letter as <u>bone</u>.
3. Write the two words that begin with the third letter in <u>bone</u>.
4. Write the word that means "to send a letter."
5. Write the word that means "a sheet of paper in a book."

B. Change the first letter of each underlined word. Write a Bonus word to finish the sentence.

6. Sue gave a pear to the ________.
7. I got a sail in the ________.
8. The crow made the best ________.
9. Draw a cage on the first ________.

bear	mail	neck	nest	page	robin

Name

Spelling and Language

UNIT 1

Read each sentence. Write the word from the box that fits in the sentence. It must begin with the same letter as the underlined word.

band	mad	neat	pan	real
bag	men	next	pat	rest

1. The family ________ door is new in town.

2. Their house is ________ but noisy.

3. They all play bugles in a big brass ________.

4. Little Max plays as loud as ten ________.

5. His parents play a pot and a ________.

6. It makes my father ________.

7. The ________ of us really like the sound.

8. We will ________ each player on the back.

Name ______________________

Extra Practice

This Week's Words

UNIT **2**

In the boxes below, write This Week's Words. Write each word only once. Some of the words fit together. Some letters are given to help you write the words in the right place.

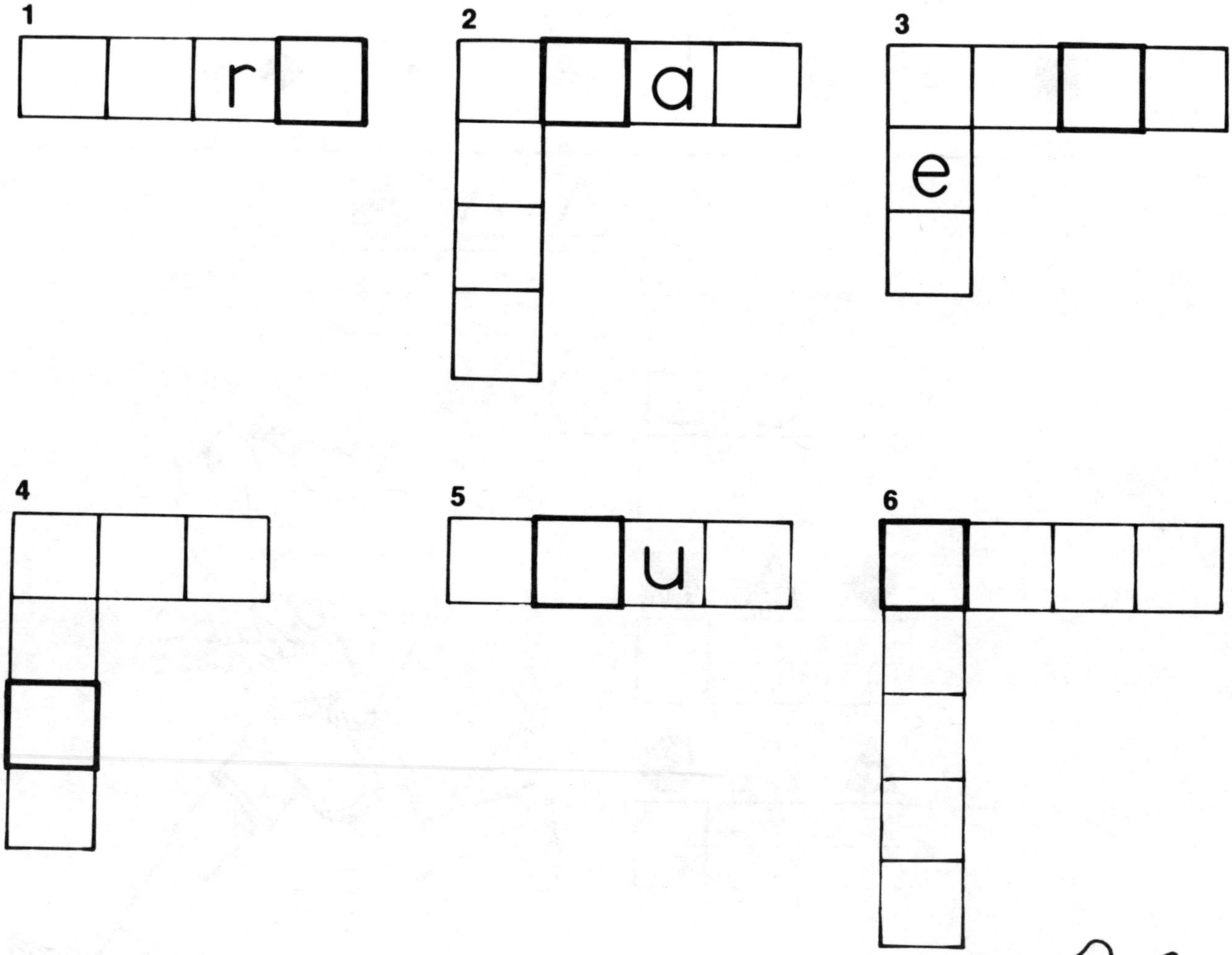

Now write the six letters in dark boxes. Write them in order by number. Spell the name of a color.

____

tell	dear	fit	very	went
your	does	woman	ten	felt

Name

Extra Practice

Mastery Words

UNIT 2

A. The shapes stand for letters. Write the letter each shape stands for. Write Mastery words.

□ = a ○ = d △ = e ◇ = f

■ = s ● = t ▲ = w ◆ = y

◇ △ △ ●

○ □ ○

◆ △ ■

▲ △ ●

B. Why did Maria win the race? To find out, write the letters in boxes in order.

She ran ______________.

dad	feet	wet	yes

Name

Extra Practice

Bonus Words

UNIT 2

A. Finish the puzzle. Use the Bonus words. The words go across and down.

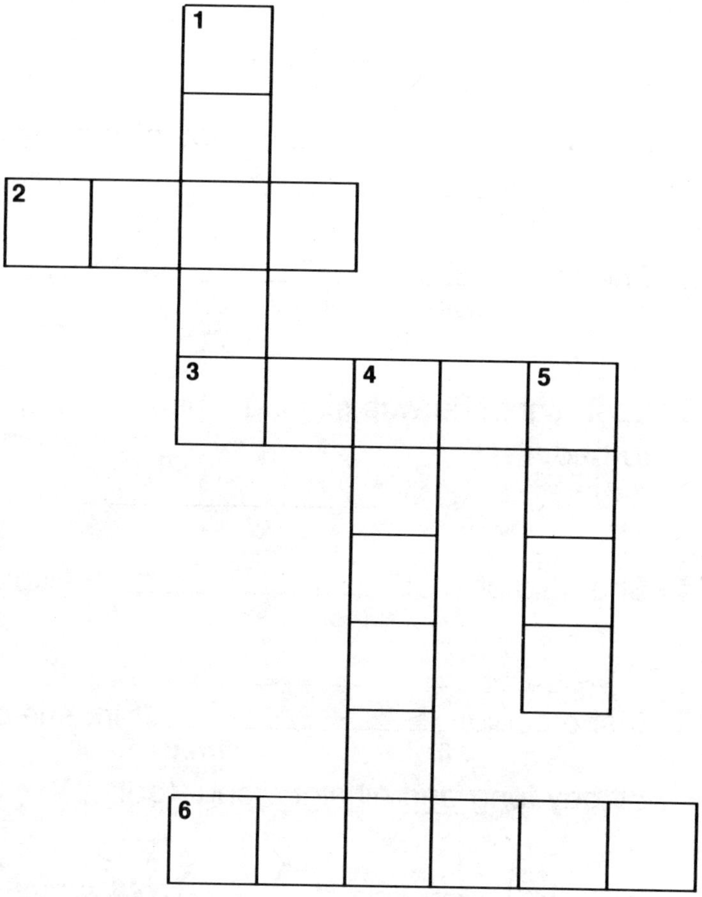

ACROSS

2. Use soap and water to clean.
3. Not yesterday or tomorrow.
6. Did not remember.

DOWN

1. Go and see someone.
4. A meal that rhymes with <u>thinner</u>.
5. Three feet long.

B. Finish the sentences. Use the Bonus words.

7. Did you remember to ________________ the dirty dishes?

8. No, I ________________.

9. What dishes will we use for ________________?

dinner	forgot	today	visit	wash	yard

Name

Spelling and Language

UNIT 2

tell
ten
dear
does
felt
fit
very
went
woman
your

A. Read each sentence. Choose the right word to finish each one.

1. Let me ______ you about my sister.
   tell **told**

2. She really ______ like to sing.
   does **do**

3. Last night she was singing when she ______ to bed.
   goes **went**

4. She said she just ______ like singing.
   feel **felt**

5. If she could ______ it in, she'd sing all day long and all night long, too!
   fit **fitted**

B. Use three of the words in the box. Write sentences that tell about someone in your family.

Name ______________________________

Extra Practice

This Week's Words | **UNIT 3**

A. Finish this "word chain." Use This Week's Words.

j ___ t (1)
a
l
l ___ ___ e (2)
v
e
j ___ r (3)
u
s
l ___ ___ t (4)
e
s
s ___ ___ d (5)
o
g ___ ___ e (6)
g ___ ___ d (7)
a
m
e
h ___ s (8)
e
a
d
s ___ ___ n (9)
a
y
s
h ___ ___ l (10)
e
n

B. Finish this message. Use words from the puzzle.

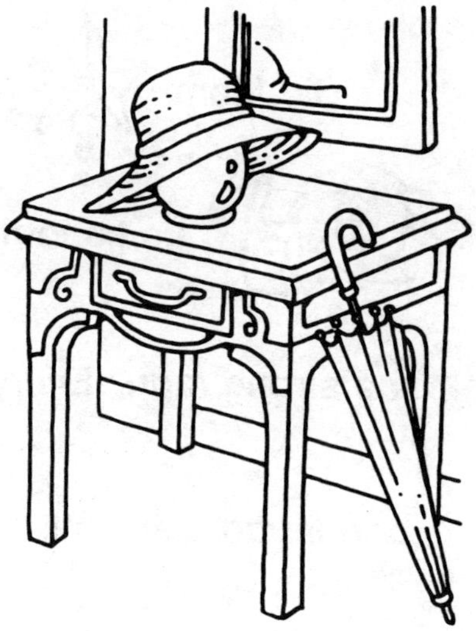

The ______ (7) ______ (3)

is ______ (6)! Who ______ (8)

taken it? We ______ (4) it in

the ______ (10).

gold	gone	hall	has	jar
jet	left	live	seed	soon

Name

UNIT 3

Extra Practice

Mastery Words

A. Change the first letter in each word. Use the first letter in the picture name in its place. Write a Mastery word.

1. day

2. me

3. get

4. bee

B. Finish this story. Use the words that begin with the same sounds as the picture words. Write your answers below.

Did Mom  5 we could go? Will she

 6 us go to the circus? I want to  7

the strong man. Everybody says  8

can lift an elephant.

5.

6.

7.

8.

he
let
see
say

Name

Extra Practice

Bonus Words

UNIT 3

A. Which word goes with each sentence clue? Write one of the Bonus words.

1. It's a funny story.

2. It means "big."

3. It's not cloudy.

4. It rhymes with bird.

5. It's not sad.

6. It's not badness.

B. Finish the sentences. Use the Bonus word that goes with the picture.

7. Alice is ______.

8. Billy's dog is very ______.

9. The day was warm and ______.

goodness	happy	heard	joke	large	sunny

Name ______________________ ______________________

Spelling and Language

UNIT
3

Write a sentence to go with each picture. Connect two groups of words shown in the box to make each sentence.

on runway six.	Soon the seed will be
The gold jar is	The jet left
to live in Portland.	in the hall.
a pretty flower.	She has gone

gold
gone
hall
has
jar
jet
left
live
seed
soon

1.
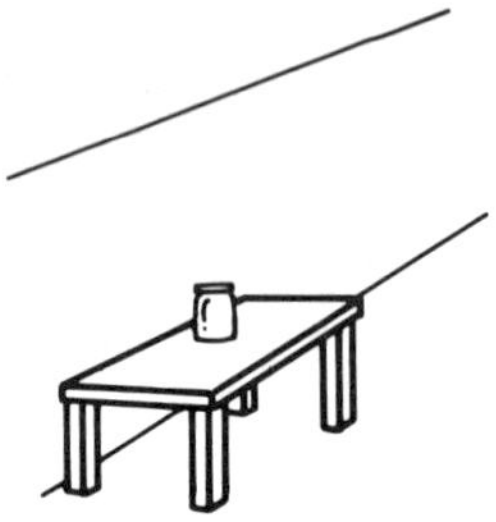

2.

3.

4.

Name

Extra Practice

This Week's Words

UNIT 4

Find the three things in the picture with names that have the sound /k/. Write each picture word in one of the boxes under the picture. Write the three words in ABC order.

Now write each of This Week's Words under the word that has the same letter or letters for /k/. Two words have two different spellings for /k/. Write each of these words twice.

keep	cat	duck	cow	kite
pick	cup	sick	cake	cook

Name

UNIT 4

Extra Practice

Mastery Words

Follow the directions.

1. Start with the word bat.
   Change a to u. Write the word.

   Now change the word so that it begins with /k/. Write the word.

2. Start with the word pen.
   Change e to a. Write the word.

   Change the word so that it begins with /k/. Write the word.

3. Start with the word gate.
   Change t to m. Write the word.

   Change the word so that it begins with /k/. Write the word.

4. Start with the word fun.
   Change u to a. Write the word.

   Change n to r. Write the word.

   Now change the word so that it begins with /k/. Write the word.

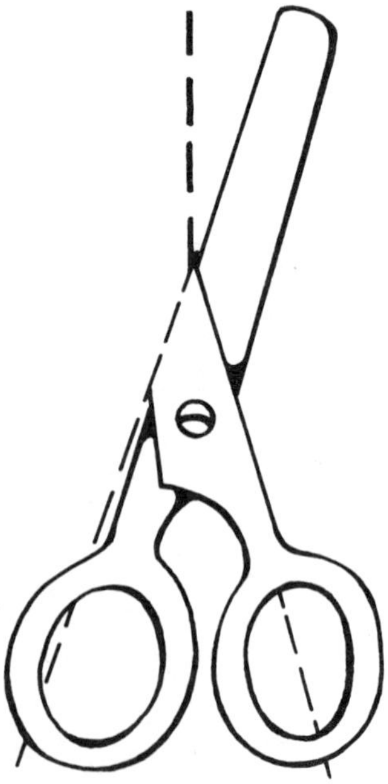

came	can	car	cut

Name

Extra Practice

Bonus Words

UNIT 4

A. Add the letter or letters that spell /k/ to finish the Bonus words. Write the words.

1. ___ ave

2. ___ oo ___ ie

3. ___ ey

4. ___ itten

5. ___ i ___ ___

6. lu ___ ___ y

B. Find four things that begin with /k/ in this picture. Write the Bonus words.

7. ______

8. ______

9. ______

10. ______

cave	cookie	key	kick	kitten	lucky

Name

UNIT 4

Spelling and Language

A. Add s to some of these words. Some words do not need s. Write This Week's Words to go with the pictures.

keep	cat	duck	cow	kite
pick	cup	sick	cake	cook

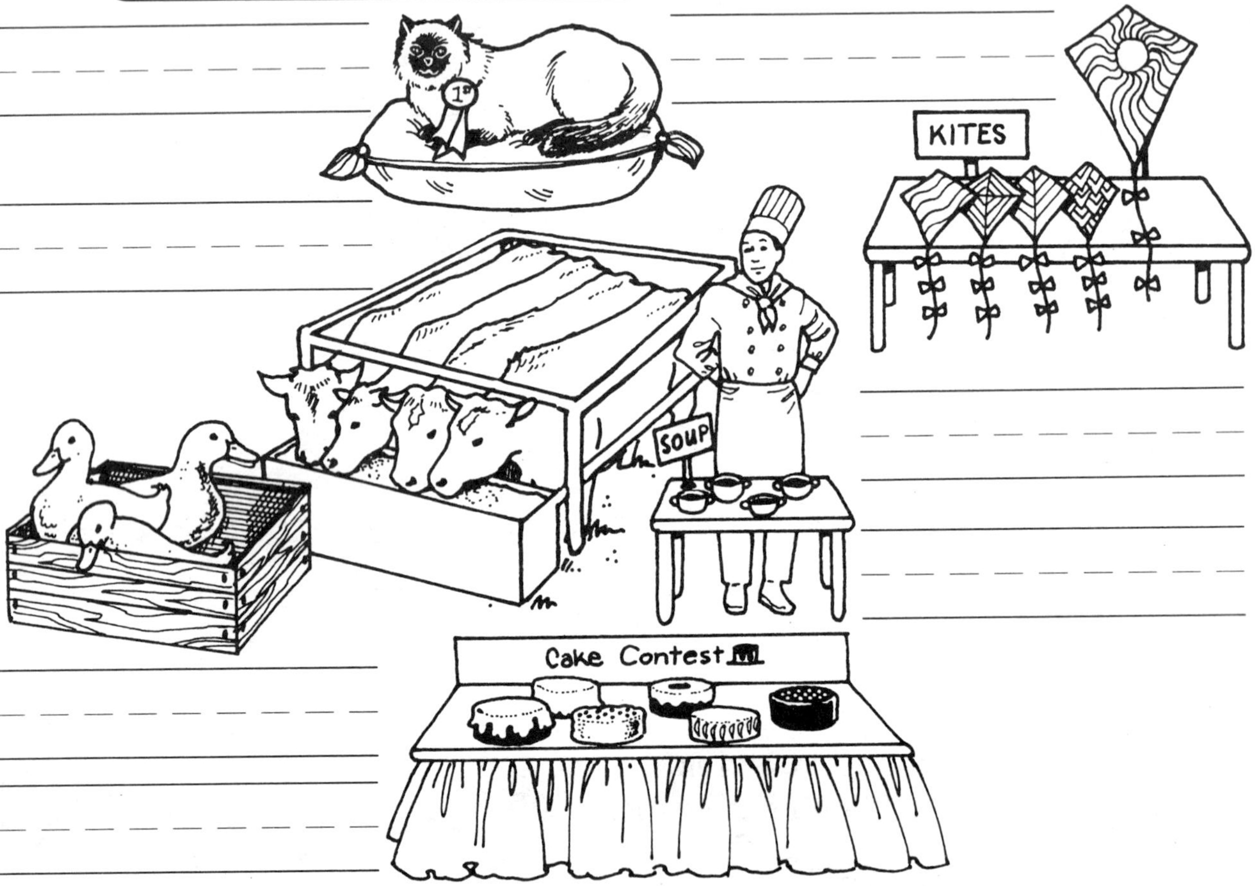

B. Use three of the words above to write sentences about the pictures. Tell how many of each thing you see.

Name

Extra Practice

This Week's Words

UNIT 5

A. Finish the sentences. Use This Week's Words. Write the words across in the boxes next to the sentences.

1. Is a turtle ___ slow as a snail?

2. How ___ can you count to ten?

3. Who is ___ in line?

4. We walked ___ the new zoo.

5. An ___ is very small.

6. I like the colors red ___ green.

7. Which ___ do you write with?

8. That ___ is a bus driver.

9. The milk tastes ___.

10. Too much food can make you ___.

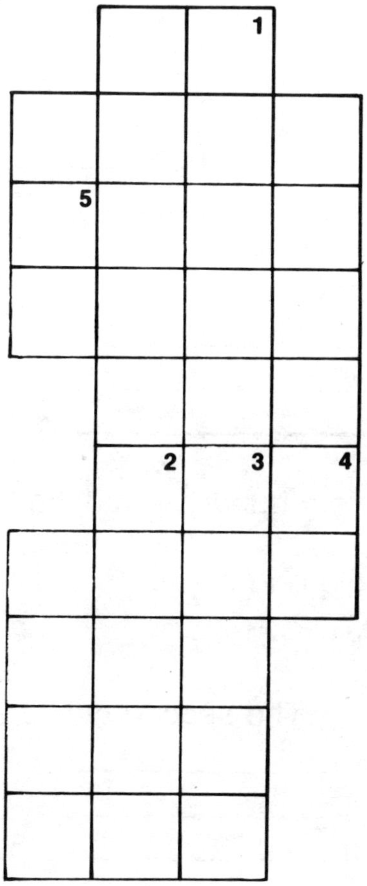

B. Two rhyming words answer this riddle. To find the answer, follow these directions. First find the numbers in the boxes above. Then write the letter you put in the box on the line that has the same number.

What can you call a beach?

___ ___ ___ ___   ___ ___ ___ ___
1 2 3 4   5 2 3 4

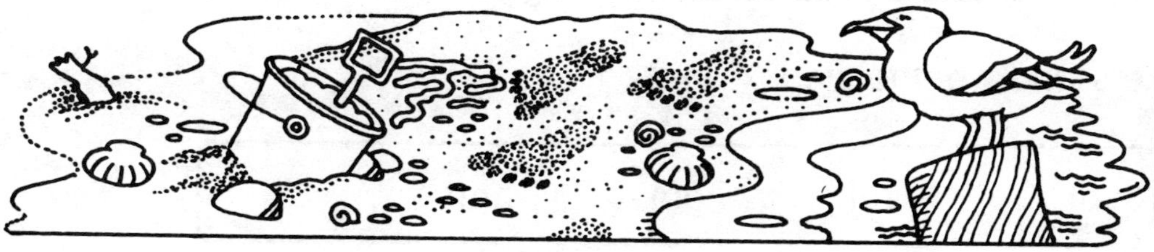

and	last
fast	bad
hand	ant
as	fat
past	man

Name ______________________________

Extra Practice

Mastery Words

UNIT 5

Read the story. Some of the words are missing. Use the Mastery words to finish the story.

Three cats ____________ ____________ a table. The first cat ____________ very big eyes. "I ____________ very hungry," said the biggest cat. So it took the biggest pie and ate it.

The second cat ____________ next to the first one. It ____________ big eyes. "I ____________ hungry, too," said the big cat. So it took the big pie and ate it.

The third cat ____________ by itself ____________ the end of the table. It ____________ little eyes. "I ____________ not hungry at all," it said. "I ____________ the biggest pie for lunch!" So it licked its whiskers and went to sleep.

at	sat	am	had

Name ___

Extra Practice

Bonus Words | **UNIT 5**

A. Finish the sentences. Use the Bonus words.

1. My ______ are too short.
2. Our car had a ______ tire.
3. We ate cotton ______ at the fair.
4. I'd like an ______, not an orange.
5. Ann found a crab in the ______.
6. You can ______ your hands now.

B. Add a letter or letters to these words to make Bonus words. Write the whole word.

7. ant ______
8. lap ______
9. rap ______
10. and ______

C. Write the Bonus word for each picture.

11.  ______

12.  ______

apple	candy	clap	flat	pants	trap

Name ______________________ ______________________

Spelling and Language

UNIT 5

A. Write a word from the box to name each picture.

ant
past
man
and
as
bad
fast
fat
hand
last

1.  ______________________

2.  ______________________

3.  ______________________

Now put the words you wrote in ABC order. Write them on the lines.

4. ______________ **5.** ______________ **6.** ______________

B. Write the underlined words in the sentence in ABC order.

The <u>bad</u> <u>man</u> ran <u>fast</u>.

7. ______________ **8.** ______________ **9.** ______________

C. Use a word from the box to write a sentence about one of the pictures.

____

____

Name

Review A: Units 1–2

UNIT 1
bag
next
real
men
pan
UNIT 2
does
went
woman
your
very

A. UNIT 1 Name the picture. Write a word that begins with the same sound. Use words from Unit 1. One word is used two times.

1. 

2. 

3. 

4. 

5. 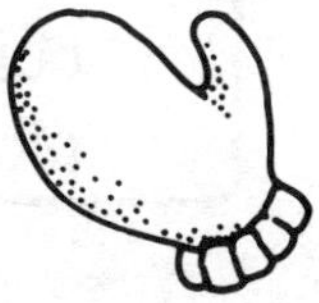

6. 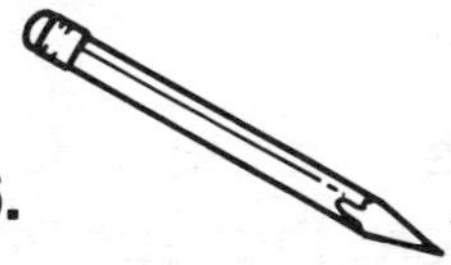

B. UNIT 2 Look at each picture. Cross out the letters that spell the picture word. The letters that are left spell one of the words from Unit 2. Write the word.

7.  w b e a b n y t

8.  w y h a o u l e r

9.  d h o e a s t

10.  v c o e a r y t

11.  b w i o m k a e n

Name ______________________

Review B: Units 3–4

UNIT 3
gone
left
has
soon
jet
UNIT 4
cook
keep
duck
cup
pick

A. UNIT 3 Make a spelling word from each group of letters. Write the word from Unit 3.

1. lfet ______________ **2.** sha ______________

3. osno ______________ **4.** etj ______________

5. egno ______________

B. UNIT 4 Look at the letters that stand for /k/ in the underlined word. Write a word that spells /k/ the same way. Use a word from Unit 4.

6. The ______________ is stuck in the tree.

7. The ______________ looks at his book.

8. Carrie wants a ______________ of milk.

9. ______________ the kite up high.

10. She will ______________ the plums and pack them.

Name

UNIT 6

Review C: Unit 5 • Test Exercise

A. UNIT 5 Write the words that fit together. Some letters are given to help you. Use all the words from Unit 5.

UNIT 5
bad
last
hand
fast
man

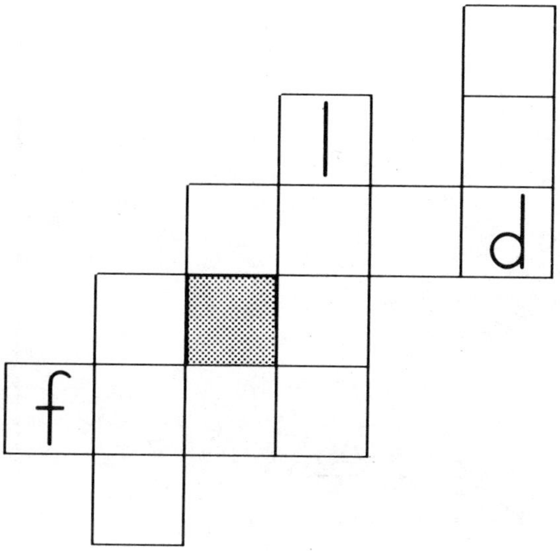

B. UNITS 1–5. Fill in the circle below the word that is spelled wrong.

1 very ⓐ next ⓑ pann ⓒ

2 letf ⓐ cook ⓑ pick ⓒ

3 dab ⓐ man ⓑ fast ⓒ

4 real ⓐ kepe ⓑ does ⓒ

5 last ⓐ hand ⓑ yor ⓒ

6 men ⓐ gone ⓑ rael ⓒ

7 haas ⓐ jet ⓑ soon ⓒ

8 cup ⓐ pik ⓑ woman ⓒ

Name ____________________

UNIT 6

Language Study

Here are all the letters of the alphabet in ABC order.

a b c d e f g h i j k l m
n o p q r s t u v w x y z

A. Write these groups of words in ABC order.

1. man
last
fast

2. next
bag
pan

3. very
does
went

4. soon
gone
jet

next
pan
bag
very
does
went
jet
gone
soon
cup
cook
pick
duck
keep
man
fast
last

B. Draw a line. Connect the words in ABC order.

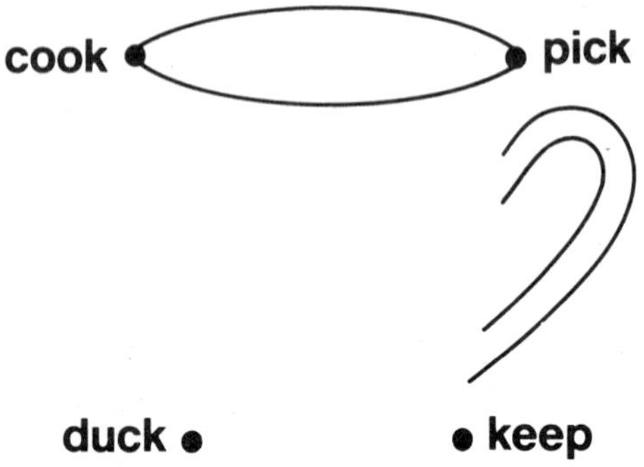

5. Write the name of the picture you drew.

Name

Review: Units 1–5

Mastery Words

UNIT 6

A. Finish the sentences. Use words from Unit 1.

1. The ________ ________ home.

2. It wanted to ________ on time.

B. Write a word from Unit 2 that begins with the same sound as each picture name.

3.  ________

4.  ________

C. Write a word or words from Unit 3 that rhyme with each picture name.

5.  ________ ________

6.  ________

7.  ________

D. Change the first letter in each word. Write a word from Unit 4.

8. but ________

9. man ________

E. Finish the puzzles to spell words from Unit 5.

10. 

11. 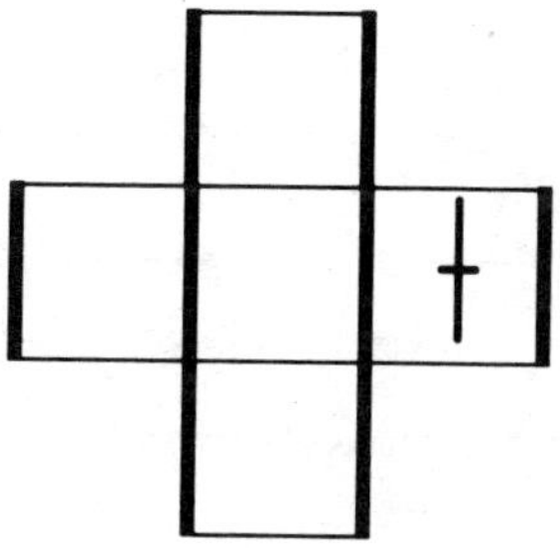

UNIT 1
be
no
pig
ran
UNIT 2
dad
feet
wet
yes
UNIT 3
he
let
say
see
UNIT 4
came
can
car
cut
UNIT 5
am
at
had
sat

Name

Review: Units 1–5

Bonus Words

UNIT **6**

A. Write the words that have double consonants. An example of this kind of word is summer.

B. Write all the words with the sound of /k/. Use words you did not use above. Circle the letter or letters that spell /k/.

C. Write the words that start with the sound you hear at the beginning of the word that names the picture. Write words you did not use above. Circle each word that has the short a sound.

1. 

2. 

3. 

UNIT 1

bear next
mail page
neck robin

UNIT 2

dinner
forgot
today
visit
wash
yard

UNIT 3

goodness
happy
heard
joke
large
sunny

UNIT 4

cave
cookie
key
kick
kitten
lucky

UNIT 5

apple
candy
clap
flat
pants
trap

Name

Extra Practice

This Week's Words

UNIT 7

Finish the puzzle. Write the word that fits each sentence. A * tells you that the word is one of This Week's Words. The other words are also words you know.

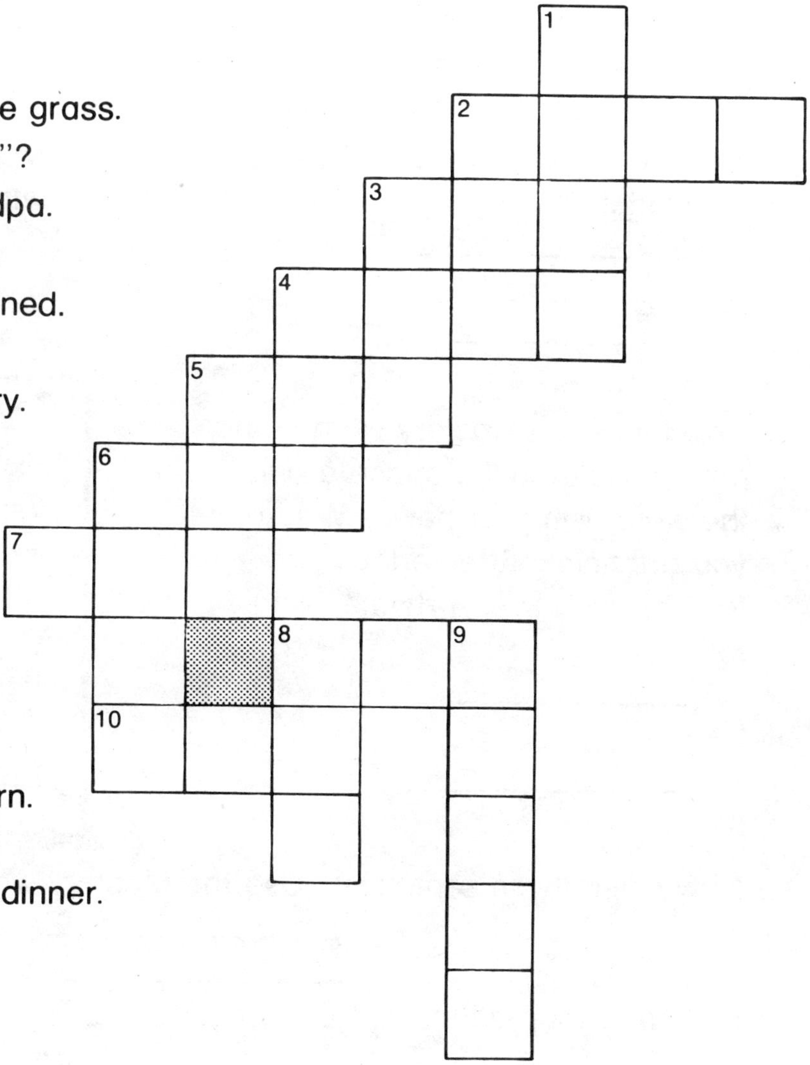

ACROSS

*2. Dad needs ___ cutting the grass.
3. Did you say "___" or "no"?
*4. Bob ___ a letter to Grandpa.
*5. A cat makes a good ___.
6. Maria got ___ when it rained.
7. Five and five make ___.
*8. This is the ___ of the story.
*10. The puppy hurt its ___.

DOWN

*1. Ken is the ___ dancer in our class.
2. The red ___ ate some corn.
*3. Is it five o'clock ___?
*4. Michael ___ the table for dinner.
5. The ___ ran out of ink.
*6. Luis did ___ on the test.
8. Don't drop the ___.
*9. Linda wore a green ___ to the party.

leg	set	pet	end	best
sent	yet	dress	well	help

Name

Extra Practice

Mastery Words — **UNIT 7**

A. Follow the directions.

1. Write the Mastery word that rhymes with <u>red</u>.

2. Write the Mastery word that rhymes with <u>pen</u>.

3. Write the word that rhymes with <u>let</u>.

4. Write the word that rhymes with <u>fell</u>.

B. Now find each Mastery word in the puzzle. Color in the space around the word with your pencil. When you are finished, write the word for what you see. It rhymes with <u>tell</u>.

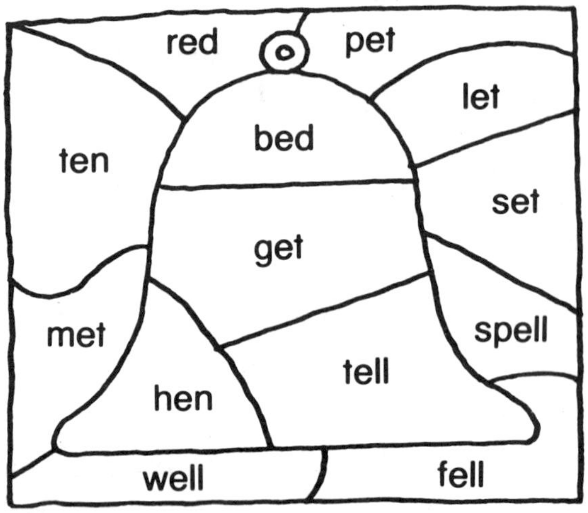

C. Now finish these sentences. Use the Mastery words.

5. The farmer fed the red ______________.

6. It is time for ______________.

7. What did you ______________ for your birthday?

8. Please ______________ me that story again.

tell
hen
bed
get

Name

Extra Practice

Bonus Words

UNIT 7

A. Write the word in each group that rhymes with the underlined word.

1. <u>letter</u> better butter
2. <u>tell</u> spell tall
3. <u>bend</u> mind spend
4. <u>pep</u> stop step
5. <u>rest</u> test rust

B. Write the Bonus word for the picture.

6. 

C. Answer each question. Use the Bonus words.

7. What do you do with money?
8. What is one part of the stairs?
9. What does a teacher give to find out what you have learned?

spell	better	spend	desk	step	test

Name ______

Spelling and Language

UNIT 7

The underlined word in each sentence below does not make sense. Change one letter to make a new word that does make sense in each sentence. Use This Week's Words.

pet
best
dress
end
help
leg
sent
set
well
yet

1. My dog was in a set show. ______
2. It did very bell. ______
3. I got to kelp with the show. ______
4. I did my rest to keep the dogs in line. ______
5. But a funny part came near the and of the show. ______
6. There was a dog with a press and hat. ______
7. It stood on one beg and barked. ______
8. And the show was not over jet. ______
9. At the end, a boy pet a mouse loose. ______
10. That was when I rent for help! ______

Name

Extra Practice

This Week's Words

UNIT 8

A. Write This Week's Words to fit in the puzzles. Some letters are given to help you.

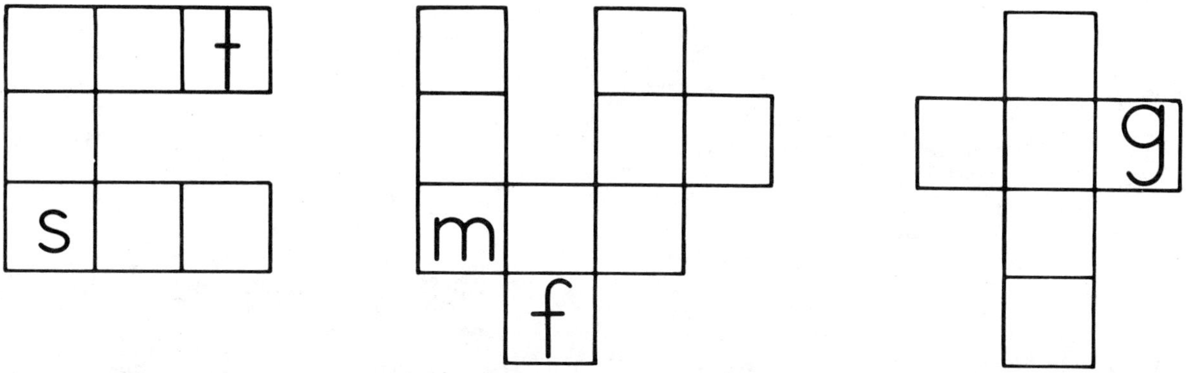

B. Finish each sentence. Write a word that begins with the same letter as the underlined word.

1. Pepper started to ________________ in the dirt.

2. Henry is wearing ________________ new shoes.

3. Frank will ________________ the pool with water.

4. Mom is going to ________________ the fan.

5. Please ________________ on the sofa.

6. That bug ________________ one inch long.

7. I will go ________________ Inez goes.

8. Millie will ________________ up pancake batter.

fix
dig
fill
him
his
hit
if
is
mix
sit

Name

Extra Practice

Mastery Words

UNIT 8

A. Draw a line under each Mastery word that has the sound /i/. Write each word as you find it.

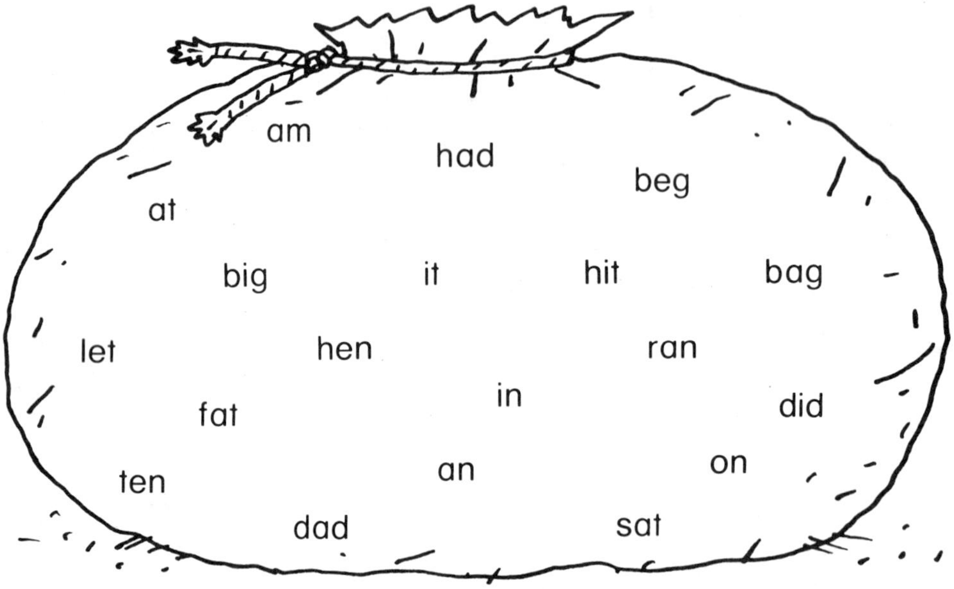

B. Now use the words you found to finish the sentences.

1. Glenn put his foot ______ the shoe.
2. Louise ______ not like that book.
3. Is ______ raining?
4. An elephant is a very ______ animal.

big
did
in
it

Name

Extra Practice

Bonus Words

UNIT 8

A. Which word goes with each sentence clue? Write one of the Bonus words.

1. It means "to carry with you." __________

2. It comes between the beginning and the end. __________

3. It is a place where lots of people live. __________

4. It means "to pick up." __________

5. It is a white drink that comes from cows. __________

6. It goes with <u>treat</u> on Halloween. __________

B. Write a Bonus word that begins with the same sounds as each picture word.

7. 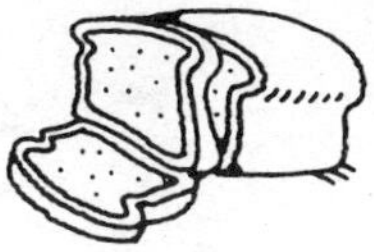 __________

8.  __________

C. Write the two Bonus words that begin with the same letter.

9. __________

10. __________

D. Write the Bonus word that fits each word shape.

11. 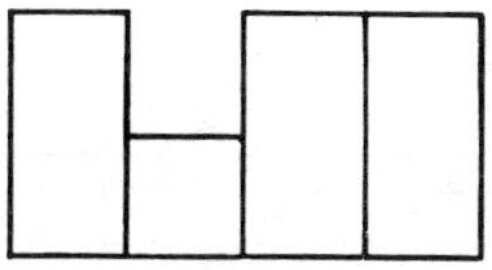

12. 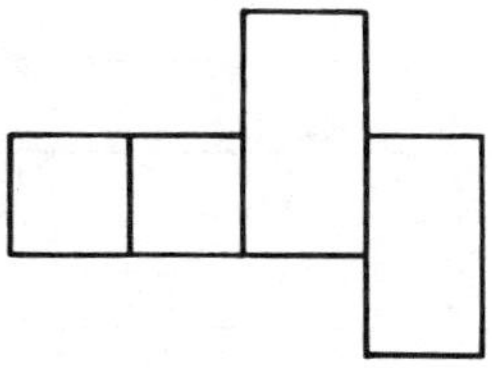

bring
city
lift
middle
milk
trick

Name

Spelling and Language

UNIT 8

A. Choose the right word to finish each sentence. Write it in the blank.

fill
dig
fix
him
his
hit
if
is
mix
sit

1. Kim is going to plant a tree.

   First she ______ a big hole.
   dig **digs**

2. Then she ______ the dirt with some sand.
   mix **mixes**

3. After she puts the tree in, Kim ______ in the hole.
   fill **fills**

4. Then she ______ back to look at her work.
   sit **sits**

5. She ______ one spot to make it just right.
   fix **fixes**

B. Write two sentences about this picture. Use some of This Week's Words that you did not write in **A**. You may add s or es to verbs.

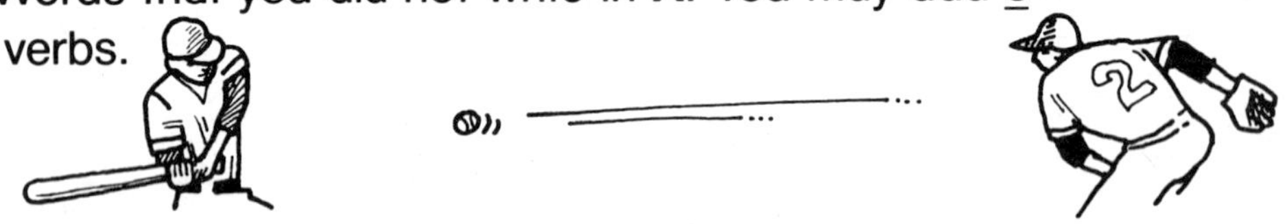

Name

Extra Practice

This Week's Words

UNIT 9

Follow the directions and write This Week's Words.

1. Start with tab. Change t to r. Change a to u. Write the new word.

2. Start with list. Change l to j. Change i to u. Write the new word.

3. Start with back. Change b to l. Change a to u. Write the new word.

4. Start with brick. Change b to t. Change i to u. Write the new word.

5. Start with lamp. Change l to j. Change a to u. Write the new word.

6. Start with dig. Change d to b. Change i to u. Write the new word.

7. Start with fun. Take away f. Write the two letters. Then take s and one l away from still. Write these three letters after the first two.

8. Start with glove. Take away gl. Put c at the beginning. Change v to m. Write the new word.

9. Start with love. Change the l to s. Change the v to m. Write the new word.

10. Start with one. Add d to the beginning of the word. Write the new word.

truck	come	just	bug	until	done	rub	luck	jump	some

Name

Extra Practice

Mastery Words

UNIT **9**

Write the letter that begins each underlined word.
Write Mastery words.

1. The cat ran under the new chair.

2. My uncle sings in a band.

3. The rain fell until noon.

4. No one is unhappy at a parade.

fun	up	run	us

Name

Extra Practice

Bonus Words

UNIT 9

A. Draw a line under the word that is spelled wrong in each sentence. Then write the word the right way.

funny
month
son
summer
won
wonder

1. Our team wun five games. ____________
2. March is a windy munth. ____________
3. Wanda told us a fonny story. ____________
4. Billy is Aunt Ella's sun. ____________
5. We go swimming every sommer. ____________
6. I wunder where Albert is. ____________

B. Write the two Bonus words that have double letters.

7. ____________ 8. ____________

C. Write the two Bonus words that rhyme with bun.

9. ____________ 10. ____________

D. Finish this sentence with two Bonus words.

11. I ____________ who ____________ the race.

Name

UNIT 9

Spelling and Language

Complete each poem with words that rhyme. Choose words from the box.

jump
rub
bug
just
truck
luck
until
come
done
some

1. Give this lamp a bit of a rub.
   See if it helps your ___.

   Wish for a shiny silver tub
   Or a big red moving ___.

2. A rabbit can ___
   Over a bump.

   And before it is ___,
   It will jump more than one.

3. When they passed the pie,
   I said, "Please, I'd like ___."

   But when they passed me by,
   I said, "Why did I ___?"

Name

Extra Practice

This Week's Words

UNIT **10**

Finish the puzzle. Use This Week's Words. Some letters are given to help you. Use each word once only. After you write the word in the puzzle, write it again below. You will write one word that is not one of This Week's Words.

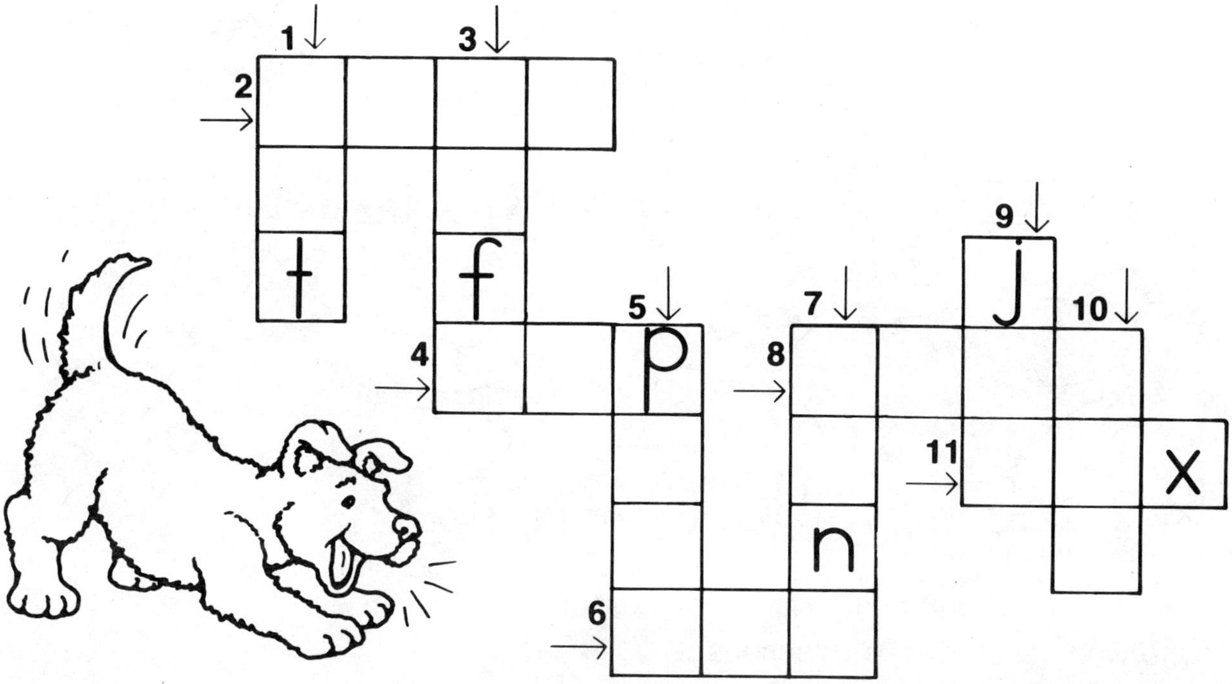

1. ____________
2. ____________
3. ____________
4. ____________
5. ____________
6. ____________
7. ____________
8. ____________
9. ____________
10. ____________
11. ____________

top	dog	job	lot	pond
pop	shop	lost	soft	song

Name ______________________

Extra Practice

Mastery Words

UNIT 10

A. Each frog has a letter on it. Write more letters to spell Mastery words. Write each word once.

B. The frogs had a jumping race. To find out who won, follow these directions.

Write the first letter in <u>s</u>at.
Write the last letter in coa<u>t</u>.
Write the second letter in n<u>o</u>t.
Write the last letter in u<u>p</u>.

____

Find the frog that has the word you just wrote.

The winner is frog number ______________.

C. Now find out how far the winner jumped. Write the letters with stars under them in number order.

The winner jumped one ______________.

box
fox
stop
got

Name

Extra Practice

Bonus Words | **UNIT 10**

A. Draw a line from each sentence to the picture it tells about. Then write the Bonus word after the picture.

1. It is a small green animal that hops.

2. You can open it with a key.

3. It is green and grows on stones.

4. It is what you must pay for something.

B. Write the two Bonus words that have the sound /ô/ in dog.

5. ________ **6.** ________

C. Write the four Bonus words that have the sound /o/ in top.

7. ________ **8.** ________

9. ________ **10.** ________

clock
cost
drop
frog
lock
moss

Name

Spelling and Language

UNIT **10**

Write a word to complete each picture riddle. Use This Week's Words. Add s if the word stands for more than one.

top
dog
job
lot
pond
pop
shop
lost
soft
song

1.  Not cats, but ________.

2.  Not hard, but ________.

3.  Not lakes, but ________.

4.  Not found, but ________.

5.  Not hops, but ________.

6.  Not bottom, but ________.

7.  Not singers, but ________.

8.  Not houses, but ________.

9.  Not a little, but a ________.

10.  Not workers, but ________.

Name

UNIT 11

Extra Practice

This Week's Words

Find each word that ends with two consonant letters that are alike. Draw lines to connect the dots that go with the words. Use ABC order to go from one word to the next. Start with across. Write each word as you find it.

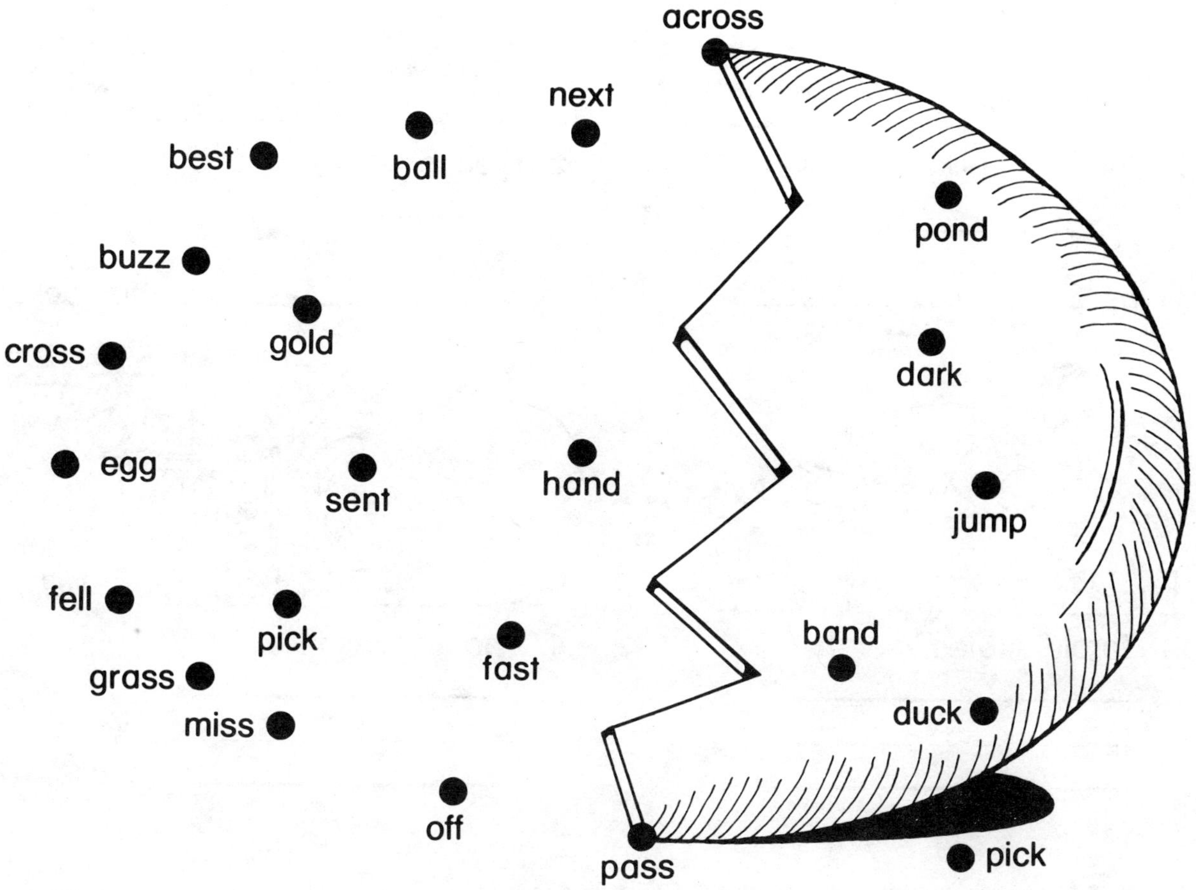

1. ____________ 2. ____________ 3. ____________

4. ____________ 5. ____________ 6. ____________

7. ____________ 8. ____________ 9. ____________

10. ____________

Name ______________________________

Extra Practice

Mastery Words | **UNIT 11**

A. Use Mastery words to finish the sentences.

1. Teri and Lucky ran down

____

the ______________________ .

2. Please

____

______________________ the bucket.

3. Harold skates very

____

______________________ .

4. The elf lives in a

____

______________________ house.

B. Write Mastery words where they fit in the puzzle. The sentence numbers above will help you.

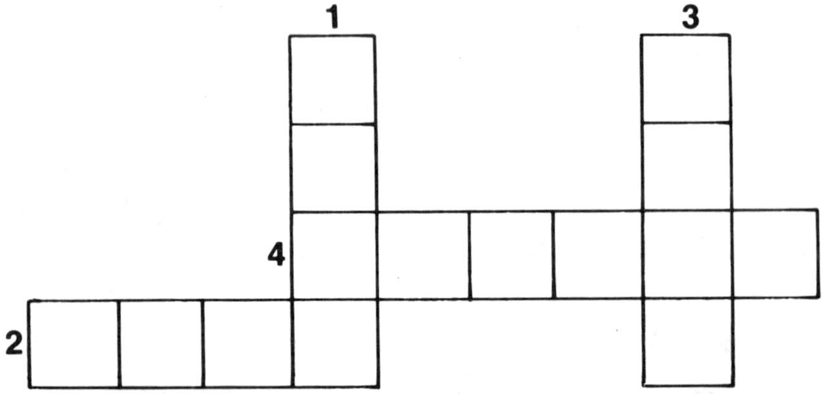

fill
well
little
hill

Name ______________________________

Extra Practice

Bonus Words

UNIT 11

Read the sentences about Bobby. Look at the two underlined words. The first letters are the double letters in the missing words. Here is an example.

Bobby does not live on low land.

He lives on a hill.

The two l's in low land tell you that the missing word has ll.

1. Bobby has no nickels.

He just has a ______________.

2. Bobby does not have a baby bunny.

He has a ______________.

3. Bobby has five footballs.

Bobby has a lot of ______________.

4. Bobby likes tasty toast.

He likes it best with ______________.

5. Bobby likes looking for things.

He found a ______________ on the beach.

6. Bobby earned a dollar dusting.

He will ______________ it to the money in his bank.

add
butter
penny
rabbit
shell
stuff

Name

Spelling and Language

UNIT 11

buzz
across
ball
egg
cross
fell
grass
miss
off
pass

A. Read each sentence below. Then write the underlined word under the correct heading.

1. We passed the red car.
2. The bee buzzes in the garden.
3. The man crosses the street with the green light.
4. I missed one question on the test.

is happening now	already happened

B. Write sentences about this picture. Use some of This Week's Words that you did not use above.

Name

Review A: Units 7–8

UNIT 12

UNIT 7
best
help
well
sent
yet
UNIT 8
him
if
sit
his
is

A. UNIT 7 Write the word from Unit 7 that rhymes with each word below.

1. rest

2. rent

3. bell

4. yelp

5. jet

B. UNIT 7 Add a letter to make a word from Unit 7.

6. bet

7. set

C. UNIT 8 Write the words from Unit 8 that begin with the same sound as the picture name.

8. 

9. 

10. 

Name ______________________

Review B: Units 9–10

UNIT 9
just truck some until done
UNIT 10
job lost song dog shop

A. UNIT 9 Write each group of words from Unit 9 in ABC order.

1. some ______
done ______
truck ______

2. just ______
done ______
until ______

B. UNIT 10 Complete each sentence. Use words from Unit 10.

3. Lisa has a ______ after school.

4. She works in a pet ______.

5. She gives a ______ a bath.

6. She finds a ______ kitten.

7. She teaches a bird a pretty ______.

Name ______

UNIT 12

Review C: Unit 11 • Test Exercise

A. UNIT 11 Add double letters to each group of letters. Write words from Unit 11.

UNIT 11
across
off
grass
ball
fell

1. gra __ __ ______ **2.** o __ __ ______

3. fe __ __ ______ **4.** acro __ __ ______

5. ba __ __ ______

B. UNITS 7–11 Listen to the words. Fill in the circle below the word that is spelled wrong.

1	best	jobe	song
	ⓐ	ⓑ	ⓒ
2	off	sit	acros
	ⓐ	ⓑ	ⓒ
3	jus	sent	ball
	ⓐ	ⓑ	ⓒ
4	truck	yet	shopp
	ⓐ	ⓑ	ⓒ
5	help	som	lost
	ⓐ	ⓑ	ⓒ
6	grase	well	dog
	ⓐ	ⓑ	ⓒ
7	just	across	hime
	ⓐ	ⓑ	ⓒ
8	untill	if	lost
	ⓐ	ⓑ	ⓒ

Name ______________________________

Language Study

UNIT **12**

A. Change one letter to make a new word. Use the words in the box.

best
well
sent
yet
sit
is
just
truck
job
ball
fell

1. nest → rest → ______

2. went → tent → ______

3. bit → pit → ______

4. it → if → ______

5. fall → call → ______

6. must → dust → ______

7. let → pet → ______

8. bell → tell → ______ ______

B. Add s to make a word that names more than one.

9.  job ______

10.  truck ______

Name

Review: Units 7–11

Mastery Words

UNIT **12**

UNIT 7	UNIT 8	UNIT 9	UNIT 10	UNIT 11
bed	big	fun	box	fill
get	did	up	got	hill
hen	in	run	fox	little
tell	it	us	stop	well

A. Write a word that rhymes with each word below. Use words from the box. Do not use the same word twice.

1. red ________ **2.** pen ________

3. tell ________ **4.** will ________

5. fox ________ **6.** bill ________

7. pig ________ **8.** lot ________

B. Add the same vowel to each pair of words to make words from the box.

9. st __ p ________ **10.** g __ t ________

f __ x ________ t __ ll ________

11. r __ n ________ **12.** d __ d ________

__ s ________ l __ ttle ________

13. __ t ________ **14.** f __ n ________

__ n ________ __ p ________

Name

Bonus Words UNIT **12**

Review: Units 7–11

A. Write the word from the box that names each picture.

1. 

2. 

3. 

4. 

5. 

6. 

7. 

8. 

9. 

10. 

11. 

12. 

13. $\begin{array}{r} 2 \\ +2 \\ \hline \end{array}$

14. 

B. Write six words that have /u/ in the middle.

C. Write three words that spell /e/ with an e.

UNIT 7
spell
better
spend
desk
step
test
UNIT 8
bring
city
lift
middle
milk
trick
UNIT 9
funny
month
son
summer
won
wonder
UNIT 10
clock
cost
drop
frog
moss
lock
UNIT 11
add
butter
penny
rabbit
shell
stuff

Name

Extra Practice

This Week's Words

UNIT 13

Finish the puzzle. Write one of This Week's Words that rhymes with each word given.

ACROSS

3. face
4. hand
5. ant
6. pass
8. toast
9. sees

DOWN

1. dust
2. sad
4. hill
7. more

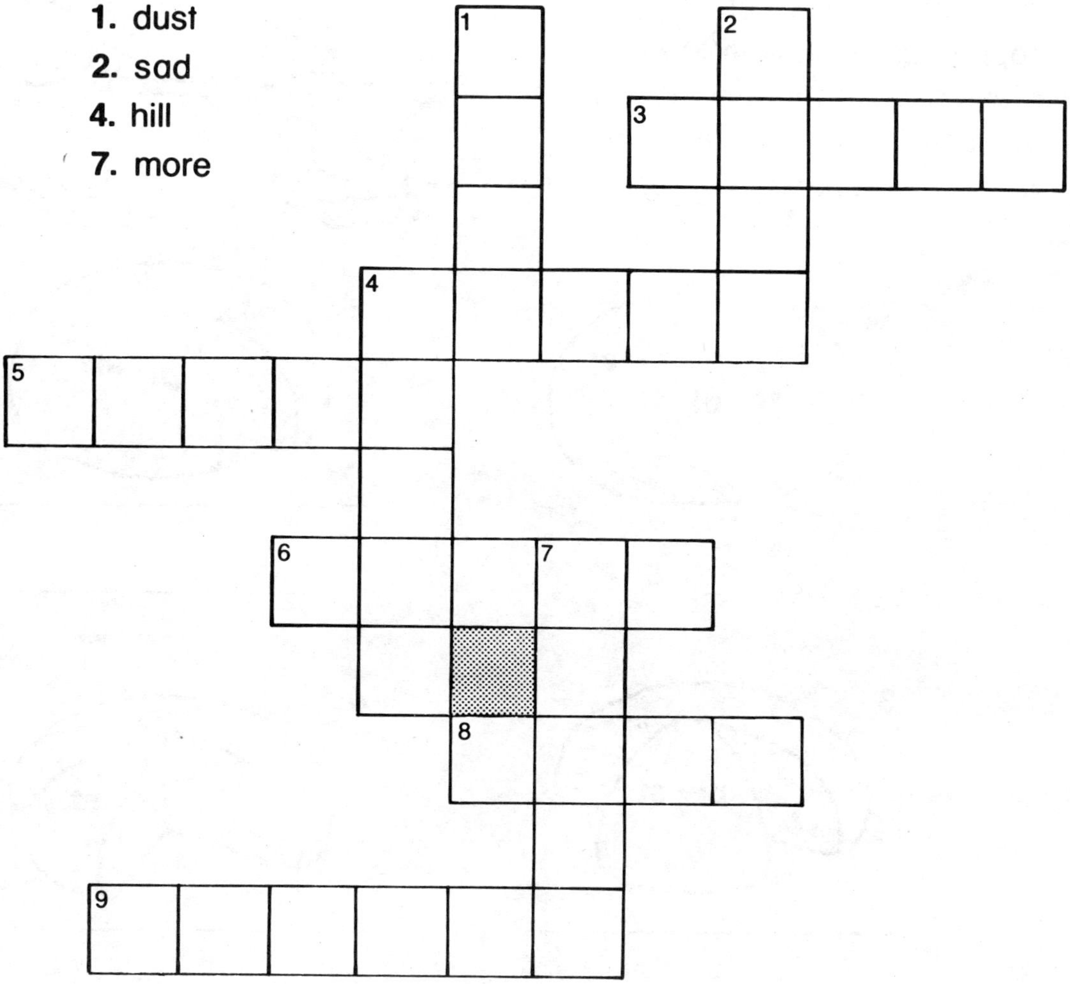

stand
still
store
glad
glass
place
plant
please
most
must

Name

Extra Practice

Mastery Words

UNIT 13

The elf baked a strange loaf of bread. There are consonant clusters on the crust! Each time the elf cuts a piece of bread, a consonant cluster is gone.

Look at each picture in order. Which consonant cluster has disappeared each time? Write a Mastery word that begins with that cluster. The last cluster left comes at the end of a word.

1

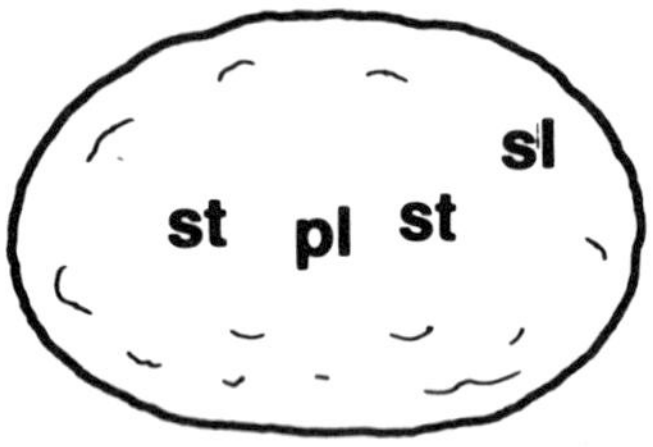

2

3

4

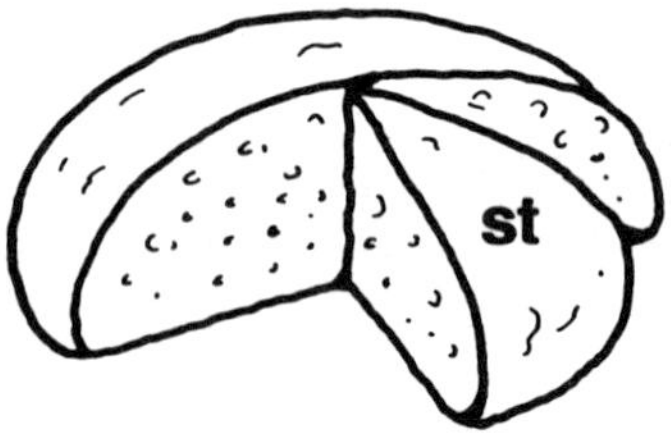

5

play
sleep
story
best

Name

Extra Practice

Bonus Words

UNIT **13**

A. Write the same two letters in each pair of boxes. Then write the Bonus words.

1. ☐ ☐ i c k
2. t r u ☐ ☐
3. ☐ ☐ a r e
4. d u ☐ ☐
5. ☐ ☐ e e p

B. Answer the questions. Write the Bonus words.

6. Where do you go to have fun?

7. What has to be wiped off the furniture?

8. What do tape and paste do?

9. What do you do when you look hard at something?

10. What is a hill that is hard to climb?

stare	steep	stick	dust	trust	playground

Name

Spelling and Language

UNIT 13

A. Read the sentences below. Write the underlined word on the line. If the underlined word is a noun, write **n** after it. If the underlined word is a verb, write **v** after it.

1. There is a flower stand next door.
2. Next to it is a big store.
3. The store has windows of glass.
4. It is a busy place.
5. The owner wants to plant flowers in front of the store.

B. Complete each of the sentences about going to the store. Write the whole sentence on the line.

6. I must buy ___.
7. What I want most is ___.
8. Please look for ___.

stand	still	store	glad	glass
place	plant	please	most	must

Name

Extra Practice

This Week's Words

UNIT 14

Look at each picture. Cross out the letters that spell the picture word. The letters that are left spell one of This Week's Words. Write the word.

1.  s f w i i s m h ____________

2.  s d p o o g t ____________

3.  s c m a a l t l ____________

4.  p f i r o g m ____________

5.  k b r i o t t h e e r ____________

6.  c g r o e a a t t ____________

7.  c t a r r u e ____________

8.  f h r o a n t t ____________

9. 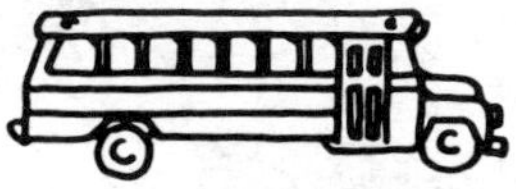 f b r i u e s n d ____________

10.  c p r a e t k t e y ____________

friend	brother	swim	front	small
spot	great	true	pretty	from

Name

Extra Practice

Mastery Words

UNIT 14

Use your pencil and go from START to FINISH in the puzzle. When you come to a word, decide if it begins with a consonant cluster. If it does, make your line go toward **Y** for yes. Then write the word below. If it does not begin with a consonant cluster, make your line go toward **N** for no.

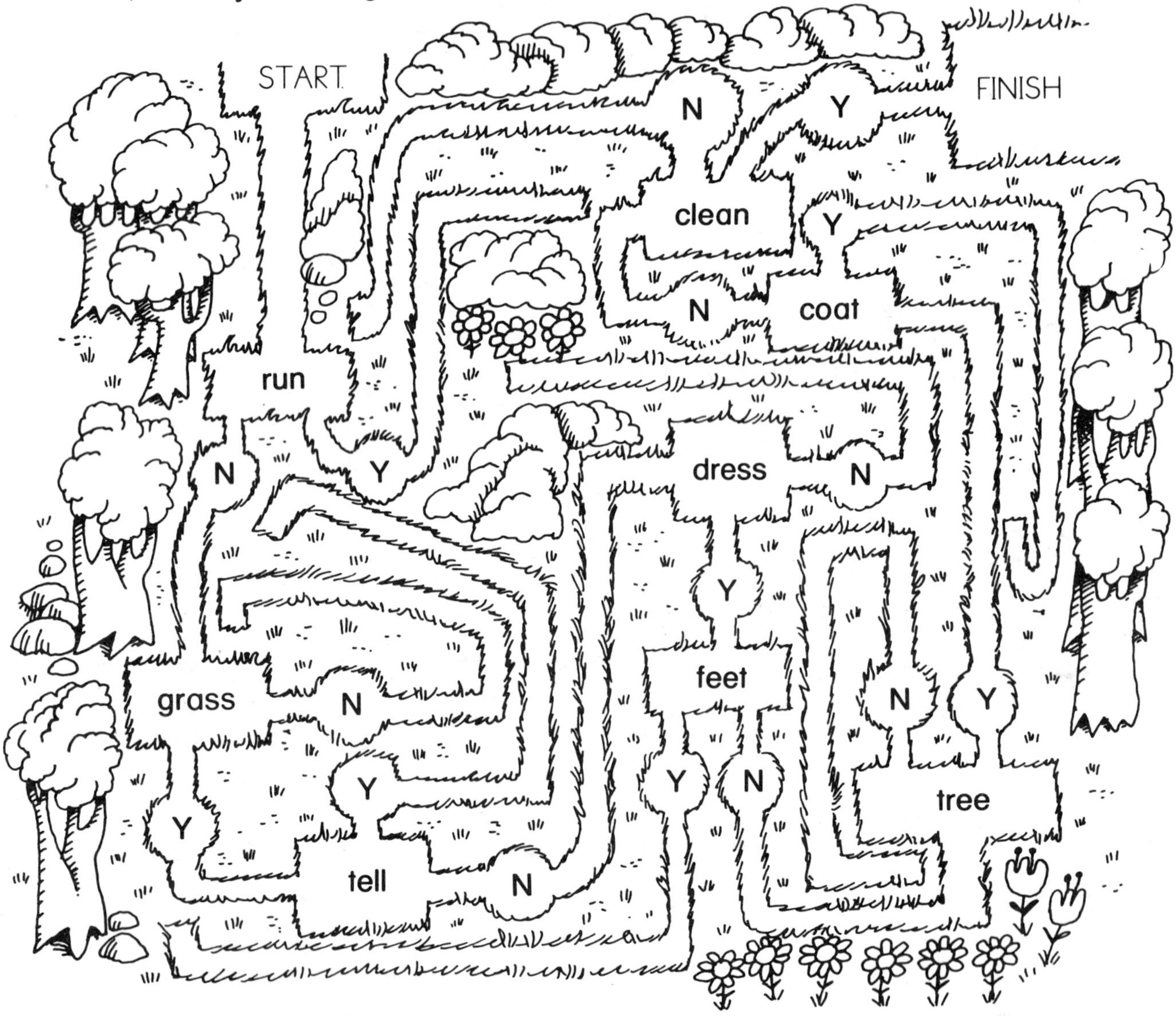

1. ____________

2. ____________

3. ____________

4. ____________

Name

Extra Practice

Bonus Words

UNIT 14

A. Write the Bonus word that begins like the first word and rhymes with the second word.

1. great band ________
2. proud size ________
3. brown head ________
4. train pack ________
5. swan feet ________
6. small tile ________

B. Finish the puzzle. Use the Bonus words. The words go across and down.

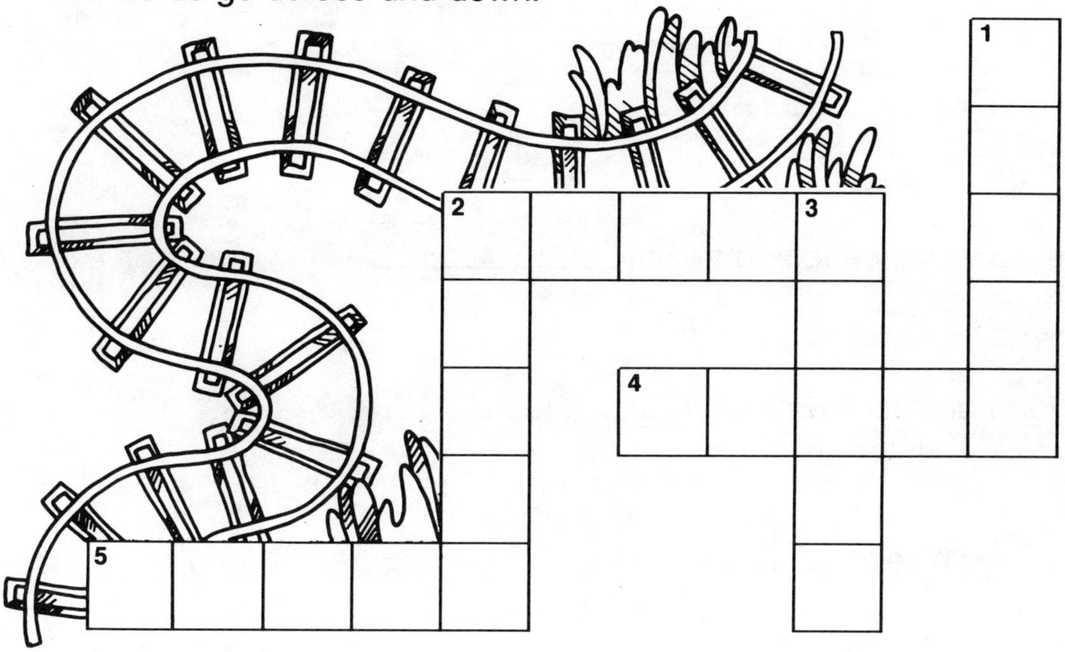

ACROSS

2. Not sour.
4. Important.
5. The winner gets one.

DOWN

1. It comes in a loaf.
2. What you do when you are happy.
3. A train moves on this.

grand	track	smile	bread	sweet	prize

Name ____________________

Spelling and Language

UNIT 14

Read each sentence. Look for the underlined letters. These letters are in the wrong order. Write the misspelled word again. Spell it the right way.

small
from
spot
front
swim
great
brother
pretty
friend
true

1. My borther and I like to swim. ____________
2. We know of a good sopt. ____________
3. The water there is graet. ____________
4. The trees are pertty. ____________
5. Last time we went, we took a freind. ____________
6. He was form another town. ____________
7. He likes to siwm, too. ____________
8. He brought his samll dog. ____________
9. It swam in fornt of him. ____________
10. That dog is a treu pet. ____________

Name

Extra Practice

This Week's Words

UNIT 15

A. Which word goes with each sentence clue? Write one of This Week's Words in the blanks.

1. These are animals. (◯) (◯) (◯) ___ ___
2. To want something to happen. (◯) ___ ___ ___
3. You use these to chew food. ___ ___ (◯) ___ ___
4. You use this word when you get a gift. ___ ___ ___ (◯) ___
5. A word that means "to close." ___ ___ ___ (◯)
6. Another word for <u>end</u>. (◯) ___ ___ ___ ___ ___
7. A plate is this. ___ (◯) ___ ___
8. Touch to make something move. ___ ___ (◯) ___
9. You wear this on your foot. ___ (◯) ___ ___
10. Add this word to <u>any</u> or <u>some</u> to make a bigger word. ___ ___ (◯) (◯) (◯)

B. Now find out what Laura did this morning. Write the circled letters in order. You will spell three words. Begin with a capital letter and end with a period.

____

shoe	shut	dish	finish	push
sheep	wish	thank	thing	teeth

Name

Extra Practice

Mastery Words

UNIT 15

A. Do some "word math" and write the Mastery words.

1. f o x − o x + i n − n + d i s h − d i = ____

2. s h i p − i p + w e − w = ____

3. w e l l − e l l + i s − s + b a t h − b a = ____

4. s h u t − u t + h o p − h = ____

B. Add sh before each group of letters. Write some new words.

5. __ __ a p e

6. __ __ a l l

7. __ __ o w

8. __ __ o r t

9. __ __ o e

she	fish
shop	with

Name

Extra Practice

Bonus Words

UNIT 15

Finish the story. Use the Bonus words. Write the words below.

Tiny Alfie was a little elf. He was no bigger than your __1__.

Tiny Alfie lived near a __2__ in a garden. Often he heard loud crunching sounds. (The sounds were made by people walking by. But Alfie did not know this.)

One day he heard the loud crunching sounds. Then he heard something __3__ to the ground. Something had fallen to __4__. It was round. It was flat. Alfie saw it __5__ in the sun. He thought it was a flying saucer. He started to __6__ for help.

What did Alfie see?

1. ______________ 2. ______________ 3. ______________

4. ______________ 5. ______________ 6. ______________

path shine thumb crash earth shout

Name

Spelling and Language

UNIT 15

A. Find each word below that stands for more than one. Circle it. Then write the word on the line.

sheep
shoe
shut
dish
finish
push
wish
thank
thing
teeth

1. Did you finish brushing your teeth?

2. I put the dishes on the table.

3. The good fairy gave me three wishes.

4. She gave her thanks for her birthday present.

5. There will be many things in the room.

6. Do you push your shoes under your bed?

7. Are the sheep shut in the barn?

B. Answer one of the questions above. Write a complete sentence.

Name

Extra Practice

This Week's Words

UNIT 16

Finish the puzzle with This Week's Words. Some letters are given to help you. Use each word only once. After you write the word in the puzzle, write it again below.

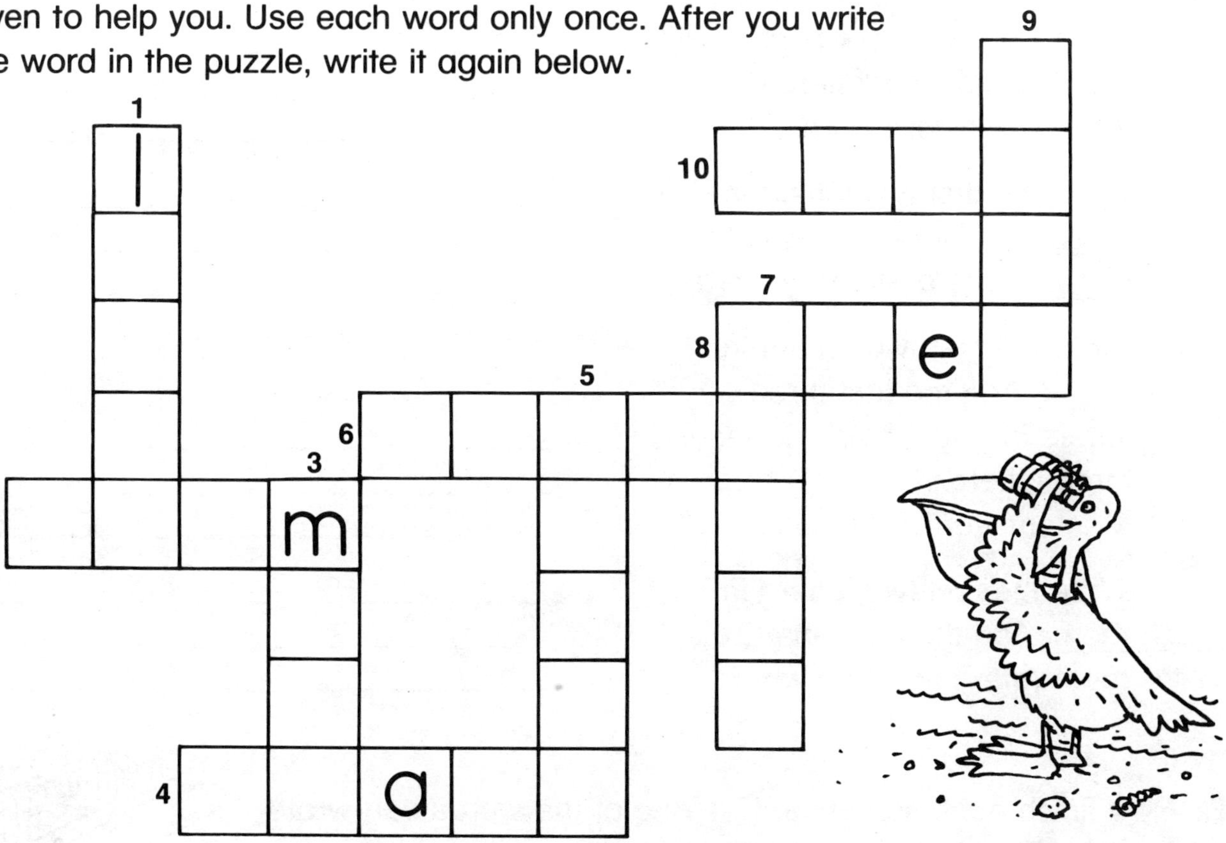

1. ____________ 2. ____________ 3. ____________

4. ____________ 5. ____________ 6. ____________

7. ____________ 8. ____________ 9. ____________

10. ____________

watch	them	than	their	then
these	chair	each	lunch	much

Name ______________________

Extra Practice

Mastery Words

UNIT 16

A. Follow the directions.

1. Write the last two letters in with. Add the last two letters in his. Write a Mastery word. ______________________
2. Write the first two letters in these. Add the last two letters in hat. Write a Mastery word. ______________________
3. Write the first two letters in cheek. Add the last three letters in wild. Then add the first three letters in rent. Write a Mastery word. ______________________
4. Write the first two letters in them. Add the last letter in me. Write a Mastery word. ______________________

B. Now finish each sentence. Use one of the words you wrote for **1–4**. The number under the line shows you which word to write.

5. Do you want ______ (1) apple or ______ (2) one?
6. Mr. Stevens took ______ (4) ______ (3) to Toy Town.

that	the	this	children

Name

Extra Practice

Bonus Words

UNIT 16

A. Write the missing letters in the boxes to finish each Bonus word. Then write the whole word.

1. ☐ ☐ t h ☐ ☐

2. ☐ ☐ ☐ ☐ t h ☐ ☐

3. ☐ ☐ ☐ t h ☐ ☐

4. ☐ ☐ t c h

5. c h ☐ ☐ c h

6. ☐ ☐ t c h ☐ ☐

B. Write the Bonus word that goes with each group of words.

7. rain snow wind

8. sink stove table

9. ball glove grab

10. Sunday bell building

bother	catch	together	church	weather	kitchen

Name

Spelling and Language

UNIT
16

Choose the word in dark print that fits the sentence. Circle it. Then write the whole sentence.

their
chair
than
them
then
these
each
lunch
much
watch

1. Would you rather sit in that chair **than then** watch the show?

2. Each of these lunches is much better **than then** any of those.

3. **Than Then** tell them to come over.

4. They ate their lunches and **than then** went out to play.

Name

Extra Practice

This Week's Words

UNIT 17

A. Find the word in each box that is spelled right. Write the word.

1 **wen when wehn**	2 **again agen agin**
3 **wheer where wher**	4 **been bene ben**
5 **heer heere here**	6 **uys uss use**
7 **whant want wannt**	8 **theer theere there**
9 **wat waht what**	10 **wher were wer**

there
here
were
what
when
where
want
again
been
use

B. Letters are missing from each word. Add the letters. Write some of This Week's Words.

11. w__ nt

12. th__ __ __

13. __h__t

14. w____e

15. h__ __ __

16. w__ __ __e

Name

Extra Practice

Mastery Words

UNIT 17

A. Each picture stands for a letter. Write the letters for each group of pictures. You will write four Mastery words.

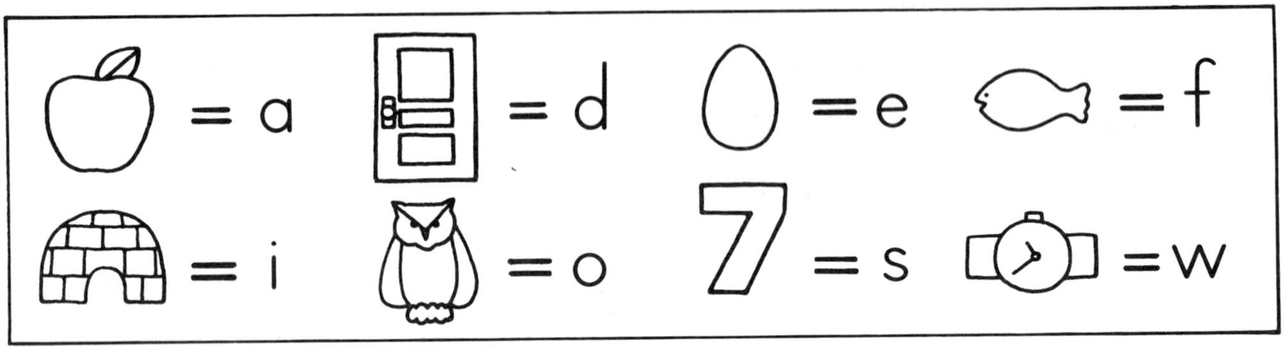

1. ______

2. ______

3. ______

4. ______

B. Finish the second sentence in each pair. Use three of the words you just wrote.

5. What did Mr. Green say?
   He ___, "How are you?" ______

6. Where is Tommy?
   He ___ here a minute ago. ______

7. I do my work carefully.
   Alice ___ her work carefully, too. ______

does
of
said
was

Name ______________________

Extra Practice

Bonus Words

UNIT 17

A. Draw a line under the word that is spelled wrong in each sentence. Then write the word the right way.

1. I thawt I knew the answer. ______________
2. But my answer was rong. ______________
3. Please lissen to me. ______________
4. My famly went to the zoo. ______________
5. The monkeys made us laff. ______________
6. Eddie sat bitween Karen and Paul. ______________

B. Finish each second sentence. Write a Bonus word.

7. Mom, Dad, Billy, and I like carrots.

   My whole ______________ likes carrots.

8. Enid is on one side, and Mandy is on the other.

   Pat sits ______________ Enid and Mandy.

9. Jack made a left turn and got lost.

   Jack went the ______________ way.

wrong   between   listen   family   laugh   thought

Name

Spelling and Language

UNIT 17

there
here
were
what
when
where
want
again
been
use

A. Write each group of words in ABC order.

1. there
again
here

2. use
been
want

3. what
there
again

4. where
here
there

B. Write each group of words in ABC order. Put them in order by the second letter.

5. what
want
were

6. win
when
want

Name ______________________

UNIT 18

Review A: Units 13–14

UNIT 13
please
stand
must
store
glad
UNIT 14
brother
friend
swim
great
true

A. UNIT 13 Complete each sentence with a word from Unit 13. Use a word that begins with the same sound as most of the other words in the sentence.

1. Mary ____________ make the most of Mrs. Mitchell's money.
2. Gertie is ____________ that Gary got a glass goose.
3. Steve will ____________ still and stare.
4. ____________ tell Pam to pick a picture.
5. Sam sells seeds at his sister Stella's ____________.

B. UNIT 14 Write a word that starts with the same consonant cluster as the word that names the picture. Use a word from Unit 14.

6.  ____________

7.  ____________

8. 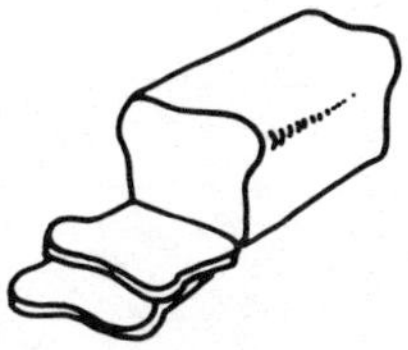 ____________

9.  ____________

10.  ____________

Name

UNIT 18

Review B: Units 15–16

UNIT 15
shoe
thing
wish
thank
finish

UNIT 16
chair
watch
their
these
much

A. UNIT 15 Read each sentence. Write the word that fits. Use a word from Unit 15.

1. You might do this while looking at a star.
2. If this fits, you should wear it.
3. Be sure to do this to someone who does something nice for you.
4. You can not do this until after you start.
5. If it is not a person or place, it might be this.

B. UNIT 16 Listen for the sound at the end of the picture name. Write words from Unit 16 that have the letters that make that sound.

6. 

7. 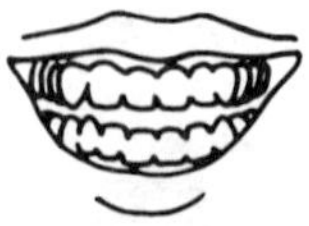

Name

Review C: Unit 17 • Test Exercise

UNIT 18

UNIT 17
again
been
were
there
here

A. UNIT 17 Write a word that rhymes with each word. Use words from Unit 17.

1. her ____________ **2.** dear ____________

3. where ____________

B. Follow the directions. Use words from Unit 17.

4. Write the word that will finish the sentence.

Paulo has ____________ here before.

5. Write the word that means "one more time." ____________

C. UNITS 13–17 Fill in the circle under the word that is spelled correctly.

1	pleese ⓐ	pleaze ⓑ	please ⓒ	plese ⓓ
2	finish ⓐ	finnish ⓑ	finsh ⓒ	finishe ⓓ
3	shuw ⓐ	shew ⓑ	shue ⓒ	shoe ⓓ
4	agen ⓐ	aggain ⓑ	again ⓒ	agin ⓓ
5	theyr ⓐ	their ⓑ	ther ⓒ	thair ⓓ
6	watsh ⓐ	wach ⓑ	wasch ⓒ	watch ⓓ
7	friend ⓐ	frend ⓑ	freind ⓒ	frennd ⓓ
8	binn ⓐ	been ⓑ	bien ⓒ	benn ⓓ

Name

Language Study

UNIT 18

Each underlined word is spelled wrong. Write the sentence over. Spell all the words correctly.

1. I wish to thank you again for a <u>grate</u> time.

2. Will you <u>wach</u> my brother swim?

3. I was <u>gald</u> to see him.

4. Please <u>finnish</u> your work before you come here.

5. It is <u>treu</u> that the store has been there a long time.

please
stand
must
store
glad
brother
friend
swim
great
true
shoe
thing
wish
thank
finish
chair
watch
their
these
much
again
been
were
there
here

Name

Review: Units 13–17

Mastery Words

UNIT **18**

UNIT 13
play sleep story best
UNIT 14
clean grass dress tree
UNIT 15
fish she shop with
UNIT 16
that the this children
UNIT 17
does of said was

A. Write each group of words in ABC order.

1. play sleep best

2. does of children

3. story dress was

4. grass clean tree

B. Listen for the sound at the beginning of the picture name. Write the words that have the letters that make that sound.

5. 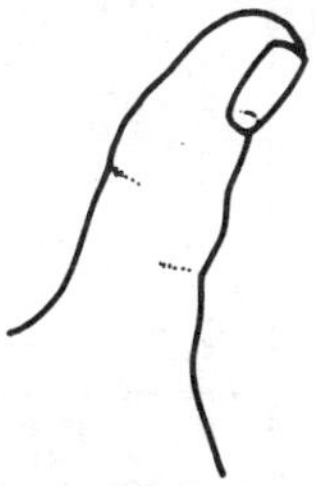

6. 

Name

UNIT 18

Review: Units 13–17

Bonus Words

A. Write a word from the box that goes with each word.

1. hill	**2.** swings
3. win	**4.** sun
5. grin	**6.** loud
7. candy	**8.** pray
9. ball	**10.** right
11. around	**12.** dirt
13. race	**14.** loaf

B. Listen for the sound at the end of the picture name. Write the words that have the letters that make that sound.

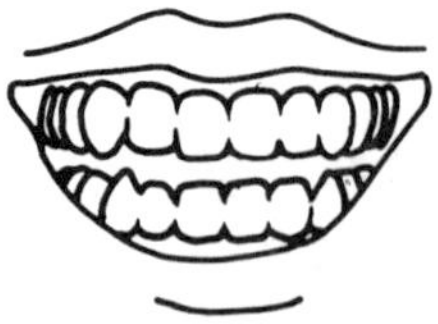

UNIT 13	UNIT 14	UNIT 15	UNIT 16	UNIT 17
stare	grand	crash	bother	wrong
steep	track	earth	catch	between
stick	smile	path	together	listen
dust	bread	shine	church	family
trust	sweet	shout	weather	laugh
playground	prize	thumb	kitchen	thought

Name

Extra Practice

This Week's Words

Write This Week's Words in ABC order. Start by writing ate in the first blank. Two of This Week's Words begin with the same two letters. Use the third letter in these words to put them in ABC order.

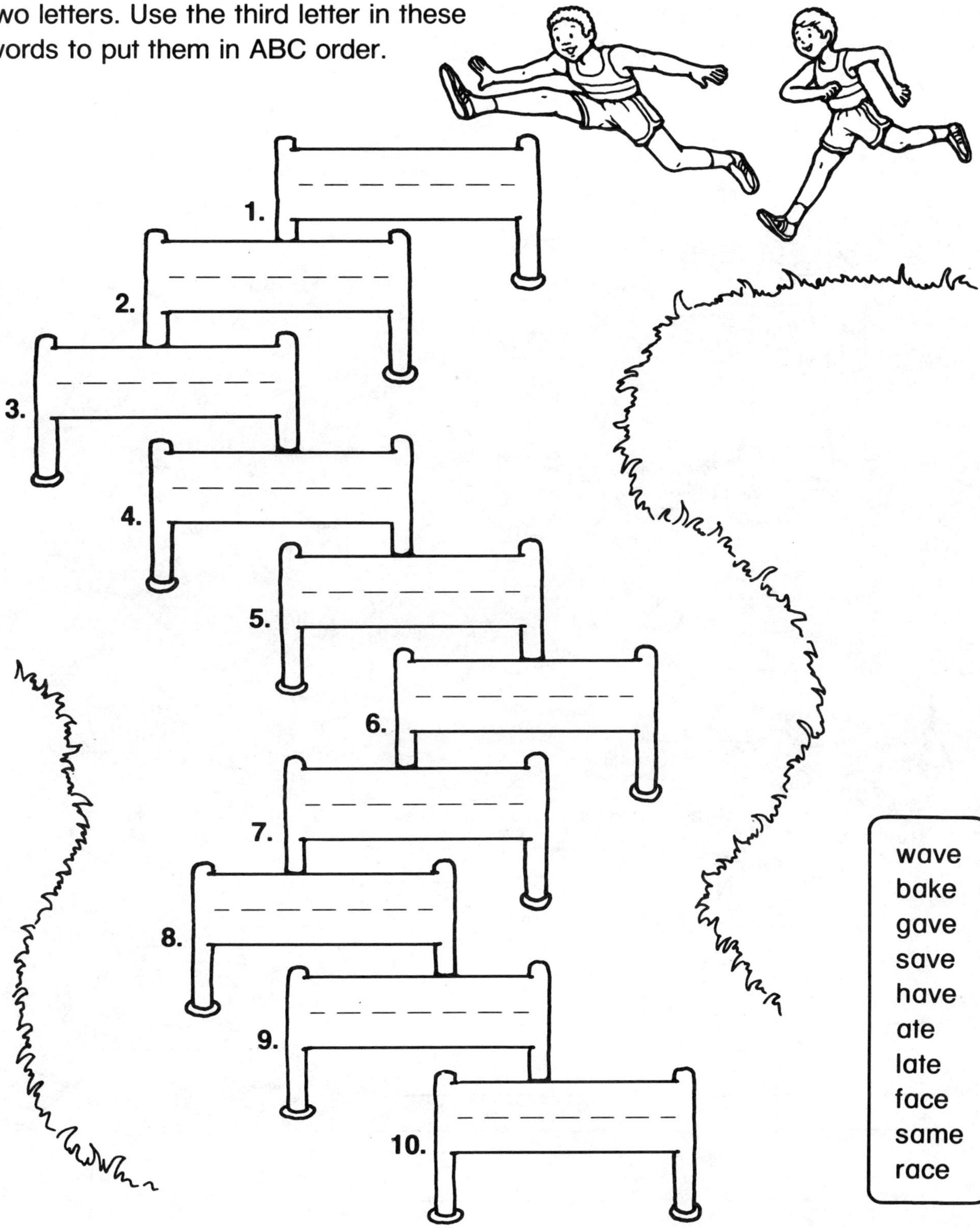

wave
bake
gave
save
have
ate
late
face
same
race

Name

Extra Practice

Mastery Words

UNIT **19**

Help David and Kay get to Sailfish Bay. Use your pencil to go from START to FINISH. When you come to a word that has a long a, as in day, make your line go toward **Y** for yes. Write the word below. If the word does not have long a, make your line go toward **N** for no.

1. ____________

2. ____________

3. ____________

4. ____________

Name

Extra Practice

Bonus Words

A. Choose one consonant or consonant cluster from Box **A** and one word part from Box **B.** Write ten words. Six words are Bonus words. Four words are not. Circle the Bonus words.

A			
sk	br	l	s
	sn	sh	

B	
ate	ake
ave	afe

brave
lake
safe
shake
skate
snake

1. ______ 2. ______ 3. ______
4. ______ 5. ______ 6. ______
7. ______ 8. ______ 9. ______
10. ______

B. Answer each question. Use a Bonus word that rhymes with the underlined name.

11. What kind of boy is Dave? ______

12. What does Kate like to do? ______

13. What kind of pet does Jake have? ______

14. What does Blake do when he is very cold? ______

15. Where does Mr. Drake like to swim? ______

Name

Spelling and Language

UNIT 19

A. Start with the word in dark print. Change or drop one letter each time to make This Week's Words. Write the new words. The • shows you which letter to change first.

wave
ate
bake
face
gave
late
race
same
save
have

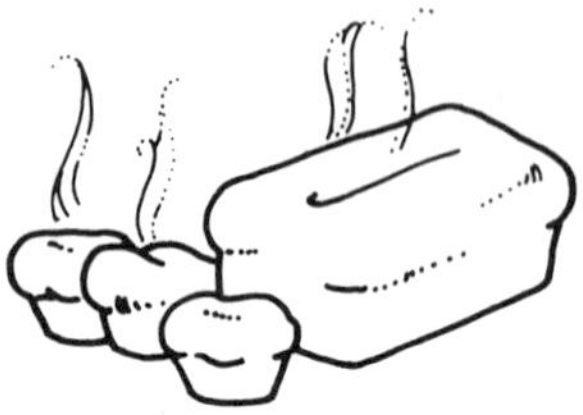

1. **make**

2 **mate**

3. **game**

B. Complete the sentence below. Use words that rhyme.

At the end of the ______,

he was red in the ______.

Name ______________________________

Extra Practice

This Week's Words

UNIT 20

Write This Week's Words where they fit in the puzzles. Some letters are given to help you. Then write the letters that spell /ā/ in the words you used.

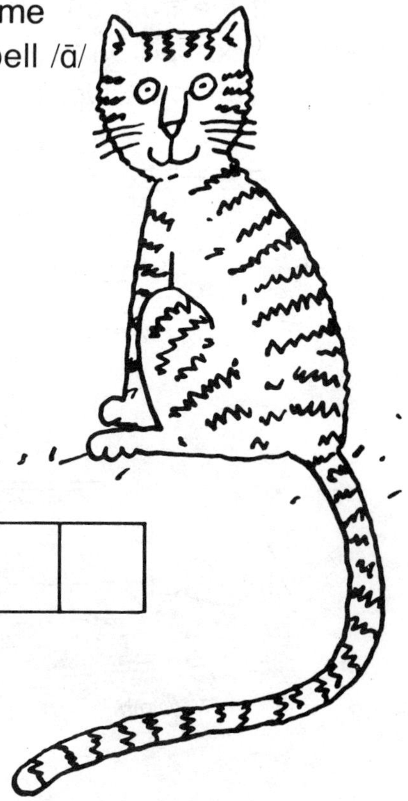

1.

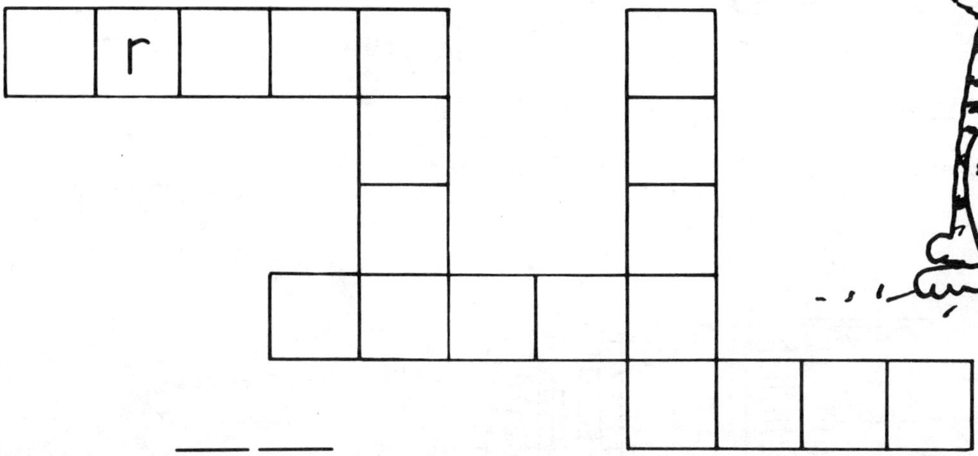

The letters ____ ____ spell /ā/ in these words.

2.

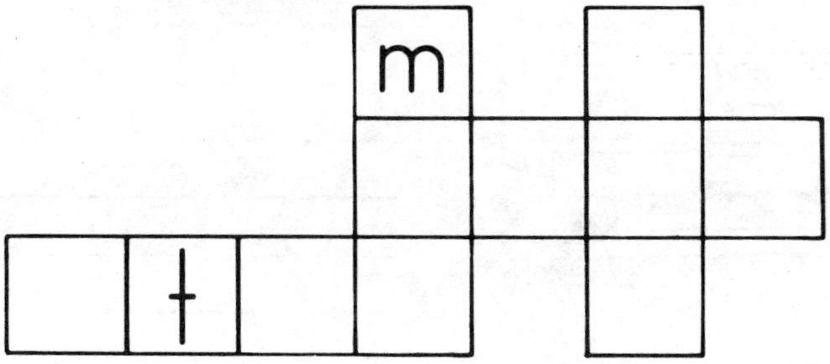

The letters ____ ____ spell /ā/ in these words.

3.

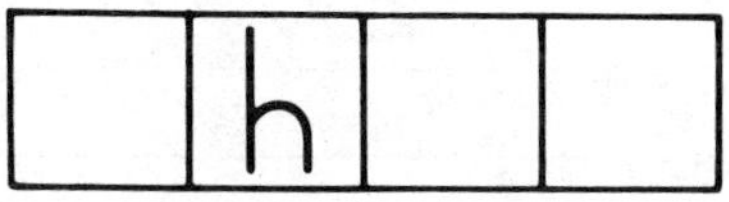

The letters ____ ____ spell /ā/ in this word.

pay
plain
away
nail
they
tail
stay
train
may
paint

Name

Extra Practice

Mastery Words

UNIT 20

Look at the train on each track. Next to the train, write the letters you see on the cars. Then add the letters for long a. Write a Mastery word.

1. 

2. 

3. 

4. 

way	rain	wait	day

Name ______________________

Extra Practice

Bonus Words

UNIT **20**

A. Write the Bonus words where they fit in ABC order.

______	**made**	**sail**
brave	**make**	______
______	______	**tail**
day	**nail**	**they**
______	**name**	______

B. Two words are spelled wrong in each sentence. Also, two other things are missing. Write the sentences correctly.

we were afrayd to hike on that trale

____

maybee we can make a horse with klay

____

it rained for ate days straght

____

clay maybe trail eight afraid straight

Name

Spelling and Language

UNIT 20

train
nail
paint
plain
tail
away
may
pay
stay
they

A. Add ing or ed to one of the words in the box to complete each sentence.

nail	paint	pay
stay	train	

1. Dad is __________ workers to fix up our house.
2. First, the workers __________ up new boards.
3. Then they __________ the house.
4. While they worked, we __________ with friends.
5. Now, Mom is __________ flowers to grow by the door.

B. Write two sentences about the picture below. Use words from the list.

Name

Extra Practice

This Week's Words

UNIT 21

Add the letters that spell /ē/ to these consonants. Finish This Week's Words. Write the whole word.

1. str _ _ t
2. f _ _ l
3. l _ _ ve
4. thr _ _
5. m _ _ n
6. man _
7. t _ _ ch
8. fr _ _
9. d _ _ p
10. _ _ sy

street	easy	deep	mean	many
feel	teach	three	free	leave

Name

Extra Practice

Mastery Words

UNIT **21**

A. The shapes in the box stand for letters. Write the right letter under each shape. Write the Mastery words.

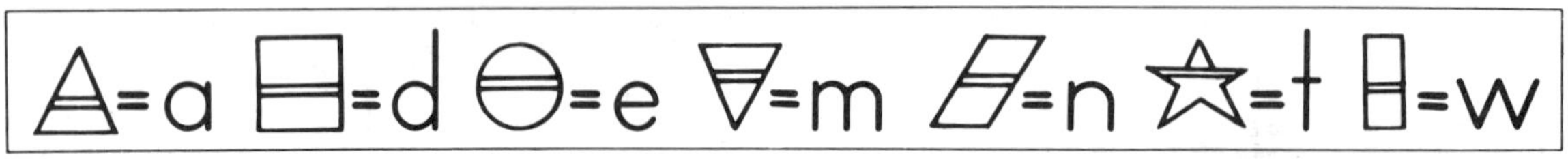

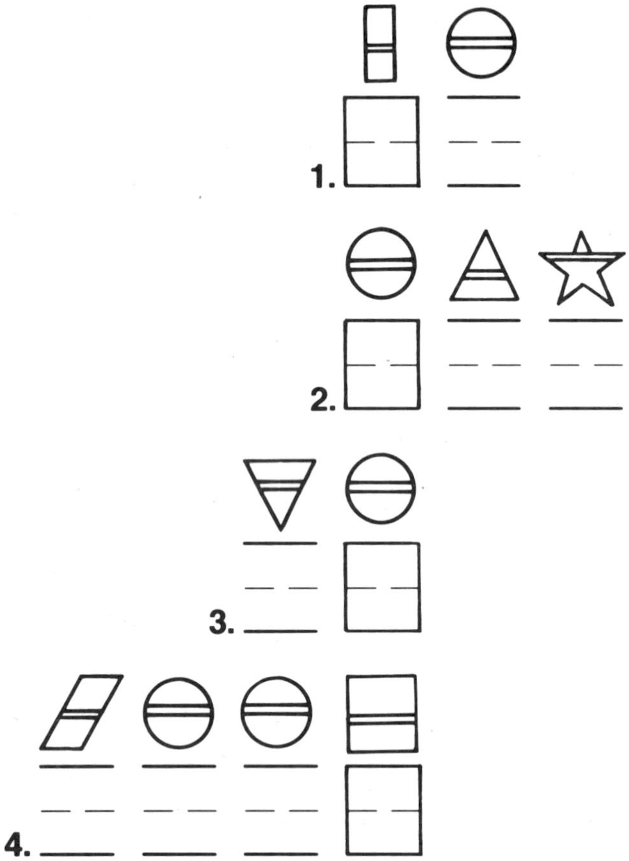

B. Danny saw something growing near the rosebush. He pulled it out of the ground. What was it? Find the letters you wrote in boxes above. Write them in the same order to spell the word.

____

Danny pulled out a ______________.

eat	need	we	me

Name

Extra Practice

Bonus Words UNIT **21**

A. Finish the puzzle. Use the Bonus words. The words go across and down.

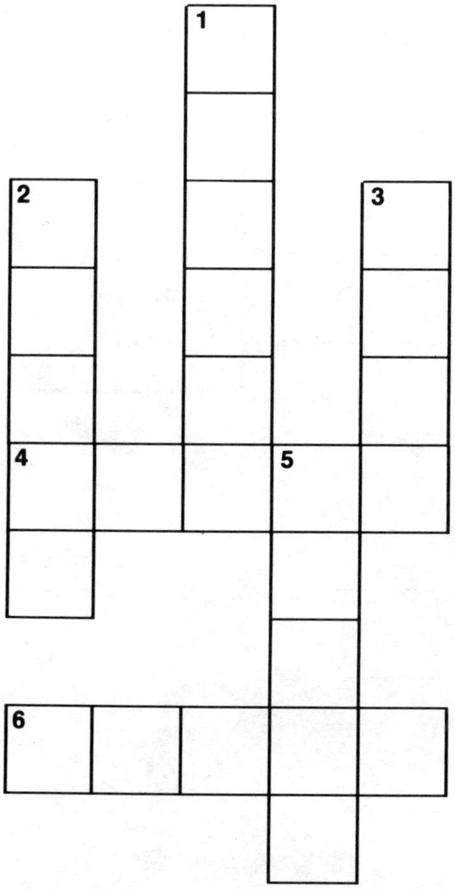

ACROSS

4. A box with nothing inside is ____.

6. You often have this when you are sleeping.

DOWN

1. What you are in the middle of the night.

2. The space on each side of your face.

3. What you are when you have a lot to do.

5. A special snack, such as a juice bar.

B. Each of these words has /ē/. See how /ē/ is spelled in each word. Write each Bonus word under the word that has /ē/ spelled the same way.

three	happy	seals

asleep busy cheek dream empty treat

Name

Spelling and Language

UNIT 21

Read each sentence. Replace the underlined words with one of This Week's Words. Write the new sentence.

deep
feel
free
street
three
mean
leave
teach
many
easy

1. There are more than two and less than four free kittens on my street.

2. A lot of people leave town on Saturday.

3. It is not hard to teach someone that game.

4. She was not nice to push him in the deep puddle.

Name

Extra Practice

This Week's Words

UNIT 22

A. Find the nine words that have long i. Write each word as you find it. Then use your pencil to fill in the space around each word with long i.

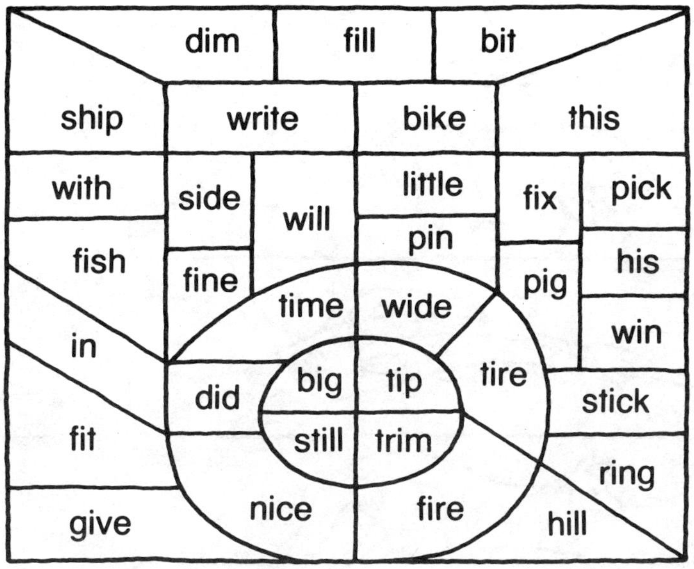

B. Finish the question with one of This Week's Words. Then use what you found in the puzzle to help you write the answer.

Andy had ten pencils. He gave half of them to Missy.

How many pencils did he ________ her?

nice	fire
side	tire
wide	bike
time	write
fine	give

Name

Extra Practice

Mastery Words

UNIT 22

A. Drop the first letter in each word. Put the first letter in the picture word in its place. Write a Mastery word.

1. hike

2. side

3. live

4. bite

B. Now drop the underlined letter in each word. Put the first letter in the picture word in its place. Write a Mastery word.

5. rice

6. fine

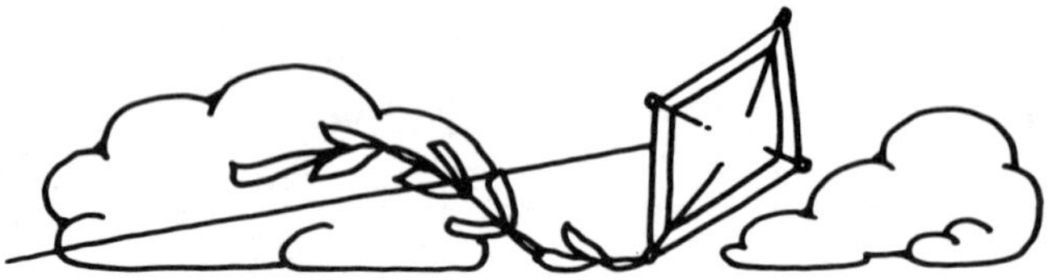

7. line

five	kite	like	ride

Name ______________________________

Extra Practice

Bonus Words

UNIT 22

A. Finish each second sentence with a Bonus word.

1. Steve's bat is not in the house.

He must have left it ____________.

2. I'm tired of the swings.

Let's play on the ____________.

3. Grandpa knows many things.

He is very ____________.

4. We ran behind the bushes.

We wanted to ____________ from Gail and Rory.

5. Mom washed my jeans two times. She had to wash them ____________ because they were very dirty.

6. Callie was born in Garfield.

She has lived here all her ____________.

hide
life
outside
slide
twice
wise

Harcourt Brace School Publishers

B. Write the words that go with these words.

7. ____________ and seek

8. slip and ____________

9. once or ____________

Name

Spelling and Language

UNIT 22

Circle the group of words that is in ABC order. Then write the words.

1. fire	fire	side
bike	give	tire
give	time	give

2. tire	nice	bike
bike	bike	fine
wide	wide	side

3. nice	tire	nice
tire	wide	tire
wide	nice	write
write	write	wide

write
bike
fine
fire
nice
side
time
tire
wide
give

Name ______________________

Extra Practice

This Week's Words

UNIT 23

A. Here are This Week's Words. But the letters that spell long i are missing. Match the shape in each word to a shape in the box. Replace the shape with the letter or letters that spell long i. Write the word.

y ★	**i** ●	**igh** ▲	**ie** ■

1. h▲ ______________
2. tr★ ______________
3. k●nd ______________
4. sk★ ______________
5. r▲t ______________
6. t■ ______________
7. f●nd ______________
8. dr★ ______________
9. n▲t ______________
10. wh★ ______________

B. Now use the shapes again. Write some new words.

11. br▲t ______________
12. l■ ______________
13. m●nd ______________
14. fr▲ten ______________

sky	dry	try	why	find
kind	high	night	right	tie

Name

Extra Practice

Mastery Words UNIT **23**

Finish the sentences. Use the Mastery words.

1. Today ________ am eight.

2. This is ________ kitten, Fluffy.

3. How high will the kite ________?

4. That book is ________ my uncle.

5. ________ will go with you to the store.

6. Do you hear the ________ buzzing?

7. ________ think ________ left ________ umbrella on the bus.

8. Meet us ________ the big tree.

I	fly	my	by

Name

Extra Practice

Bonus Words

UNIT 23

A. Write the Bonus words in ABC order. Then write the words in the puzzle. Write each word after the right number.

1. ______
2. ______
3. ______
4. ______
5. ______
6. ______

B. Add the letters for long i. Write the Bonus words.

7. sh ___ ______
8. fr ___ ten ______
9. t ___ ger ______
10. l ___ on ______
11. s ___ t ______
12. m ___ self ______

shy	lion	tiger
frighten	sight	myself

Harcourt Brace School Publishers

Name

Spelling and Language

UNIT 23

Read each sentence. In place of the underlined word, use a word that means the opposite. Write the sentence using the new word.

sky
dry
try
why
find
kind
high
night
right
tie

1. The bird flies high in the ground.

2. It is dark at day.

3. Why can't I lose my tie?

4. She was kind to give you the wrong time.

5. Try to stay wet.

Name

UNIT 24

Review A: Units 19–20

A. UNIT 19 Change the underlined letter to make a word from Unit 19. Write the word.

1. sa<u>v</u>e ______
2. <u>g</u>ave ______
3. <u>l</u>ace ______
4. a<u>p</u>e ______
5. la<u>m</u>e ______

UNIT 19
ate
same
have
face
late
UNIT 20
train
away
they
tail
stay

B. UNIT 20 Choose the correct spellings and finish the sentences.

6. We met my aunt and uncle when ______ (**thay** / **they**) came to visit.

7. The ______ (**trane** / **train**) looked like a snake with a long ______ (**tail** / **tayl**).

8. Mom told us to ______ (**stay** / **stai**) ______ (**awae** / **away**) from the train tracks.

Name ______

Review B: Units 21–22

UNIT 24

UNIT 21
three
leave
many
street
easy
UNIT 22
time
write
give
fire
wide

A. UNIT 21 Finish the rhyming lines for each poem. Use words from Unit 21.

1. Jim said, "Let's buy a treat

   At that store down the ______!"

   I said, "Have you a penny?"

   He said, "Yes, I have ______."

   Then he gave some to me

   'Cause I only had ______.

2. It's not always ______

   When you're feeling sneezy.

   Sometimes I believe

   It's best to just ______.

B. UNIT 22 Put each group of letters in the right order to make a word from Unit 22. Write the word.

3. wrtie ______
4. iwde ______
5. itme ______
6. egvi ______
7. eirf ______

Name ______________________________

UNIT 24

Review C: Unit 23 • Test Exercise

UNIT 23
kind
right
why
sky
night

A. UNIT 23 Follow the directions. Use words from Unit 23.

1. Write the word that asks a question. ______________
2. Write the word that means the opposite of each word.

   wrong ______________ mean ______________
3. Write two words that tell about the picture.

______________ ______________

B. UNITS 19–23 Fill in the circle below the word that is spelled correctly.

	a	b	c	d
1	streat	strete	street	streete
2	nigt	night	nite	nihte
3	rite	wite	writ	write
4	trane	trayn	train	traine
5	late	lait	layte	laite
6	kinde	kind	kynd	kiend
7	leve	leeve	leav	leave
8	fire	fier	fyre	fyer
9	wye	whye	why	whigh

Name

Language Study

UNIT 24

A. Read each sentence. Write a word that means the opposite of each underlined word.

same
late
tail
stay
deep
many
easy
give
fire
wide
sky
kind
night
tie

1. The kitten's <u>head</u> was in the dish. ____________

2. It is not <u>hard</u> to ride a bike well. ____________

3. We cooked the fish over the <u>water</u>. ____________

4. Hurry up, or you will be <u>early</u> for the bus. ____________

B. Write the opposite of each word.

5. different ___ ___ (○) ___

6. go ___ ___ (○) ___

7. mean ___ ___ (○) ___

8. earth ___ ___ (○)

Now use the letters you wrote in the circles to finish this sentence.

The opposite of <u>few</u> is ____________.

Name

Review: Units 19–23

Mastery Words

UNIT 24

A. Write the word that names the picture. Then write one more word that spells the long vowel sound the same way.

1. 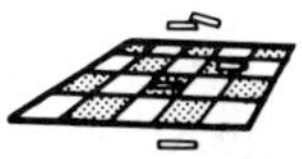

2. 

3. 

4. 

5. 

6. 

UNIT 19
cake game made make
UNIT 20
rain wait day way
UNIT 21
eat me need we
UNIT 22
five kite like ride
UNIT 23
I fly my by

B. Finish the sentence. Use words you did not write above. Use the vowel sounds to help you.

(/ī/) ______ (/ē/) ______ to

(/ē/) ______ three times a day.

Name ______________________________

Review: Units 19–23

Bonus Words

UNIT 24

Write the words that will finish each sentence. Use the vowel sounds to help you.

1. It is not /ā/ ____________ to /ā/ ____________ on the /ā/ ____________.

2. The boy climbed /ā/ ____________ up the /ā/ ____________ -mile /ā/ ____________.

3. After a /ē/ ____________ day, the girl fell /ē/ ____________ and began to /ē/ ____________.

4. The cat went /ī/ ____________ to /ī/ ____________ under the /ī/ ____________.

5. Did the people /ī/ ____________ the /ī/ ____________ /ī/ ____________?

UNIT 19
- brave
- lake
- safe
- shake
- skate
- snake

UNIT 20
- afraid
- trail
- clay
- maybe
- straight
- eight

UNIT 21
- asleep
- busy
- cheek
- dream
- empty
- treat

UNIT 22
- hide
- life
- outside
- slide
- twice
- wise

UNIT 23
- frighten
- lion
- myself
- shy
- sight
- tiger

Name

Extra Practice

This Week's Words | **UNIT 25**

A. Help Pokey look for the bones. Under each bone is a clue. Write the word that fits the clue.

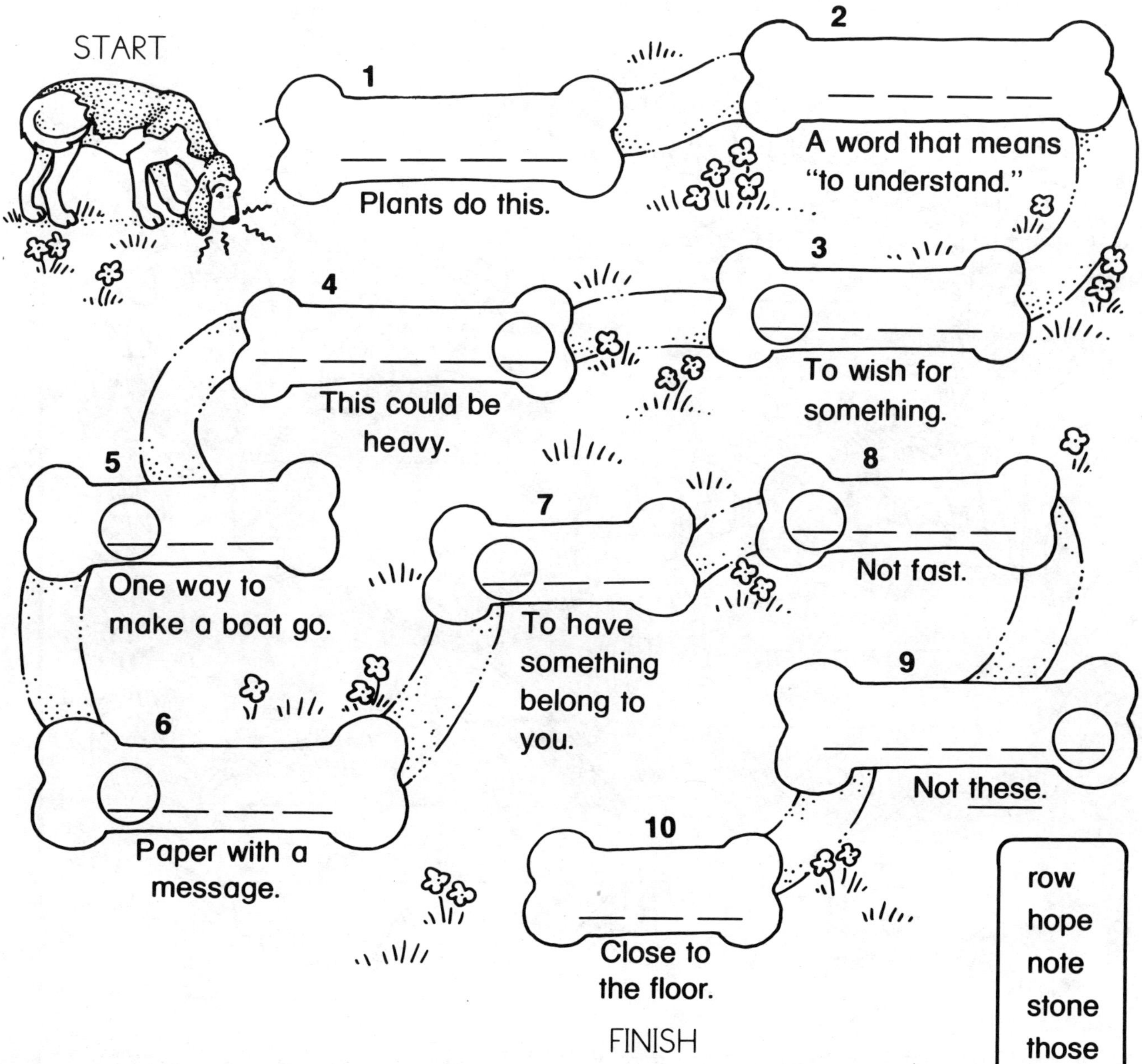

row
hope
note
stone
those
grow
know
low
slow
own

B. What did Pokey follow to find the bones? Write the circled letters in order. You will write two words.

Name

Extra Practice

Mastery Words

UNIT 25

A. Rose found four big stones on her walk. Each stone had a letter on it. Help Rose solve the puzzle. Find the Mastery word to which each of the letters belongs. Write the words in the blanks.

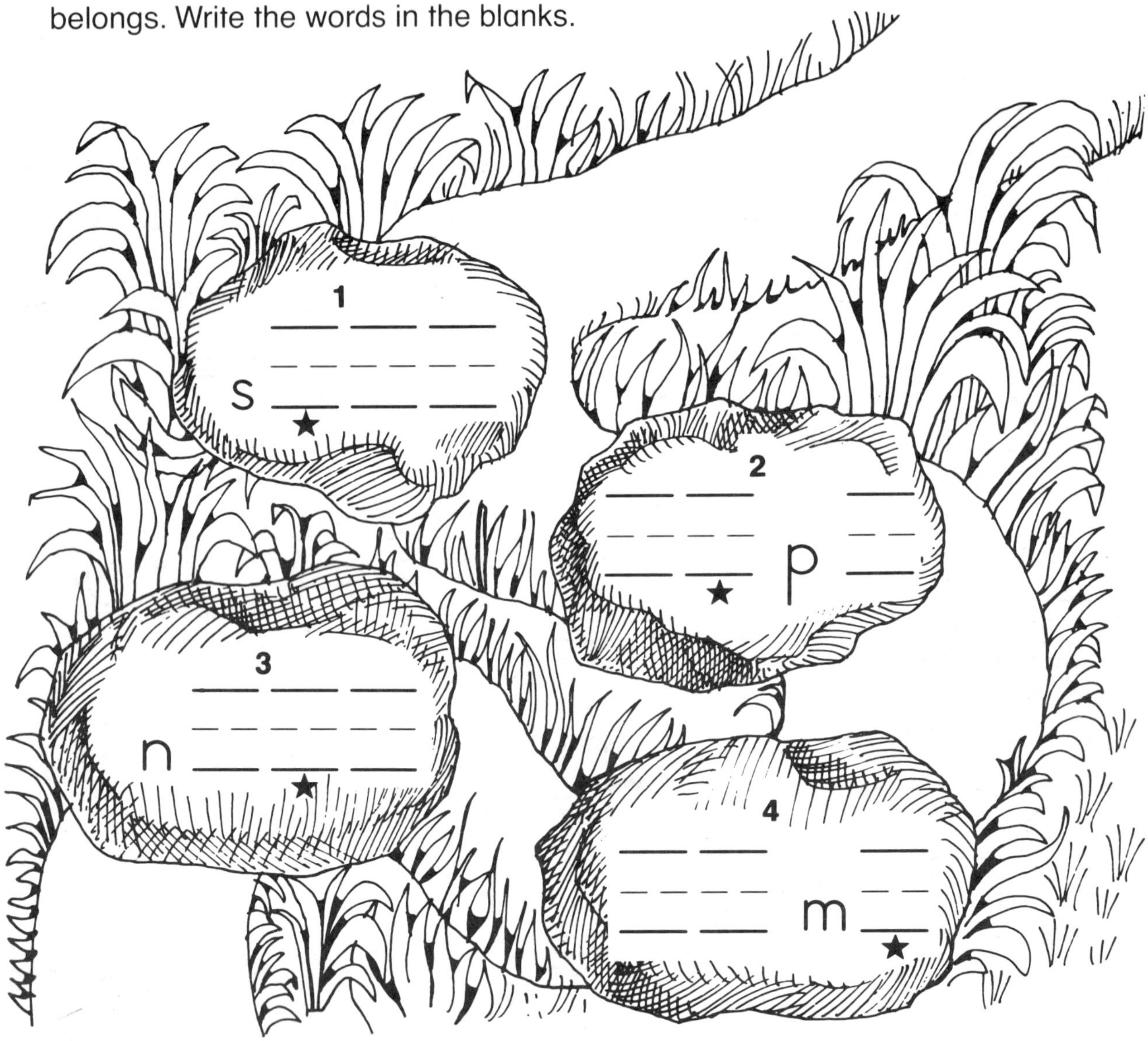

B. What else did Rose see in the garden? To find out, write the letters that have stars under them. Write them in number order.

She saw a garden ____________.

home
nose
rope
show

Name

UNIT 25

Extra Practice

Bonus Words

A. Which word goes with each sentence? Write the Bonus word.

1. You cook on it in the kitchen.
2. You can do this with a ball.
3. You look through this to see outside.
4. You did this if you said something.
5. You did this if you were asleep but you aren't asleep now.
6. You do this if you are not the leader.

woke
throw
window
stove
follow
spoke

B. Add letters to these words. The numbers show you where to put the letters and how many to add. Write Bonus words.

7. win (3)
8. (3) low
9. (1) poke
10. (2) row

C. Add the letters below to this letter pattern: s_o_e. Write two Bonus words and two new words.

11. t v
12. m k
13. p k
14. t l

Name

UNIT 25

Spelling and Language

A. Read the sentences. Write the missing words on the lines. Add s or ing if it is needed.

Dinah __1__ about plants. She __2__ cactus in her __3__ garden.

The boat is too __4__. But __5__ boys are __6__ as fast as they can.

1. ____ ____ (◯) ____ ____

2. ____ ____ ____ (◯) ____

3. ____ ____ ____ (◯) ____

4. ____ (◯) ____ ____

5. ____ ____ (◯) ____ ____

6. ____ ____ (◯) ____ ____ ____

B. Look at the letters you wrote inside the circles. They spell two of This Week's Words. Use each word to finish these sentences. Use s or ing if it is needed.

7. Teddi likes ______________ her own bike.

8. A ______________ tree branch makes a good swing.

row hope note stone those grow know low slow own

Name

Extra Practice

This Week's Words

UNIT 26

A. The word on each bowl of oatmeal has one or two letters missing. Add the letter or letters that spell /ō/.

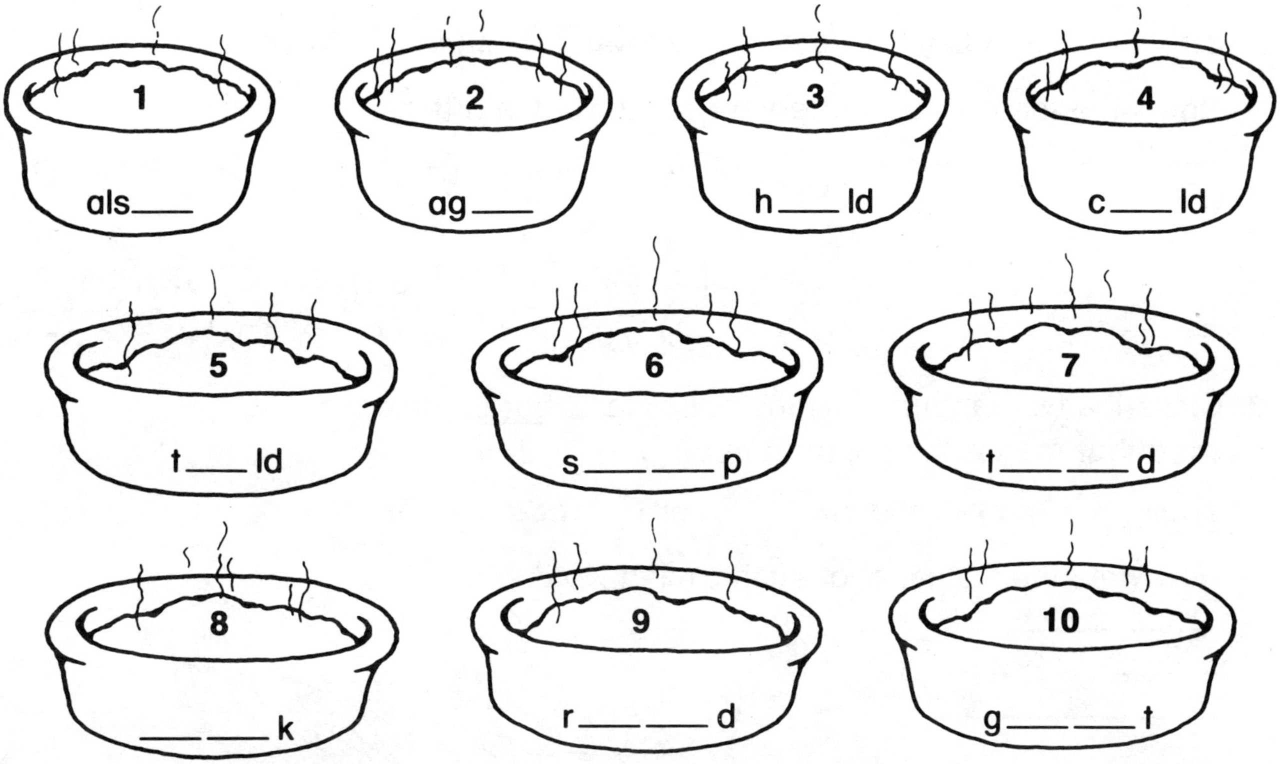

B. Now write the word from each bowl in the same number order. Read the message in the circles to find out what Linda saw on her spelling test.

1
2
3
4
5
6
7
8
9
10

cold
goat
hold
oak
told
road
ago
soap
also
toad

Name

Extra Practice

Mastery Words | **UNIT 26**

Follow the directions. Write Mastery words.

1. Circle the words that name animals.

   dress **monkey** **owl** **sheep** **milk** **tiger**

   Now write the first letter of each circled word in order.

2. Circle the word that means the opposite of <u>hard</u>. Circle the word that means the opposite of <u>off</u>.

   short **soon** **soft** **over** **odd** **on**

   Now write the first letter of each circled word in order.

3. Circle the words that name things to eat.

   berry **oats** **bed** **apple** **rope** **toast**

   Now write the first letter of each circled word in order.

4. Write the first letter of the word for the color of grass. Write the first letter of the word that means the opposite of <u>under</u>.

boat
go
most
so

Name ______

Extra Practice

Bonus Words

UNIT 26

A. The star in each word stands for /ō/. Add the letter or letters that spell /ō/. Write the whole word.

1. r★st ______
2. hell★ ______
3. b★th ______
4. ★tmeal ______
5. fl★t ______
6. t★st ______

B. Finish the sentences. Use the Bonus words.

7. When Pete made breakfast, he burned the ______.
8. Karen saw ______ movies in one day.
9. I say ______ when I answer the phone.
10. Mom put raisins in the ______.
11. Lie on your back and ______ on the water.
12. Should we ______ the meat in the oven?

both
float
hello
oatmeal
roast
toast

C. Put a consonant cluster in place of the underlined letter. Write two Bonus words.

13. roa<u>d</u> ______
14. <u>b</u>oat ______

Name ______________________

Spelling and Language

UNIT **26**

Read the poem. Look for this mark ∧. It shows that a letter needs to be added to the word. Add the missing letter. Then write the word on the line.

A frog, a to∧d (1), and a g∧at (2)
Sailed off in a little red boat.

But the sea was bold
And als∧ (3) c∧ld (4)
When they fell in and had to float.

But very soon after their dip,
An ∧ak (5) branch floated by like a ship.
So they quickly grabbed h∧ld (6)
And, so I am t∧ld (7),
Went merrily on with their trip.

1. ______________________
2. ______________________
3. ______________________
4. ______________________
5. ______________________
6. ______________________
7. ______________________

cold	toad	told	ago	also
goat	oak	road	soap	hold

Name

Extra Practice

This Week's Words

UNIT 27

A. Finish the "word chain." Use This Week's Words. Use each word only once.

```
                              s
s __1__ g                     t r ___ _3_ ___
        o                     i               i
        o                     c               t
        d ___ _2_ ___ k                       t
                                              e
                                   h _4_ n ___
                                   u
                         r __5__ g
                         u
                         s
                     ___ h ___ _6_ ___
     b               e
     a ___ _7_ n ___
     l
     l __8__ g
              r                   b ___ _10_ ___
              a                   a
              y ___ _9_ ___ g
```

B. Finish the message. Use words from the puzzle.

"I ______ (6) the ______ (5)

is in the ______ (3)," said Ada. "It has been

here a ______ (8) time."

long
trunk
along
hang
ring
young
bank
drink
think
sing

Name

Extra Practice

Mastery Words

UNIT 27

A. Find the Mastery words in the puzzle. The words go across and down. Circle the words you find.

r	g	b	a	n	d	p	l
k	m	x	l	s	q	z	i
y	e	i	o	a	j	o	n
j	n	h	w	e	n	t	x

B. Finish the sentences with Mastery words. Write each Mastery word in the boxes next to the right number.

1. Joanne plays in the ___.
2. There are nine ___ on the team.
3. Britt lives ___ Summer Street.
4. Dad and Ricky ___ to the store.

1 ☐☐☐☐

2 ☐☐☐

3 ☐☐

4 ☐☐☐☐

C. Now look at the words you wrote in the boxes. They make a word going down. Circle the word. Then write it here.

____

on	went	band	men

Name

Extra Practice

Bonus Words

UNIT 27

A. Use the Bonus words to finish the puzzle. Some letters are given to help you. Begin by writing the picture word.

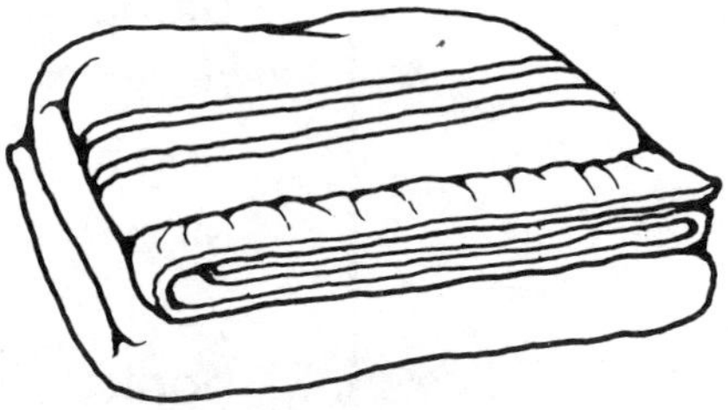

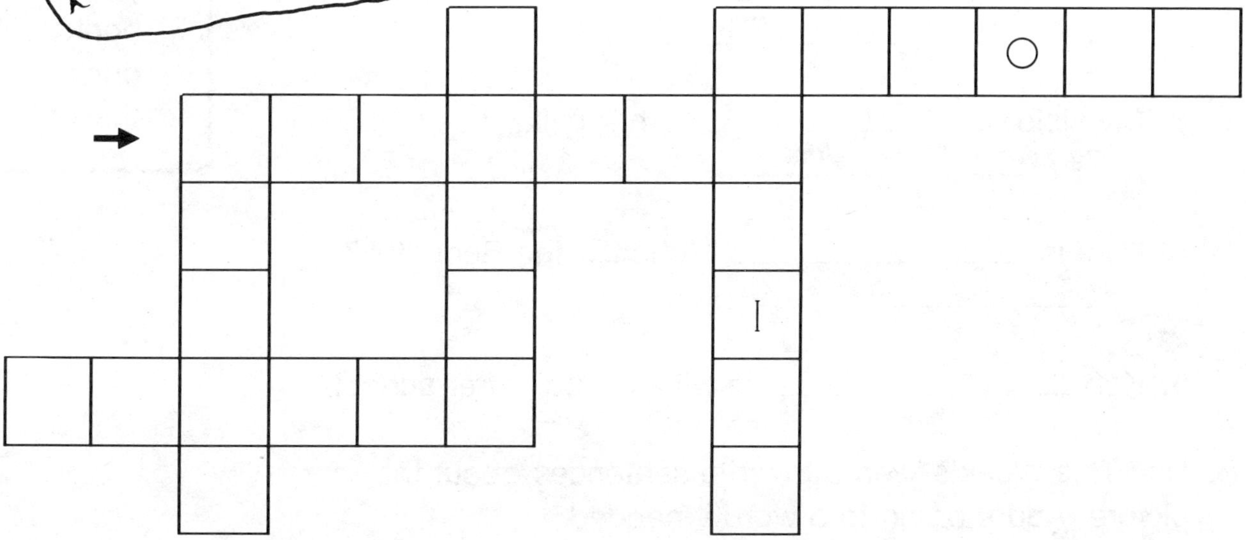

B. Follow the directions. Use Bonus words.

1. Write the word that rhymes.

bring ____________ wink ____________

2. Write the word that means the same.

mad ____________ cover ____________

starved ____________ powerful ____________

angry	blink	strong	blanket	string	hungry

Name

Spelling and Language

UNIT 27

long
trunk
along
hang
ring
sing
young
bank
drink
think

A. Add s or ing to the word below the line. Make a word to fit the sentences.

1. The school bell is ______________.
   ring

2. The bird feeder ______________ in the tree.
   hang

3. My sister is ______________ her milk.
   drink

4. Pam is ______________ "America the Beautiful."
   sing

5. Ken ______________ he will play ball after school.
   think

B. Use This Week's Words to write sentences about the picture. Add s or ing to a word if needed.

Name

Extra Practice

This Week's Words

UNIT **28**

The pictures stand for consonant letters. Look at each picture and write the letter it stands for. Then add the letter or letters that spell /o͞o/. Write This Week's Words. Use each word once.

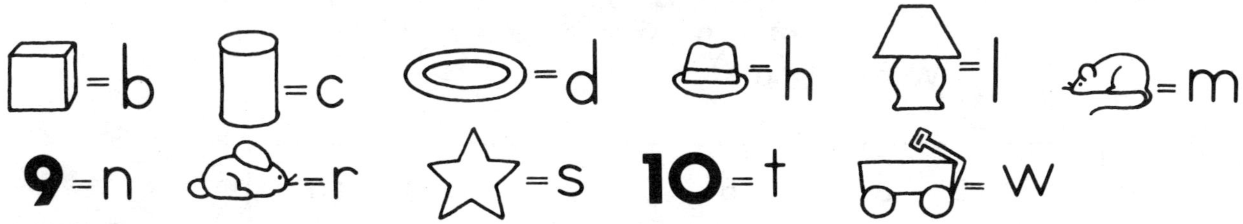

1. 

2. 

3. 

4. 10 

5.  10

6. 

7. 10

8. 10

9. 

10. 9

two	who
new	too
boot	room
to	school
do	blew

Name ______________________

Extra Practice

Mastery Words

UNIT **28**

A. Use the number code to write Mastery words. Match the numbers with the letters. Here is an example to help you.

Word in number code: **2 5 8**

2 = **h** **5** = **o** **8** = **t**

Word: hot

1	2	3	4	5	6	7	8	9	10
e	h	l	n	o	r	s	t	u	y

7 5 5 4

1. ______________________

8 6 9 1

2. ______________________

10 5 9

3. ______________________

7 2 5 1

4. ______________________

B. Now finish the sentence with the words you wrote in **A.** The number under each line tells you which word to write.

I'm sure it's ______________ that ______________
2 3

will ______________ find a
1

______________ that fits.
4

shoe
true
soon
you

Name ______________________

Extra Practice

Bonus Words | **UNIT 28**

A. Finish the puzzle. Use the Bonus words. The words go across and down.

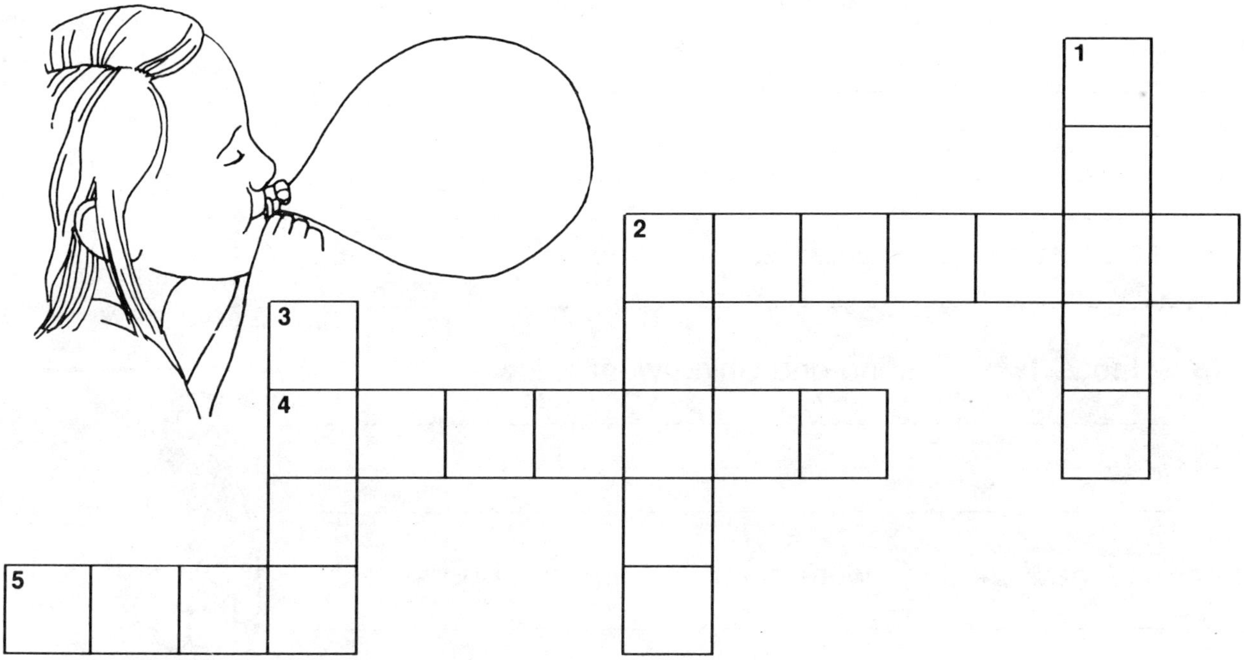

ACROSS

2. Fill it up with air.
4. This animal washes its food.
5. How the bird got from here to there.

DOWN

1. Use it to eat your soup.
2. Use it to sweep the floor.
3. If you are taller than you were, you ___.

B. Use Bonus words to finish the answers.

balloon
broom
flew
grew
raccoon
spoon

6. Where did the bird fly?

It ____________ up to the roof.

7. When did Pinocchio's nose grow?

It ____________ when he told a lie.

Name

Spelling and Language

UNIT 28

Read each sentence. Find the word in dark print that fits in the sentence. Then write the sentence with that word.

two
new
boot
to
do
who
too
room
school
blew

1. **to too two** Jane went ___ the ball game after school.

2. **to too two** Mina and Chico went, ___.

3. **knew new** Jane wore her ___ coat and boots.

4. **to too two** Mina wore ___ scarves.

5. **blew blue** But the wind ___ so hard, they left early.

Name

Extra Practice

This Week's Words

UNIT 29

Each book has all the letters for a word except the letters that spell /o͝o/. Add the letter or letters that spell /o͝o/. Then write the whole word next to the right number below.

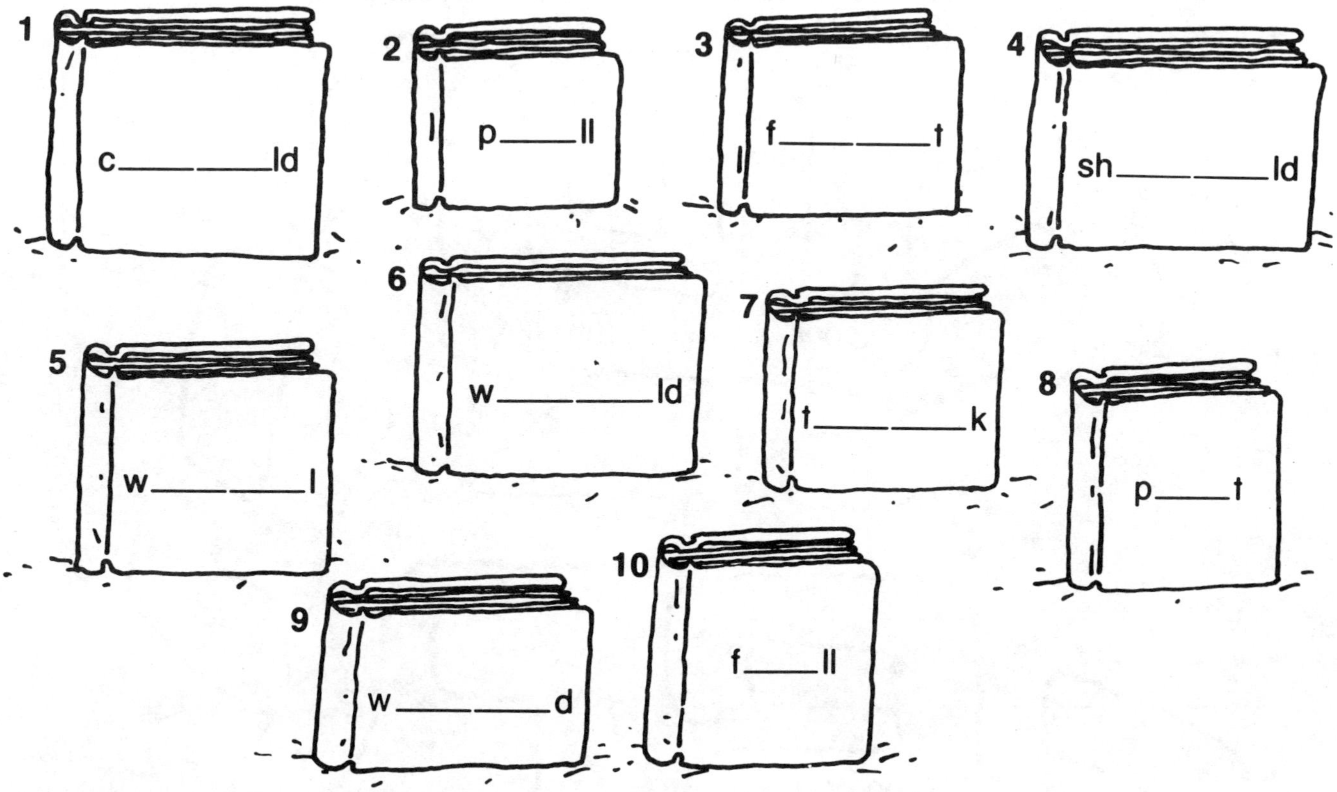

1. ____________________ 2. ____________________

3. ____________________ 4. ____________________

5. ____________________ 6. ____________________

7. ____________________ 8. ____________________

9. ____________________ 10. ____________________

wool
foot
took
wood
full
pull
put
could
should
would

Name

UNIT 29

Extra Practice

Mastery Words

Use your pencil to draw a line from START to FINISH in the puzzle. When you come to a word that has the sound /o͝o/, as in foot, make your line go toward **Y** for yes. Write the word below. If the word does not have the sound /o͝o/, make your line go toward **N** for no.

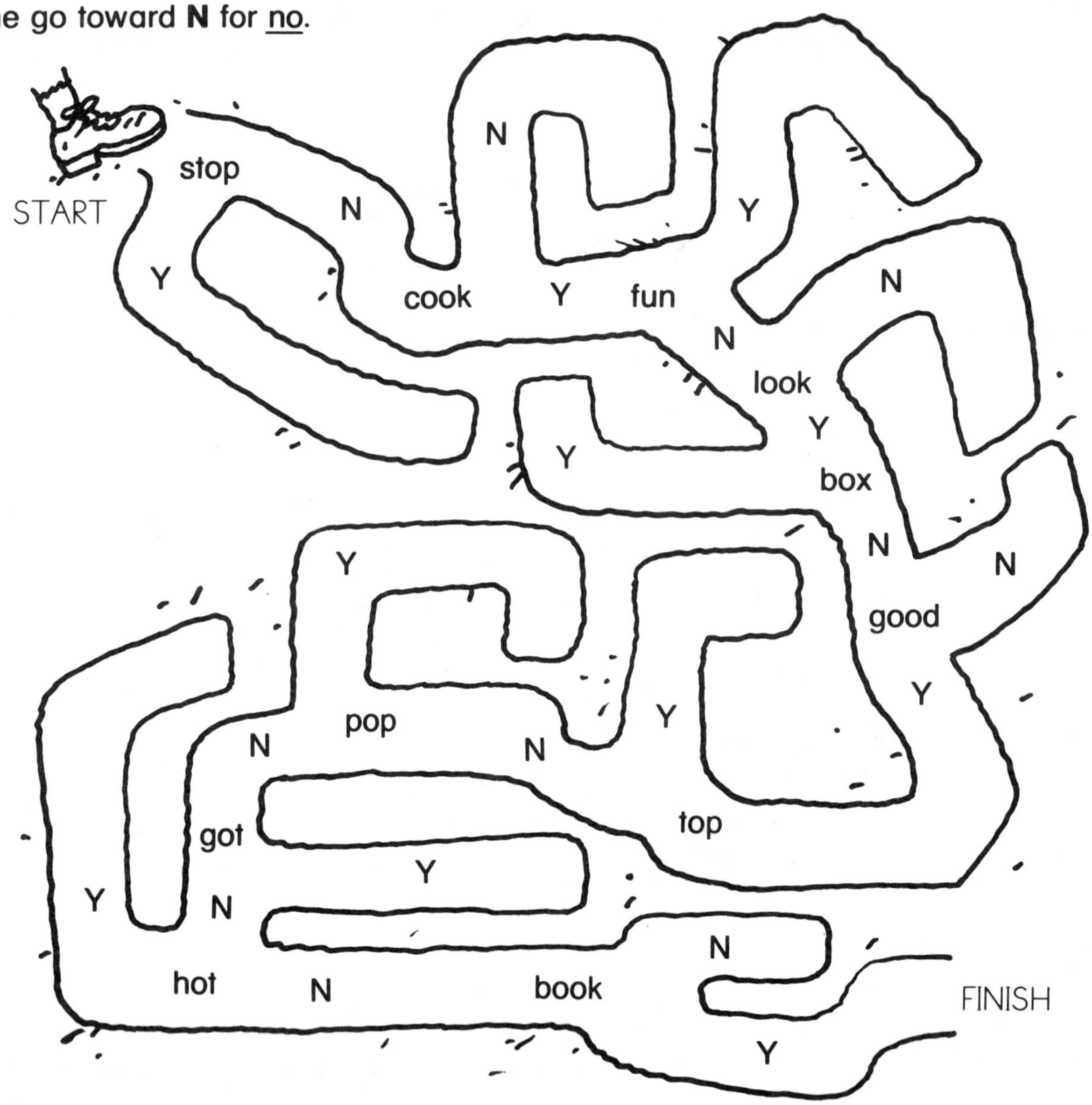

1. ______________ 2. ______________

3. ______________ 4. ______________

Name

Extra Practice

Bonus Words

UNIT 29

A. Each number stands for the letter under it. Read the sentences. Write a letter for each number and spell a Bonus word.

1 **a**	2 **b**	3 **c**	4 **d**	5 **e**	6 **f**	7 **g**	8 **h**	9 **i**	10 **j**	11 **k**	12 **l**	13 **m**
14 **n**	15 **o**	16 **p**	17 **q**	18 **r**	19 **s**	20 **t**	21 **u**	22 **v**	23 **w**	24 **x**	25 **y**	26 **z**

1. We had a picnic near a 2 18 15 15 11. ______
2. A large willow tree 19 20 15 15 4 near the shore. ______
3. Jimmy brought his 2 21 12 12 4 15 7 with him. ______
4. Kerry saw something move in the 2 21 19 8 5 19. ______
5. Jimmy's dog barked and 19 8 15 15 11 its tail. ______
6. It was Gina in the bushes. She was looking for her 6 15 15 20 2 1 12 12. ______

B. Put the picture words together. Write two Bonus words.

7. 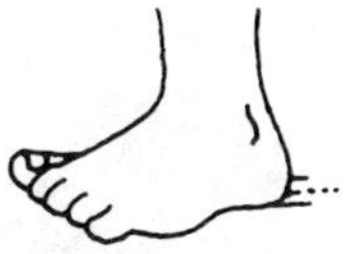 +  = ______

8.  +  = ______

brook	bulldog	bushes	football	shook	stood

Name

UNIT 29

Spelling and Language

Write each group of letters in ABC order. You may need to look at the second or third letter.

pull
full
put
foot
took
wood
wool
could
should
would

1. put
   foot
   pull

2. took
   would
   wool

3. full
   could
   foot

4. wood
   should
   would

5. took
   pull
   foot
   should

6. full
   could
   wood
   put

Name

Review A: Units 25–26

UNIT 30

A. UNIT 25 Read what is being said in each picture. Write the missing word or words. Use a word from Unit 25.

1.

2.

3.

4.

UNIT 25

- grow
- know
- those
- slow
- note

B. UNIT 26 Read each word. Then write the word or words from Unit 26 that spell /ō/ the same way.

5. ago

6. gold

7. boat

UNIT 26

- told
- also
- soap
- cold
- road

Name ______

Review B: Units 27–28

UNIT 30

UNIT 27
along
think
young
sing
drink
UNIT 28
who
school
new
do
room

A. UNIT 27 Make a word from Unit 27. First unscramble each group of letters. Then add ng or nk. Write the word.

1. ouy__ __ ______
2. idr__ __ ______
3. is__ __ ______
4. oal__ __ ______
5. ith__ __ ______

B. UNIT 28 Choose the correct spelling and finish each sentence. Use words from Unit 28.

6. Amy is going to a ______ (**noo** / **new**) ______ (**schewl** / **school**) this year.
7. She wonders ______ (**woo** / **who**) her teacher will be.
8. She will be in Mrs. Fong's class in ______ (**room** / **rom**) 6.
9. How ______ (**do** / **due**) you think she will like her new school?

Harcourt Brace School Publishers

Name ______________________________

UNIT 30

Review C: Unit 29 • Test Exercise

A. UNIT 29 Add the letter or letters that spell the vowel sound /ŏŏ/ in each word. Write words from Unit 29.

UNIT 29
took
pull
could
would
put

1. w ___ ___ ld ______________

2. p ___ t ______________

3. p ___ ll ______________

4. t ___ ___ k ______________

5. c ___ ___ ld ______________

B. UNITS 25–29 Fill in the circle below the word that is spelled correctly.

1 cud (a) coud (b) could (c)

2 those (a) thos (b) thoze (c)

3 alon (a) allong (b) along (c)

4 sope (a) soap (b) solp (c)

5 yung (a) youn (b) young (c)

6 took (a) tuc (b) tuk (c)

7 aslo (a) alsoe (b) also (c)

8 skool (a) scool (b) school (c)

Name

Language Study

UNIT 30

Two words in each sentence are spelled wrong. Find the words and circle them. Then write each sentence again. Spell all the words correctly.

grow
those
note
told
soap
cold
road
along
think
young
sing
drink
who
school
new
room
took
would
put

1. Would you water thos flowers to make them groe?

2. Let's seng as we walk along the rode.

3. What rom are you in at sckool?

4. I tuke the dish and poot it on the table.

Name

Review: Units 25–29

Mastery Words

UNIT 30

UNIT 25
home nose rope show
UNIT 26
boat go most so
UNIT 27
band men on went
UNIT 28
soon shoe true you
UNIT 29
book cook good look

A. Write a Mastery word to go with each picture. Then write other words that spell the vowel sound the same way.

1. 

2. 

3. 

B. Write the Mastery word that means the opposite of each word.

4. stop

5. off

6. hide

7. false

8. few

9. me

10. later

Harcourt Brace School Publishers

Name ______________________________

Review: Units 25–29

Bonus Words

UNIT 30

Follow the directions. Use Bonus words.

1. Write the words that show that the following actions have already happened.

speak ______ wake ______ shake ______

2. Write the words that mean the opposite of these words.

sink ______ weak ______

lead ______ goodbye ______

3. Add the missing letters. Write the words.

r __ __ st ______ br __ __ m ______ b __ shes ______

a __ __ ry ______ bla __ __ et ______ gr __ __ ______

b __ th ______ st __ v __ ______ sp __ __ n ______

UNIT 25
woke
throw
window
stove
follow
spoke
UNIT 26
both
float
hello
oatmeal
roast
toast
UNIT 27
angry
blink
strong
blanket
string
hungry
UNIT 28
balloon
broom
flew
grew
raccoon
spoon
UNIT 29
brook
bulldog
bushes
football
shook
stood

Name

Extra Practice

This Week's Words

UNIT 31

1. Circle the five words that have /ô/ spelled <u>a</u>.
2. Draw a box around the three words that have /ô/ spelled <u>aw</u>.
3. Draw a line under the two words that have /ô/ spelled <u>au</u>.

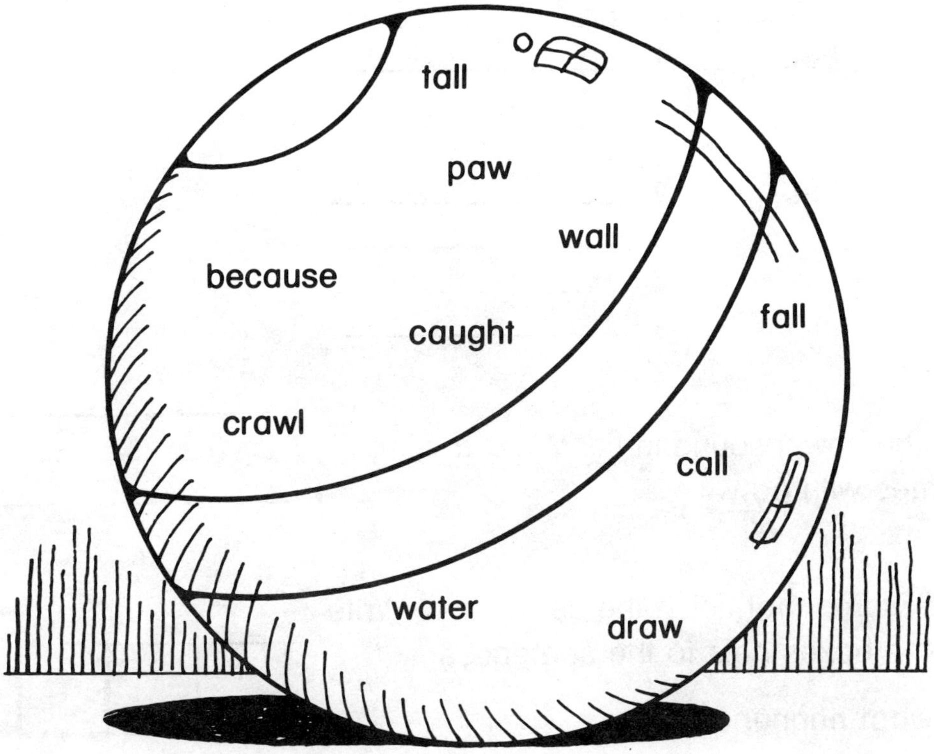

4. Write the five words you circled.

5. Write the three words you drew a box around.

6. Write the two words you drew a line under.

Name

Extra Practice

Mastery Words

UNIT 31

A. Change the vowel sound in each of these words. Write three words that rhyme with call.

bell 1. ____________

fell 2. ____________

ill 3. ____________

B. Change the vowel sound in so. Write a word that rhymes with paw.

4. ____________

C. Write the words that finish the sentences. Write them in the boxes next to the sentences.

5. I ___ what happened.

6. We were ___ going out to play.

7. Amos had the ___.

8. He dropped it in the ___.

D. What did the floor meet at the corner? The four letters you put in the dark boxes spell the answer. Write the word.

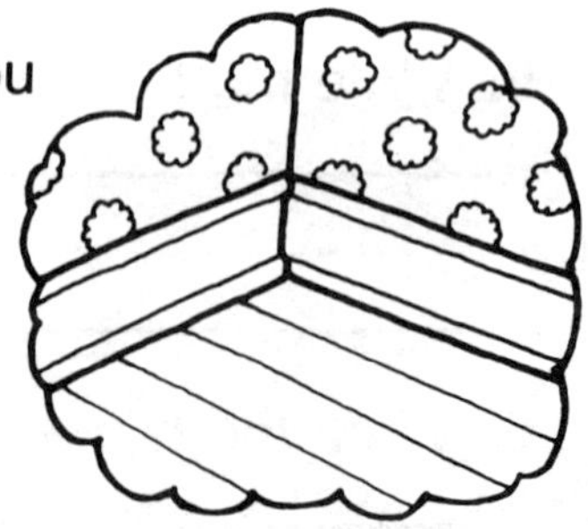

The floor met the ____________.

all ball hall saw

Name

Extra Practice

Bonus Words

A. Finish the sentences. Use the Bonus words.

1. I drink milk with a ____________.

2. I ____________ tell the truth.

3. I like to ____________ on the telephone.

4. When I'm sick, I feel ____________.

5. I ____________ my brother how to count.

6. Let's take a ____________ in the park.

always
talk
walk
awful
straw
taught

B. Write the two Bonus words that rhyme.

7. ____________ **8.** ____________

C. Add two letters to each word. Write a Bonus word.

9. ways ____________ **10.** raw ____________

D. Follow the directions. Write the Bonus words.

11. Start with careful. Take away care.
Put the letters for /ô/ in its place. ____________

12. Start with caught. Take away /k/.
Put /t/ in its place. ____________

Name

Spelling and Language

UNIT 31

tall
call
fall
wall
water
paw
draw
crawl
because
caught

A. Find the group of words that will finish each sentence. Write the whole sentence.

he is tall.	it is so pretty.	its paw was caught.

1. The kitten cried because ___.

2. Tom could see over the wall because ___.

3. I will draw a picture of the waterfall because ___.

B. Complete this sentence. Use the word <u>because</u>.

I like Saturday ___________________________.

Name ______________________________

Extra Practice

This Week's Words

UNIT **32**

Read the story about Maxwell Mouse. Add the letters that spell /ou/ to each numbered word. Write the words below. You will use two words twice.

One day Maxwell Mouse said, "I think I will go to t___(1)n. My uncle has a big h___(2)se. I will stay with him."

Maxwell Mouse f___(3)nd his bag. He packed up his things. Then he went ___(4)t. Maxwell took T___(5)er Road. Along the way he f___(6)nd a red fl___(7)er.

At last Maxwell Mouse came to his uncle's h___(8)se. The door opened. "Papa!" cried a small mouse. "Look who is at ___(9)r door!"

"H___(10) are you, Maxwell?" asked his uncle. "Come inside right n___(11). Sit down and tell us all ab___(12)t your trip."

1. ______________ 2. ______________ 3. ______________

4. ______________ 5. ______________ 6. ______________

7. ______________ 8. ______________ 9. ______________

10. ______________ 11. ______________ 12. ______________

house	flower	about	found	our	out	how	now	tower	town

Name

Extra Practice

Mastery Words

UNIT 32

A. Write Mastery words where they fit in the puzzles. Some letters have been given to help you.

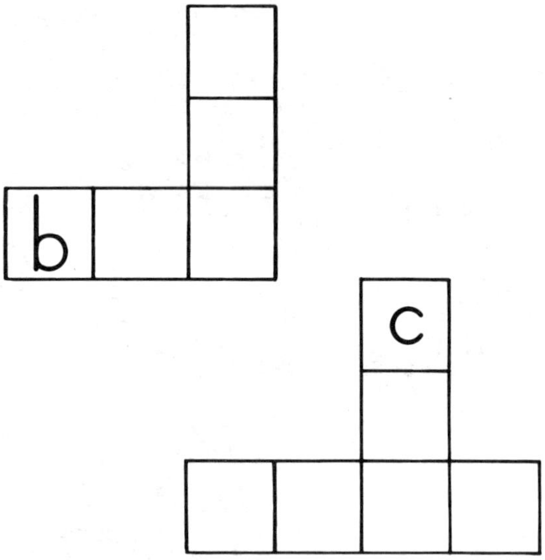

B. Now finish the sentences with the Mastery words you wrote.

1. A farmer gets milk from a ________.

2. Doreen made a ________ airplane.

3. The ________ fell off his bike.

4. Stan ran ________ the hill.

5. Billy's new watch is not a ________.

6. Mitzy walked ________ the steps.

boy
down
cow
toy

Name

Extra Practice

Bonus Words **UNIT 32**

A. Write the Bonus words in ABC order. Then draw a line under the letters that spell /ou/.

1. ____________
2. ____________
3. ____________
4. ____________
5. ____________
6. ____________

B. Write the Bonus word for each picture.

7.  ____________

8.  ____________

9.  ____________

C. Follow the directions. Use the Bonus words.

10. Write the three words that rhyme.

____________ ____________ ____________

11. Write the two words that begin with consonant clusters.

____________ ____________

ground
clown
round
owl
mouse
sound

Name

UNIT 32

Spelling and Language

A. Write words from the word list that rhyme with each picture name.

Word List
house
flower
about
found
our
out
how
now
tower
town

1. 

2. 

3. 

4. 

B. Use two words from the word list to finish the poem.

A nickel, bright and round
Was hidden in the ground.
I dug it __5__.
And with a shout,
I said, "Look at what I __6__!"

5. ______________

6. ______________

Name

Extra Practice

This Week's Words

UNIT 33

Draw a line from dot **A** to all the words that have a vowel sound followed by r. Connect the words in the right number order. Write these words below. You will end at dot **A.**

A

18 past

1 part

2 pretty

16 next

4 far

3 door

17 morning

15 more

5 cup

13 truck

6 before

14 start

7 gray

12 dress

10 arm

9 real

8 hard

11 torn

Name ____________________

Extra Practice

Mastery Words

UNIT 33

A. Finish the sentences. Use the Mastery words.

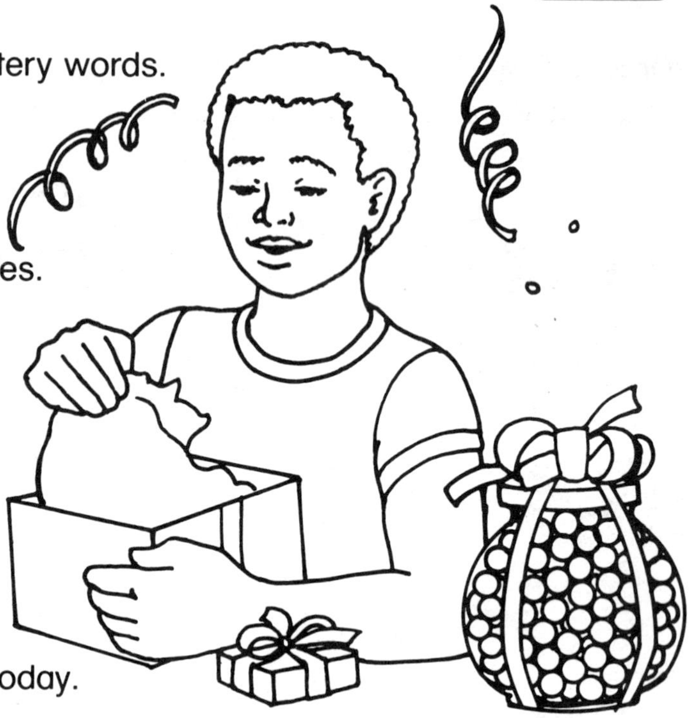

1. I brought a gift.

It is a ______ of marbles.

2. The marbles are not mine.

They are ______ you.

3. You were seven yesterday.

But you ______ eight today.

4. I've been eight for two months.

Who is older, you ______ I?

B. All the Mastery words have the letter r. Write the words in the boxes. Write them so that all the r's are under the arrow.

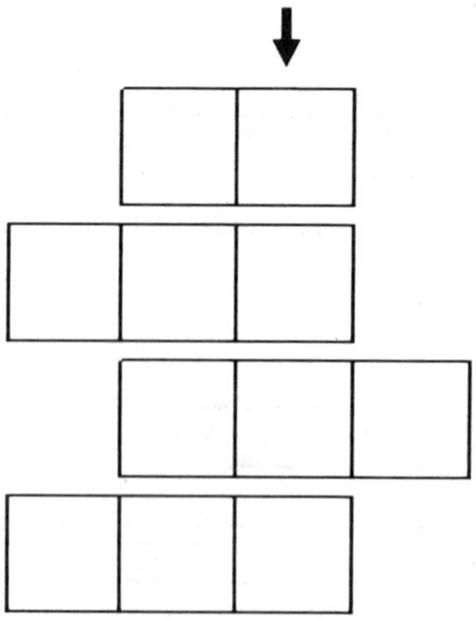

are for or jar

Name ____________________

Extra Practice

Bonus Words

UNIT **33**

A. Finish the puzzle. Use the Bonus words. The words go across or down.

ACROSS

2. Where two streets meet.
5. It goes with <u>ever</u>.
6. It has trees, grass, and benches.

DOWN

1. Where chickens and cows are raised.
3. What you do when you eat out.
4. Not tall.

corner
farm
hardly
order
park
short

B. Add letters to these words. The lines show where to add the letters. Write Bonus words.

7. ___ arm ____________________

8. hard ___ ___ ____________________

9. corn ___ ___ ____________________

10. ___ ___ or ___ ____________________

11. or ___ ___ ___ ____________________

Name

Spelling and Language

UNIT
33

part
arm
far
hard
start
morning
torn
before
more
door

A. Write one of This Week's Words that means the opposite of each word.

1. all

2. night

3. finish

4. after

5. less

6. near

7. easy

B. Read the story. Write This Week's Words that mean the opposite of the underlined words.

In the night (8), Dylan had to finish (9) his chores after (10) he left for school. Luckily for Dylan, his school was not very near (11).

8. ____________ **9.** ____________

10. ____________ **11.** ____________

Name

Extra Practice

This Week's Words

UNIT 34

A. Here are some of This Week's Words. But the letters that spell /ûr/ are missing. Write each word. Put the letters that spell /ûr/ in place of the box.

1. t☐n
2. g☐l
3. w☐d
4. h☐t
5. b☐d
6. w☐k
7. h☐

B. Add ear to these beginning letters. Write three of This Week's Words and three other words. Write the words in ABC order.

n	**f**
t	**h**
y	**cl**

8.
9.
10.
11.
12.
13.

hear	her
girl	turn
word	year
bird	work
near	hurt

Harcourt Brace School Publishers

Name

Extra Practice

Mastery Words

UNIT 34

A. Do some "word math." Write Mastery words.

1. w h y − y ＿＿ + t h e r e − t h ＿＿＿ = ＿＿＿

2. d a r e − a r e ＿ + e a t − t ＿＿ + c a r − c a ＿ = ＿＿＿

3. w a s − a s ＿ + h e r − h ＿＿ + c a m e − c a m ＿ = ＿＿＿

4. s h e − s ＿＿ + d a r e − d a ＿＿ = ＿＿＿

B. Follow the directions. Use the words you wrote for **1–4**.

5. Write the two words that rhyme.

＿＿＿ ＿＿＿

6. Write a sentence using the word you wrote for **3**. Remember to use a capital letter at the beginning and a period at the end.

＿＿＿

dear	here	were	where

Name ______________________

Extra Practice

Bonus Words | UNIT 34

A. Add the letters that spell /ûr/ to finish the Bonus words. Write the whole word.

1. ret ___ ___ n ______________

2. ___ ___ ___ ly ______________

3. l ___ ___ ___ n ______________

4. p ___ ___ son ______________

5. w ___ ___ ld ______________

6. c ___ ___ cus ______________

early
circus
learn
person
return
world

B. Add letters to these words. The number in ( ) tells how many letters to add. Write three Bonus words.

7. (1) earn ______________

8. (2) turn ______________

9. (3) son ______________

C. Write the Bonus words that go with these words.

10. around the ______________

11. ______________ clown

12. ______________ a lesson

13. get up ______________

Name ______________________

Spelling and Language

UNIT 34

A. Two words are spelled wrong in each sentence. Read each sentence. Find the words that are spelled wrong and circle them. Then write the sentence over. Spell all the words the right way.

work
bird
girl
her
hurt
turn
word
hear
near
year

1. That gril lives neer me.

____

2. I often here hir singing.

____

3. Last yer she bought a berd.

____

B. Look at the words you circled above. Write them in the puzzles. Spell all the words the right way. Some letters are given to help you.

4.

5.

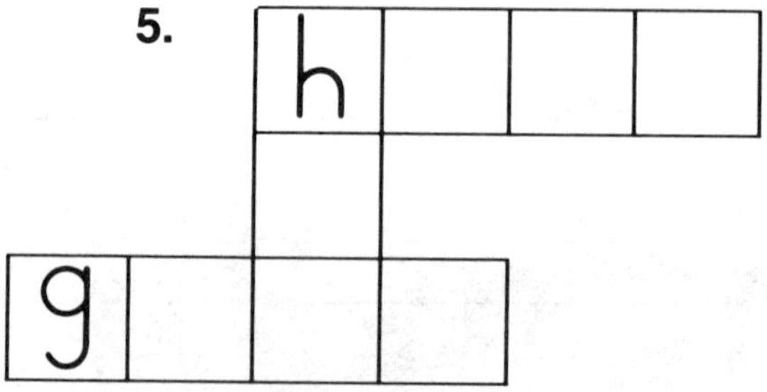

Name

Extra Practice

This Week's Word's

UNIT 35

Finish the sentences with This Week's Words. Use the code. First look at the capital letters under each blank. Then look for the same capital letters in the box. Find the small letters under them. The small letters will spell This Week's Words.

D	N	T	I	P	Y	K	Z	C	Q	S	V	U	F	E	J	O	X	A	R	H	L	B	W	M	G
a	b	c	d	e	f	g	h	i	j	k	l	m	n	o	p	q	r	s	t	u	v	w	x	y	z

1. Let's take the ____________ road.
   ERZPX

2. My ____________ loves to fish.
   YDRZPX

3. William's ____________ is a ____________.
   ACARPX IETREX

4. Did you ____________ ride a horse?
   PLPX

5. Debbie got a sled last ____________.
   BCFRPX

6. Six comes ____________ five.
   DYRPX

7. What ____________ is your new bike?
   TEVEX

8. The cat jumped ____________ the fence.
   ELPX

9. Who lost this ____________?
   IEVVDX

- winter
- father
- sister
- after
- ever
- other
- over
- color
- doctor
- dollar

Name

Extra Practice

Mastery Words

UNIT 35

You will write four sentences to answer the questions. First write a Mastery word for each picture in the box. Then put the words in order to make a sentence. Remember that a sentence starts with a capital letter and ends with a period.

mother
water
brother
flower

1. Who is Charles?

is **Charles** ______ **.** **Amy's**

2. What is a rose?

A **is** ______ **.** **rose** **a**

3. Who will drive the car?

Kim's **will** ______ **the** **drive** **car.**

4. What are you drinking?

am **drinking** ______ **.** **I**

Name

Extra Practice

Bonus Words

UNIT 35

A. Draw a line under the word that is spelled wrong in each sentence. Then write the word the right way.

1. I wrote a leter to my aunt.

2. Pat saw herself in the mirrur.

3. I want to play anuther game.

4. I like the flaver of this soup.

5. I don't use suger on my oatmeal.

6. This is my new red swetter.

B. Answer the questions. Use the Bonus words.

7. It is cold out. But it is not cold enough to wear a coat. What should you wear?

8. What can you use to read this?

ɿoɿɿim

9. You need a few of these to write your name. You write your name at the end of one. What is it?

another | flavor | letter | mirror | sugar | sweater

Name

Spelling and Language

UNIT
35

winter
father
sister
after
ever
other
over
color
doctor
dollar

A. Read each pair of sentences. Write the sentence that makes sense.

1. We visited each grandmother my winter.
Each winter, we visit my grandmother.

2. My sister and father have the same color hair.
The same sister and father have my color hair.

3. I saw the other doctor last time I was here.
The other I saw doctor last time I was here.

B. Write each group of words in a sentence. Remember: a sentence starts with a capital letter.

4. ever apples Are colors? other

5. saved I have dollar. one

Name

Review A: Units 31–32

UNIT 36

A. UNIT 31 Look at each word. Write the word or words that spell /ô/ in the same way.

1. ball
2. taught
3. paw

UNIT 31
water
because
caught
draw
tall
UNIT 32
our
about
how
house
now

B. UNIT 32 Finish each sentence. Use words that spell /ou/ in the same way as the underlined word.

4. Where is the <u>cow</u> ______?

5. The <u>mouse</u> is not ______ to leave its ______.

6. Let's <u>shout</u> for ______ team.

7. <u>Now</u> I will show you ______ to play the game.

Name ______________________________

Review B: Units 33–34

UNIT 36

UNIT 33
part
before
start
door
hard
UNIT 34
her
girl
year
work
turn

A. UNIT 33 Finish each rhyme. Use words from Unit 33.

1. I have to learn my ______________

   Before the play can ______________.

2. I have told you ______________,

   Please shut that ______________.

3. The dirt in our yard

   Is very ______________.

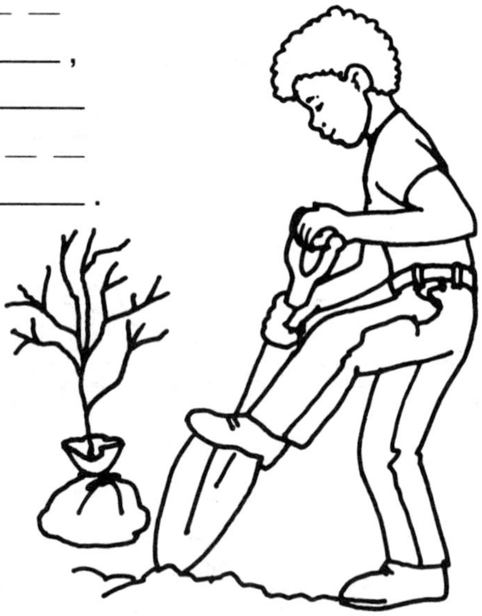

B. UNIT 34 Write each group of words in ABC order. Circle the letters in each word that spell /ûr/ or /ir/.

4. turn girl her

   ____

   ____

   ____

5. work turn year

   ____

   ____

   ____

Name

Review C: Unit 35 • Test Exercise

UNIT 36

A. UNIT 35 Write each group of words in ABC order. Circle the letters in each word that spell /ər/.

UNIT 35
after
other
color
dollar
over

1. color dollar after

2. over other dollar

B. Make a spelling word from each group of letters. Write the word.

3. lardlo

4. hreot

5. rove

6. loorc

C. UNITS 31–35 Look at the word with a line under it. Fill in **r** if the word is spelled right. Fill in **w** if the word is spelled wrong.

	Right	Wrong
1 Would you like a glass of watter?	r	w
2 Please turn off the light.	r	w
3 What coler are your eyes?	r	w
4 Is your howse on this street?	r	w
5 Let's leave befor it gets late.	r	w
6 He caught the ball in the air.	r	w

Name ______________________

UNIT 36

Language Study

A. Write a word that means the opposite of each word.

1. short ______	**2.** play ______
3. all ______	**4.** finish ______
5. land ______	**6.** boy ______
7. after ______	**8.** easy ______
9. under ______	**10.** later ______

water
tall
draw
our
now
house
part
before
start
door
hard
her
girl
year
work
after
other
dollar
over

B. Write a word that rhymes with the picture name.

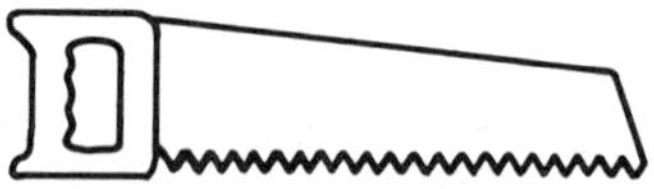

11. ______

12. ______

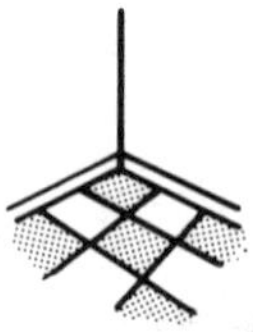

13. ______

14. ______

15. ______

Name

Review: Units 31–35

Mastery Words

UNIT **36**

Write the words that go in each sentence. Use words that have the sound given.

1. /ô/ I ___ him kick the ___.

2. /oi/ The little ___ plays with a ___ truck.

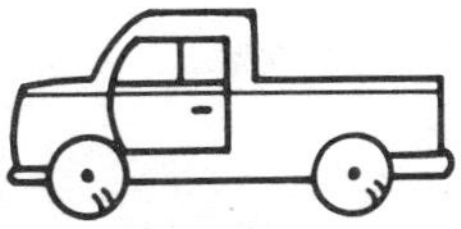

3. /ou/ Take the ___ ___ to the barn.

4. /är/ The pennies in the glass ___ ___ mine.

5. /ôr/ Are those letters ___ you ___ me?

6. /ir/ Come ___, my ___.

7. /ər/ My ___ looks like my ___.

UNIT 31
all ball hall saw
UNIT 32
boy cow down toy
UNIT 33
are for or jar
UNIT 34
dear here were where
UNIT 35
brother flower mother water

Name

Review: Units 31–35

Bonus Words

UNIT **36**

Write three words for each sound. Then circle the letters that spell the sound in each word.

1. /ô/ as in 

2. /ou/ 

3. /är/ as in 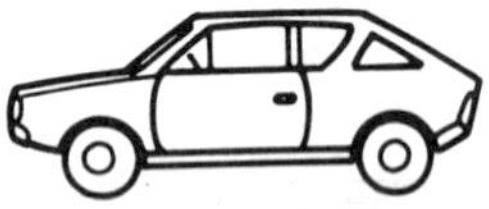

4. /ôr/ as in 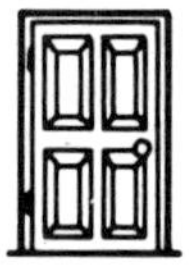

5. /ûr/ as in 

6. /ər/ as in 

UNIT 31
always
talk
walk
awful
straw
taught

UNIT 32
clown
ground
mouse
owl
round
sound

UNIT 33
corner
farm
hardly
order
park
short

UNIT 34
early
circus
learn
person
return
world

UNIT 35
another
flavor
letter
mirror
sugar
sweater

Answer Key for Extra Practice Masters

UNIT 1

Extra Practice: This Week's Words
pan, next, real, pat, neat, men, bag, rest, band, mad

Extra Practice: Mastery Words
1. no **2.** be **3.** pig **4.** ran **5.** be **6.** no **7.** ran **8.** pig

Extra Practice: Bonus Words
A. 1. robin **2.** bear **3.** neck, nest **4.** mail **5.** page
B. 6. bear **7.** mail **8.** nest **9.** page

Spelling and Language
1. next **2.** neat **3.** band **4.** men **5.** pan **6.** mad **7.** rest **8.** pat

UNIT 2

Extra Practice: This Week's Words

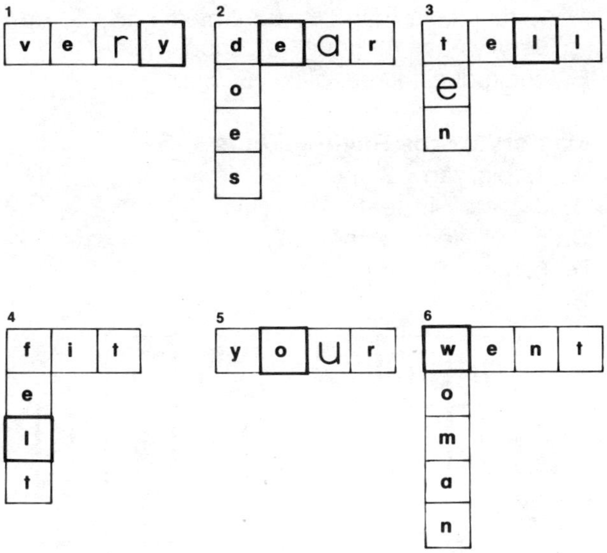

yellow

Extra Practice: Mastery Words
A. feet, dad, yes, wet
B. fast

Extra Practice: Bonus Words
A. 1-6

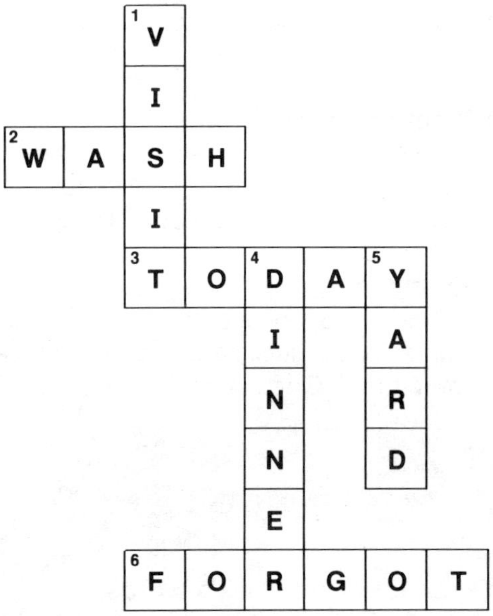

B. 7. wash **8.** forgot **9.** dinner

Spelling and Language
A. 1. tell **2.** does **3.** went **4.** felt **5.** fit
B. Example: My sister is ten. She does the dishes. She is very smart.

UNIT 3

Extra Practice: This Week's Words
A. 1. jet **2.** live **3.** jar **4.** left **5.** seed **6.** gone **7.** gold **8.** has **9.** soon **10.** hall
B. gold, jar, gone, has, left, hall

Extra Practice: Mastery Words
A. 1. say **2.** he **3.** let **4.** see
B. 5. say **6.** let **7.** see **8.** he

Extra Practice: Bonus Words
A. 1. joke **2.** large **3.** sunny **4.** heard **5.** happy **6.** goodness
B. 7. happy **8.** large **9.** sunny

Spelling and Language
1. The gold jar is in the hall. **2.** She has gone to live in Portland. **3.** The jet left on runway six. **4.** Soon the seed will be a pretty flower.

UNIT 4

Extra Practice: This Week's Words
cow: cat, cake, cup, cook; duck: pick, sick; kite: keep, cake, cook

Extra Practice: Mastery Words
1. but, cut **2.** pan, can **3.** game, came **4.** fan, far, car

Extra Practice: Bonus Words
A. **1.** cave **2.** cookie **3.** key **4.** kitten **5.** kick **6.** lucky
B. **7.** cave **8.** cookie **9.** key **10.** kitten

Spelling and Language
A. cat, kites, cows, cook, cups, ducks, cakes
B. Example: Three ducks are in a box. Six cakes are on a table. One cat won a prize.

UNIT 5

Extra Practice: This Week's Words
A. **1.** as **2.** fast **3.** last **4.** past **5.** ant **6.** and **7.** hand **8.** man **9.** bad **10.** fat
B. sand land

Extra Practice: Mastery Words
sat, at, had, am, sat, had, am, sat, at, had, am, had

Extra Practice: Bonus Words
A. **1.** pants **2.** flat **3.** candy **4.** apple **5.** trap **6.** clap
B. **7.** pants **8.** clap **9.** trap **10.** candy
C. **11.** apple **12.** flat

Spelling and Language
A. **1.** hand **2.** ant **3.** man **4.** ant **5.** hand **6.** man
B. **7.** bad **8.** fast **9.** man
C. Example: The man picked up the ant in his hand.

UNIT 6

Review A: Units 1–2
A. **1.** pan **2.** next **3.** bag **4.** real **5.** men **6.** pan
B. **7.** went **8.** your **9.** does **10.** very **11.** woman

Review B: Units 3–4
A. **1.** left **2.** has **3.** soon **4.** jet **5.** gone
B. **6.** duck **7.** cook **8.** cup **9.** Keep **10.** pick

Review C: Unit 5 and Test Exercise
A.

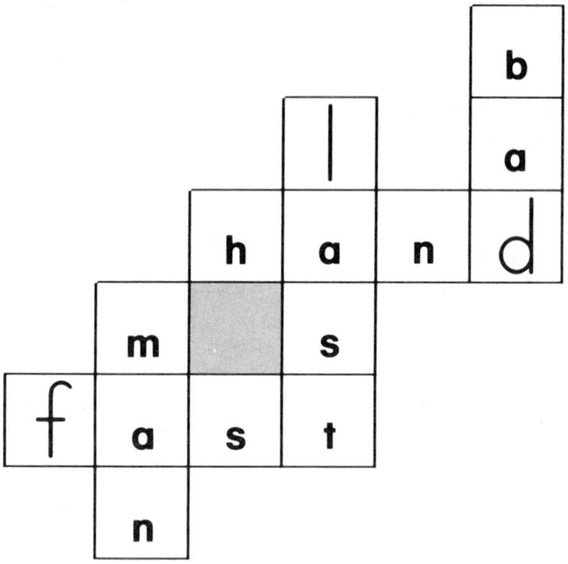

B. **1.** c **2.** a **3.** a **4.** b **5.** c **6.** c **7.** a **8.** b

Language Study
A. **1.** fast, last, man **2.** bag, next, pan **3.** does, very, went **4.** gone, jet, soon
B. cook, duck, keep, pick **5.** cup

Mastery Words Review: Units 1–5
A. **1.** pig, ran **2.** be
B. **3.** yes **4.** feet
C. **5.** he, see **6.** say **7.** let
D. **8.** cut **9.** can
E.

10. 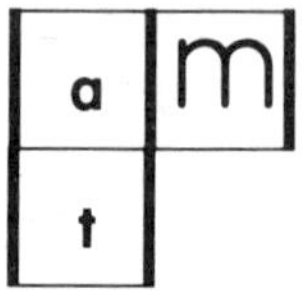

11. 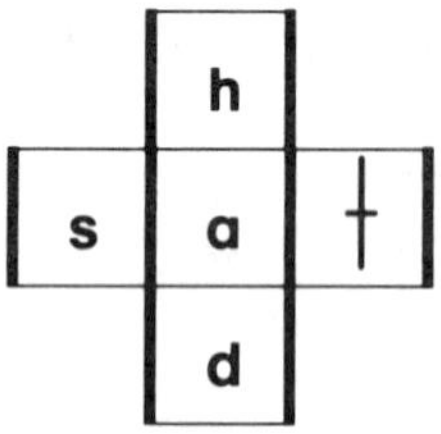

Bonus Words Review: Units 1–5
A. dinner, goodness, happy, sunny, kitten, apple
B. neck , joke, cave, cookie, key, kick , lucky, candy, clap
C. **1.** forgot, flat **2.** page, pants **3.** today, trap

UNIT 7

Extra Practice: This Week's Words

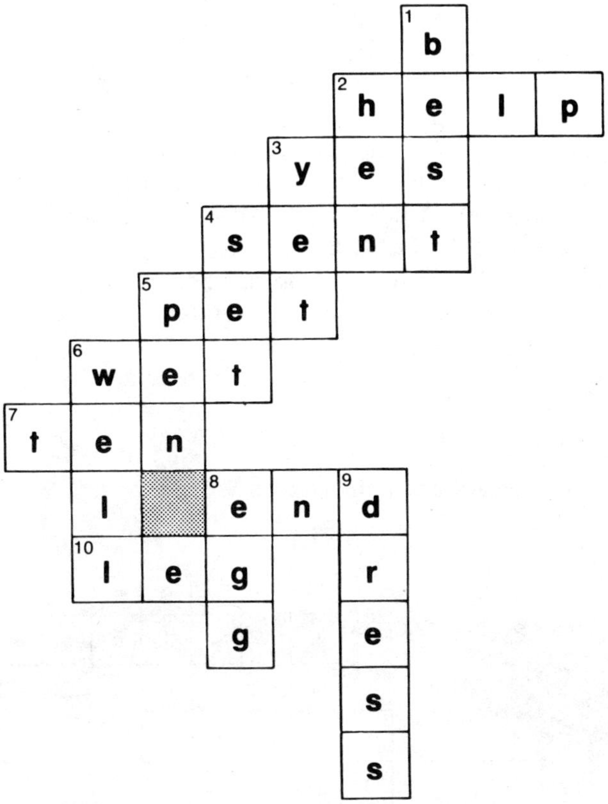

Extra Practice: Mastery Words

A. **1.** bed **2.** hen **3.** get **4.** tell
B. bell
C. **5.** hen **6.** bed **7.** get **8.** tell

Extra Practice: Bonus Words

A. **1.** better **2.** spell **3.** spend **4.** step
5. test
B. **6.** desk
C. **7.** spend **8.** step **9.** test

Spelling and Language

1. pet **2.** well **3.** help **4.** best **5.** end
6. dress **7.** leg **8.** yet **9.** set **10.** sent

UNIT 8

Extra Practice: This Week's Words

A.

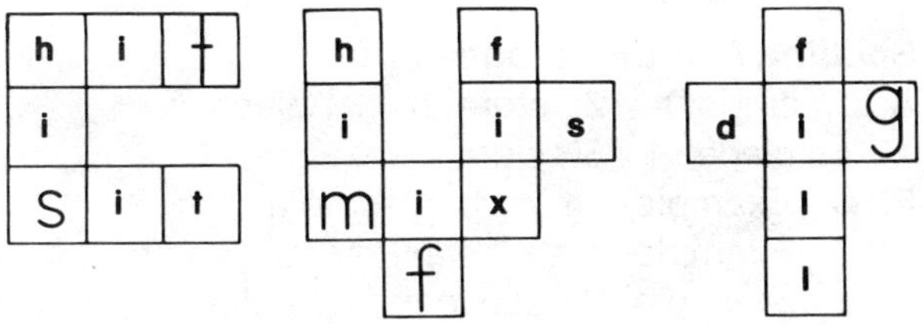

B. **1.** dig **2.** his **3.** fill **4.** fix **5.** sit **6.** is
7. if **8.** mix

Extra Practice: Mastery Words

A. big, it, in, did, hit Order will vary.
B. **1.** in **2.** did **3.** it **4.** big

Extra Practice: Bonus Words

A. **1.** bring **2.** middle **3.** city **4.** lift **5.** milk
6. trick
B. **7.** bring **8.** trick
C. **9.** middle **10.** milk
D. **11.** lift **12.** city

Spelling and Language

A. **1.** digs **2.** mixes **3.** fills **4.** sits **5.** fixes
B. Example: Will the player hit the ball? If the player hits the ball, how far will it go?

UNIT 9

Extra Practice: This Week's Words

1. rub **2.** just **3.** luck **4.** truck **5.** jump
6. bug **7.** until **8.** come **9.** some
10. done

Extra Practice: Mastery Words

1. run **2.** us **3.** fun **4.** up

Extra Practice: Bonus Words

A. **1.** won **2.** month **3.** funny **4.** son
5. summer **6.** wonder
B. **7.** funny **8.** summer
C. **9.** son **10.** won
D. **11.** wonder, won

Spelling and Language

1. luck, truck **2.** jump, done **3.** some, come

UNIT 10

Extra Practice: This Week's Words

1. lot **2.** lost **3.** soft **4.** top **5.** pond
6. dog **7.** song **8.** shop **9.** job **10.** pop
11. box

Extra Practice: Mastery Words

A. **1.** fox **2.** got **3.** box **4.** stop
B. stop, 4
C. foot

Extra Practice: Bonus Words

A. **1.** frog **2.** lock **3.** moss **4.** cost
B. **5.** cost **6.** moss
C. **7.** clock **8.** drop **9.** frog **10.** lock

Spelling and Language
1. dogs **2.** soft **3.** ponds **4.** lost **5.** pops
6. top **7.** songs **8.** shops **9.** lot **10.** jobs

UNIT 11

Extra Practice: This Week's Words
1. across **2.** ball **3.** buzz **4.** cross **5.** egg
6. fell **7.** grass **8.** miss **9.** off **10.** pass

Extra Practice: Mastery Words
A. 1. hill **2.** fill **3.** well **4.** little
B.

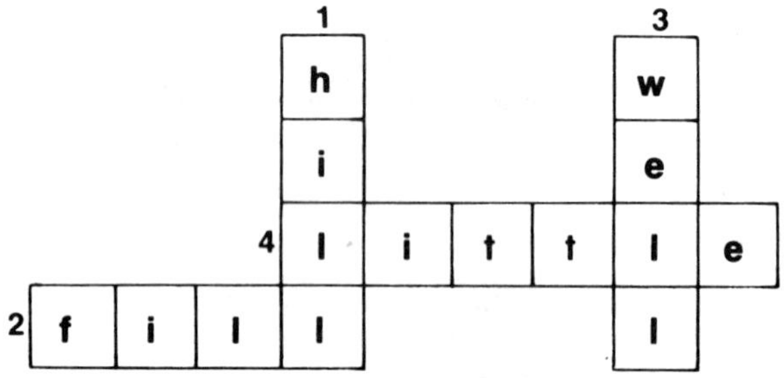

Extra Practice: Bonus Words
1. penny **2.** rabbit **3.** stuff **4.** butter
5. shell **6.** add

Spelling and Language
A. is happening now: buzzes, crosses; already happened: passed, missed
B. Example: The egg fell off her nose.

UNIT 12

Review A: Units 7–8
A. 1. best **2.** sent **3.** well **4.** help **5.** yet
B. 6. best **7.** sent
C. 8. him, his **9.** is, if **10.** sit

Review B: Units 9–10
A. 1. done, some, truck **2.** done, just, until
B. 3. job **4.** shop **5.** dog **6.** lost **7.** song

Review C: Unit 11 and Test Exercise
A. 1. grass **2.** off **3.** fell **4.** across **5.** ball
B. 1. b **2.** c **3.** a **4.** c **5.** b **6.** a **7.** c
8. a

Language Study
A. 1. best **2.** sent **3.** sit **4.** is **5.** ball
6. just **7.** yet **8.** well, fell
B. 9. jobs **10.** trucks

Mastery Words Review: Units 7–11
A. 1. bed **2.** hen **3.** well **4.** fill or hill
5. box **6.** hill or fill **7.** big **8.** got
B. 9. stop, fox **10.** get, tell **11.** run, us
12. did, little **13.** it, in **14.** fun, up

Bonus Words Review: Units 7–11
A. 1. city **2.** frog **3.** shell **4.** penny
5. desk **6.** milk **7.** clock **8.** rabbit
9. step **10.** son **11.** lock **12.** butter
13. add **14.** test
B. Possible answers: month, won, wonder, funny, summer, stuff, son, butter
C. spell, better, spend

UNIT 13

Extra Practice: This Week's Words

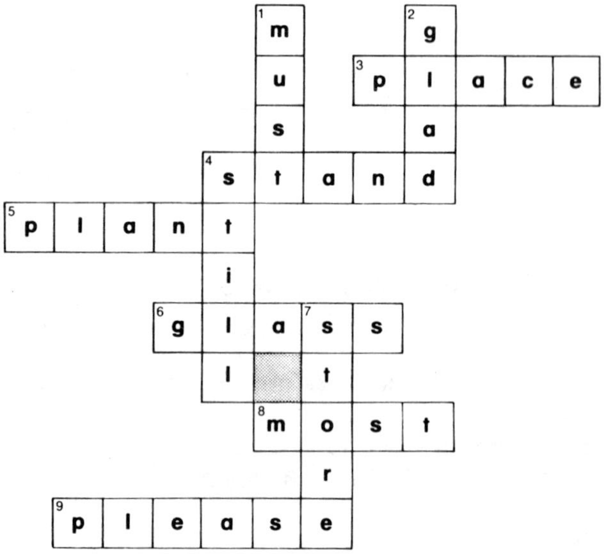

Extra Practice: Mastery Words
2. story **3.** sleep **4.** play **5.** best

Extra Practice: Bonus Words
A. 1. stick **2.** trust **3.** stare **4.** dust
5. steep
B. 6. playground **7.** dust **8.** stick **9.** stare
10. steep

Spelling and Language
A. 1. stand, n **2.** store, n **3.** glass, n
4. place, n **5.** plant, v
B. 6. Example: I must buy some milk.
7. Example: What I want most is an orange.
8. Example: Please look for apples.

UNIT 14

Extra Practice: This Week's Words
1. swim **2.** spot **3.** small **4.** from
5. brother **6.** great **7.** true **8.** front
9. friend **10.** pretty

Extra Practice: Mastery Words
1. grass **2.** dress **3.** tree **4.** clean

Extra Practice: Bonus Words
A. 1. grand **2.** prize **3.** bread **4.** track
5. sweet **6.** smile
B.

										1 B
										R
				2 S	W	E	E	3 T		E
				M				R		A
				I		4 G	R	A	N	D
				L				C		
5 P	R	I	Z	E				K		

Spelling and Language
1. brother **2.** spot **3.** great **4.** pretty
5. friend **6.** from **7.** swim **8.** small
9. front **10.** true

UNIT 15

Extra Practice: This Week's Words
A. 1. sheep **2.** wish **3.** teeth **4.** thank
5. shut **6.** finish **7.** dish **8.** push
9. shoe **10.** thing
B. She went fishing.

Extra Practice: Mastery Words
A. 1. fish **2.** she **3.** with **4.** shop
B. 5. shape **6.** shall **7.** show **8.** short
9. shoe

Extra Practice: Bonus Words
1. thumb **2.** path **3.** crash **4.** earth
5. shine **6.** shout

Spelling and Language
A. 1. teeth **2.** dishes **3.** wishes **4.** thanks
5. things **6.** shoes **7.** sheep
B. 8. Example: Yes, I finished brushing my teeth.

UNIT 16

Extra Practice: This Week's Words
1. lunch **2.** them **3.** much **4.** chair **5.** their
6. watch **7.** these **8.** then **9.** than
10. each

Extra Practice: Mastery Words
A. 1. this **2.** that **3.** children **4.** the
B. 5. this, that **6.** the, children

Extra Practice: Bonus Words
A. 1. bother **2.** together **3.** weather
4. catch **5.** church **6.** kitchen
B. 7. weather **8.** kitchen **9.** catch
10. church

Spelling and Language
1. than, Would you rather sit in that chair than watch the show? **2.** than, Each of these lunches is much better than any of those.
3. Then, Then tell them to come over.
4. then, They ate their lunches and then went out to play.

UNIT 17

Extra Practice: This Week's Words
A. 1. when **2.** again **3.** where **4.** been
5. here **6.** use **7.** want **8.** there
9. what **10.** were
B. 11. want **12.** there **13.** what **14.** were
15. here **16.** where

Extra Practice: Mastery Words
A. 1. of **2.** said **3.** was **4.** does
B. 5. said **6.** was **7.** does

Extra Practice: Bonus Words
A. 1. thought **2.** wrong **3.** listen **4.** family
5. laugh **6.** between
B. 7. family **8.** between **9.** wrong

Spelling and Language
A. 1. again, here, there **2.** been, use, want
3. again, there, what **4.** here, there, where
B. 5. want, were, what **6.** want, when, win

UNIT 18

Review A: Units 13–14
A. 1. must **2.** glad **3.** stand **4.** Please
5. store

B. **6.** swim **7.** true **8.** brother **9.** friend **10.** great

Review B: Units 15–16

A. **1.** wish **2.** shoe **3.** thank **4.** finish **5.** thing

B. **6.** chair, watch, much **7.** their, these

Review C: Unit 17 and Test Exercise

A. **1.** were **2.** here **3.** there

B. **4.** been **5.** again

C. **1.** c **2.** a **3.** d **4.** c **5.** b **6.** d **7.** a **8.** b

Language Study

1. I wish to thank you again for a great time. **2.** Will you watch my brother swim? **3.** I was glad to see him. **4.** Please finish your work before you come here. **5.** It is true that the store has been there a long time.

Mastery Words Review: Units 13–17

A. **1.** best, play, sleep **2.** children, does, of **3.** dress, story, was **4.** clean, grass, tree

B. **5.** with, that, the, this **6.** fish, she, shop

Bonus Words Review: Units 13–17

A. **1.** steep **2.** playground **3.** prize **4.** shine **5.** smile **6.** shout **7.** sweet **8.** church **9.** catch **10.** wrong **11.** between **12.** dust **13.** track **14.** bread

B. earth, path, thumb, bother, together, weather, thought

UNIT 19

Extra Practice: This Week's Words

1. ate **2.** bake **3.** face **4.** gave **5.** have **6.** late **7.** race **8.** same **9.** save **10.** wave

Extra Practice: Mastery Words

1. game **2.** made **3.** cake **4.** make

Extra Practice: Bonus Words

A. **1.** skate **2.** brake **3.** brave **4.** late **5.** lake **6.** save **7.** safe **8.** snake **9.** shake **10.** shave Order will vary.

B. **11.** brave **12.** skate **13.** snake **14.** shake **15.** lake

Spelling and Language

A. **1.** bake **2.** late, ate **3.** same, save, gave, wave, have

B. race, face

UNIT 20

Extra Practice: This Week's Words

1.

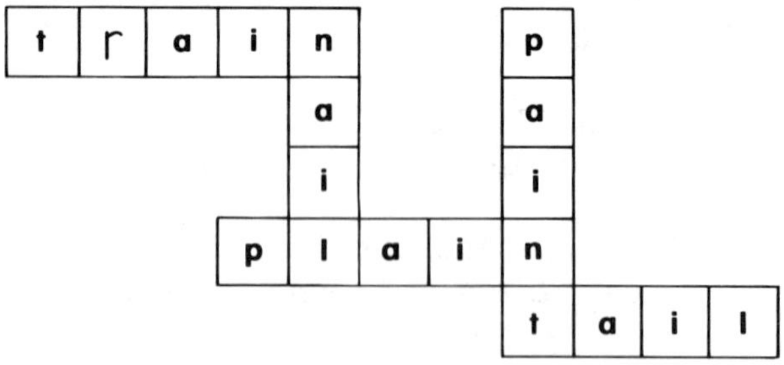

a i

2.

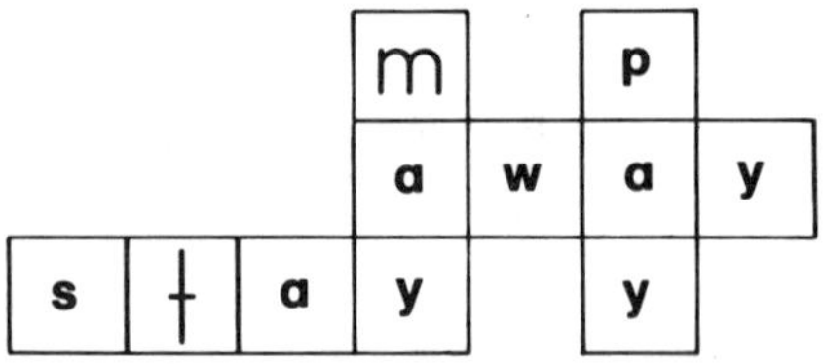

a y

3.

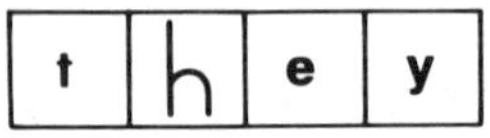

e y

Extra Practice: Mastery Words

1. w t, wait **2.** d, day **3.** r n, rain **4.** w, way

Extra Practice: Bonus Words

A. afraid, clay, eight, maybe, straight, trail

B. We were afraid to hike on that trail. Maybe we can make a horse with clay. It rained for eight days straight.

Spelling and Language

A. **1.** paying **2.** nailed **3.** painted **4.** stayed **5.** training

B. Example: The cat has a funny tail. It is using its tail to keep the bee away.

UNIT 21

Extra Practice: This Week's Words

1. street **2.** feel **3.** leave **4.** three **5.** mean **6.** many **7.** teach **8.** free **9.** deep **10.** easy

Extra Practice: Mastery Words
A. **1.** we **2.** eat **3.** me **4.** need
B. weed

Extra Practice: Bonus Words
A.

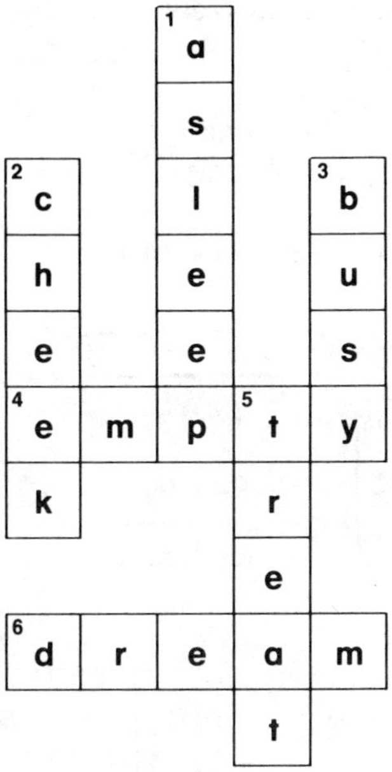

B. three: asleep, cheek; happy: busy, empty; seals: dream, treat

Spelling and Language
1. There are three free kittens on my street.
2. Many people leave town on Saturday.
3. It is easy to teach someone that game.
4. She was mean to push him in the deep puddle.

UNIT 22

Extra Practice: This Week's Words
A. write, bike, side, fine, time, wide, tire, fire, nice
B. give, five

Extra Practice: Mastery Words
A. **1.** like **2.** ride **3.** five **4.** kite
B. **5.** ride **6.** five **7.** like

Extra Practice: Bonus Words
A. **1.** outside **2.** slide **3.** wise **4.** hide **5.** twice **6.** life
B. **7.** hide **8.** slide **9.** twice

Spelling and Language
1. fire, give, time **2.** bike, fine, side **3.** nice, tire, wide, write

UNIT 23

Extra Practice: This Week's Words
A. **1.** high **2.** try **3.** kind **4.** sky **5.** right **6.** tie **7.** find **8.** dry **9.** night **10.** why
B. **11.** bright **12.** lie **13.** mind **14.** frighten

Extra Practice: Mastery Words
1. I **2.** my **3.** fly **4.** by **5.** I **6.** fly
7. I, I, my **8.** by

Extra Practice: Bonus Words
A. **1.** frighten **2.** lion **3.** myself **4.** shy **5.** sight **6.** tiger
B. **7.** shy **8.** frighten **9.** tiger **10.** lion **11.** sight **12.** myself

Spelling and Language
1. The bird flies high in the sky. **2.** It is dark at night. **3.** Why can't I find my tie? **4.** She was kind to give you the right time. **5.** Try to stay dry.

UNIT 24

Review A: Units 19–20
A. **1.** same **2.** have **3.** face **4.** ate **5.** late
B. **6.** they **7.** train, tail **8.** stay, away

Review B: Units 21–22
A. **1.** street, many, three **2.** easy, leave
B. **3.** write **4.** wide **5.** time **6.** give **7.** fire

Review C: Unit 23 and Test Exercise
A. **1.** why **2.** right, kind **3.** night, sky
B. **1.** c **2.** b **3.** d **4.** c **5.** a **6.** b **7.** d **8.** a **9.** c

Language Study
A. **1.** tail **2.** easy **3.** fire **4.** late
B. **5.** same **6.** stay **7.** kind **8.** sky; many

Mastery Words Review: Units 19–23
A. **1.** Possible answers: game, made, cake, make **2.** Possible answers: rain, wait **3.** Possible answers: kite, like, five, ride **4.** day, way **5.** Possible answers: fly, by, my **6.** me, we
B. I, need, eat

Bonus Words Review: Units 19–23
1. safe, skate, lake **2.** straight, eight, trail **3.** busy, asleep, dream **4.** outside, hide, slide **5.** frighten, shy, tiger

UNIT 25

Extra Practice: This Week's Words

A. **1.** grow **2.** know **3.** hope **4.** stone
5. row **6.** note **7.** own **8.** slow
9. those **10.** low

B. her nose

Extra Practice: Mastery Words

A. **1.** show **2.** rope **3.** nose **4.** home

B. hose

Extra Practice: Bonus Words

A. **1.** stove **2.** throw **3.** window **4.** spoke
5. woke **6.** follow

B. **7.** window **8.** follow **9.** spoke **10.** throw

C. **11.** stove **12.** smoke **13.** spoke
14. stole

Spelling and Language

A. **1.** knows **2.** grows **3.** stone **4.** slow
5. those **6.** rowing

B. **7.** owning **8.** low

UNIT 26

Extra Practice: This Week's Words

A. **1.** o **2.** o **3.** o **4.** o **5.** o **6.** o a
7. o a **8.** o a **9.** o a **10.** o a

B.

1	(a)	l	s	o	
2	a	(g)	o		
3	h	(o)	l	d	
4	c	o	(l)	d	
5	t	o	l	(d)	
6	(s)	o	a	p	
7	(t)	o	a	d	
8	o	(a)	k		
9	(r)	o	a	d	
10	g	o	a	t	

Extra Practice: Mastery Words

1. The following words should be circled: monkey, owl, sheep, tiger; most **2.** The following words should be circled: soft, on; so **3.** The following words should be circled: berry, oats, apple, toast; boat **4.** go

Extra Practice: Bonus Words

A. **1.** roast **2.** hello **3.** both **4.** oatmeal
5. float **6.** toast

B. **7.** toast **8.** both **9.** hello **10.** oatmeal
11. float **12.** roast

C. **13.** roast **14.** float

Spelling and Language

1. toad **2.** goat **3.** soap **4.** cold **5.** oak
6. hold **7.** told

UNIT 27

Extra Practice: This Week's Words

A. **1.** sing **2.** drink **3.** trunk **4.** hang
5. ring **6.** think **7.** along **8.** long
9. young **10.** bank

B. think, ring, trunk, long

Extra Practice: Mastery Words

A.

r	g	(b	a	n	d)	p	l	
k	(m	x	l	s	q	z	i	
y	e	i	o	a	j	(o	n)	
j	n)	h	(w	e	n	t)	x	

B.

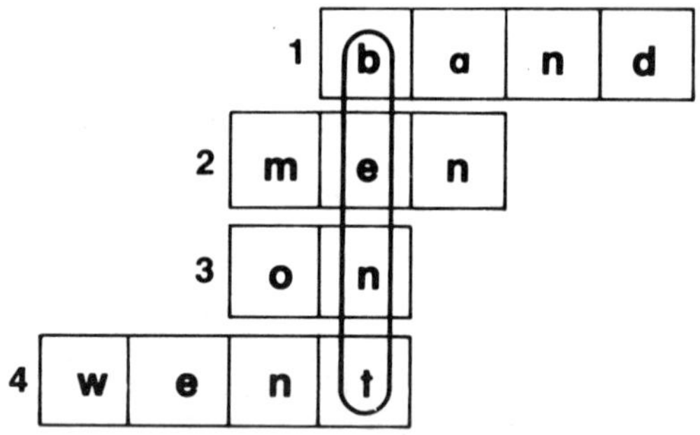

C. bent

Extra Practice: Bonus Words

A.

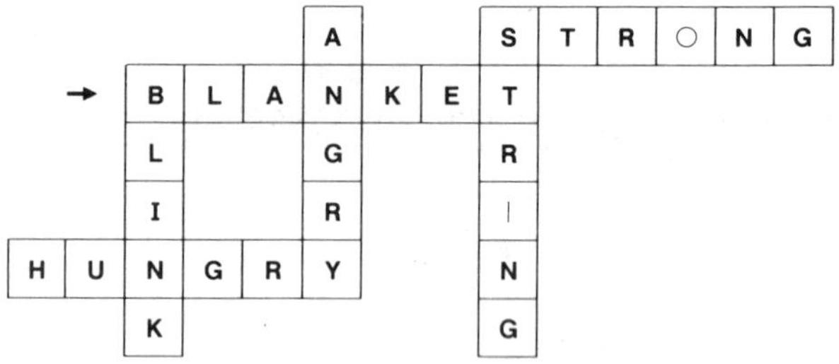

B. **1.** string, blink **2.** angry, blanket, hungry, strong

Spelling and Language

A. **1.** ringing **2.** hangs **3.** drinking
4. singing **5.** thinks

B. Example: The young elephant is holding its mother's tail with its trunk.

UNIT 28

Extra Practice: This Week's Words

1. d, do **2.** r m, room **3.** w h, who **4.** t w, two **5.** b t, boot **6.** b l, blew **7.** t, too or to **8.** t, too or to **9.** s c h l, school **10.** n, new

Extra Practice: Mastery Words

A. 1. soon **2.** true **3.** you **4.** shoe
B. true, you, soon, shoe

Extra Practice: Bonus Words

A.

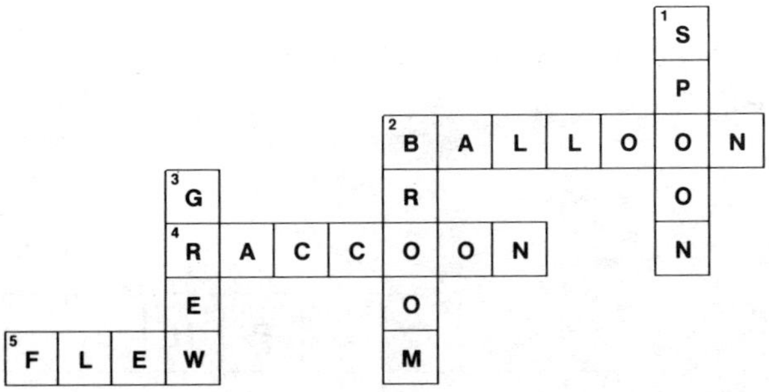

B. 6. flew **7.** grew

Spelling and Language

1. Jane went to the ball game after school. **2.** Mina and Chico went, too. **3.** Jane wore her new coat and boots. **4.** Mina wore two scarves. **5.** But the wind blew so hard, they left early.

UNIT 29

Extra Practice: This Week's Words

1. could **2.** pull **3.** foot **4.** should **5.** wool **6.** would **7.** took **8.** put **9.** wood **10.** full

Extra Practice: Mastery Words

1. cook **2.** look **3.** good **4.** book

Extra Practice: Bonus Words

A. 1. brook **2.** stood **3.** bulldog **4.** bushes **5.** shook **6.** football
B. 7. football **8.** bulldog

Spelling and Language

1. foot, pull, put **2.** took, wool, would **3.** could, foot, full **4.** should, wood, would **5.** foot, pull, should, took **6.** could, full, put, wood

UNIT 30

Review A: Units 25–26

A. 1. slow **2.** note **3.** grow **4.** know, those
B. 5. also **6.** told, cold **7.** soap, road

Review B: Units 27–28

A. 1. young **2.** drink **3.** sing **4.** along **5.** think
B. 6. new, school **7.** who **8.** room **9.** do

Review C: Unit 29 and Test Exercise

A. 1. would **2.** put **3.** pull **4.** took **5.** could
B. 1. c **2.** a **3.** c **4.** b **5.** c **6.** a **7.** c **8.** c

Language Study

1. The following words should be circled: thos, groe. Would you water those flowers to make them grow? **2.** The following words should be circled: seng, rode. Let's sing as we walk along the road. **3.** The following words should be circled: rom, sckool. What room are you in at school? **4.** The following words should be circled: tuke, poot. I took the dish and put it on the table.

Mastery Words Review: Units 25–29

A. 1. rope, nose, home **2.** book, cook, good **3.** men, went
B. 4. go **5.** on **6.** show **7.** true **8.** most **9.** you **10.** soon

Bonus Words Review: Units 25–29

1. spoke, woke, shook **2.** float, strong, follow, hello **3.** roast, broom, bushes, angry, blanket, grew, both, stove, spoon

UNIT 31

Extra Practice: This Week's Words

4. tall, wall, fall, call, water **5.** paw, crawl, draw **6.** because, caught

Extra Practice: Mastery Words

A. 1. ball **2.** fall **3.** all
B. 4. saw
C. 5. saw **6.** all **7.** ball **8.** hall
D. wall

Extra Practice: Bonus Words

A. 1. straw **2.** always **3.** talk **4.** awful **5.** taught **6.** walk
B. 7. talk **8.** walk

C. **9.** always **10.** straw
D. **11.** awful **12.** taught

Spelling and Language

A. **1.** The kitten cried because its paw was caught. **2.** Tom could see over the wall because he is tall. **3.** I will draw a picture of the waterfall because it is so pretty.
B. Example: because I can play

UNIT 32

Extra Practice: This Week's Words

1. town **2.** house **3.** found **4.** out
5. Tower **6.** found **7.** flower **8.** house
9. our **10.** How **11.** now **12.** about

Extra Practice: Mastery Words

A.

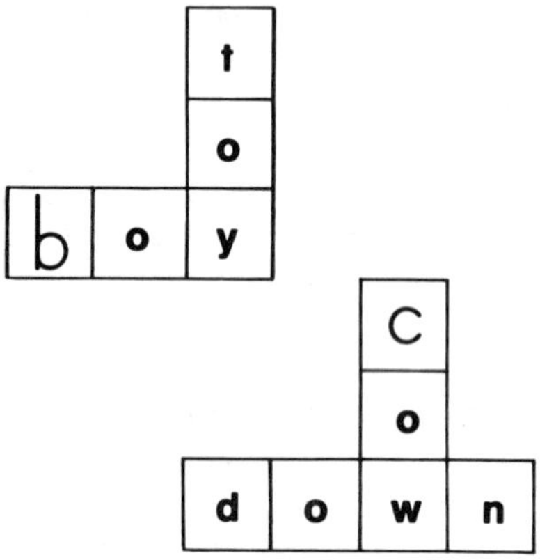

B. **1.** cow **2.** toy **3.** boy **4.** down **5.** toy **6.** down

Extra Practice: Bonus Words

A. **1.** clown **2.** ground **3.** mouse **4.** owl **5.** round **6.** sound
B. **7.** owl **8.** mouse **9.** clown
C. **10.** ground, round, sound Order may vary. **11.** clown, ground Order may vary.

Spelling and Language

A. **1.** how, now **2.** flower, tower, our **3.** house **4.** town
B. **5.** out **6.** found

UNIT 33

Extra Practice: This Week's Words

part, door, far, before, hard, arm, torn, start, more, morning

Extra Practice: Mastery Words

A. **1.** jar **2.** for **3.** are **4.** or

B.

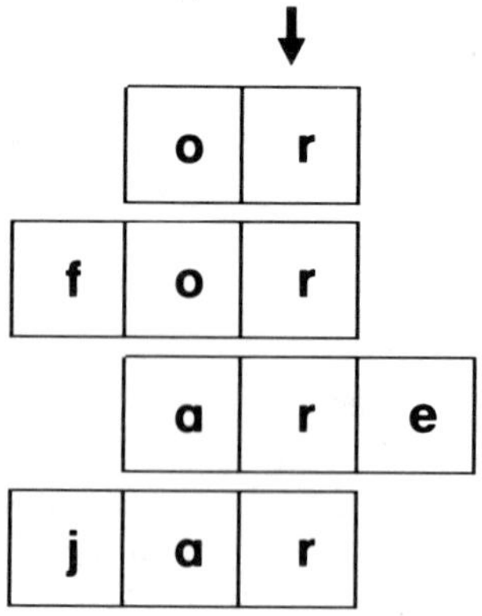

Extra Practice: Bonus Words

A.

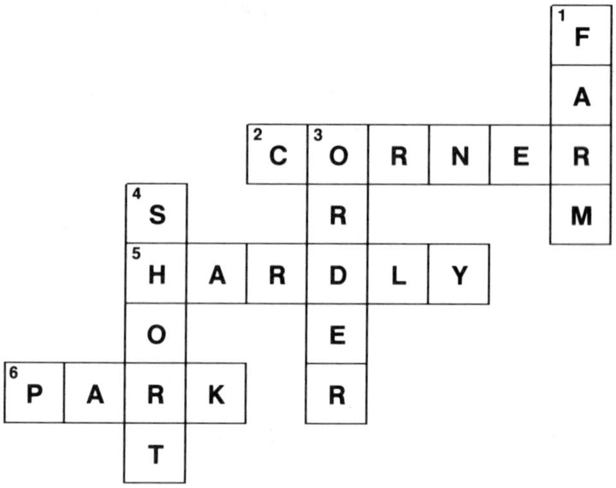

B. **7.** farm **8.** hardly **9.** corner **10.** short **11.** order

Spelling and Language

A. **1.** part **2.** morning **3.** start **4.** before **5.** more **6.** far **7.** hard
B. **8.** morning **9.** start **10.** before **11.** far

UNIT 34

Extra Practice: This Week's Words

A. **1.** turn **2.** girl **3.** word **4.** hurt **5.** bird **6.** work **7.** her
B. **8.** clear **9.** fear **10.** hear **11.** near **12.** tear **13.** year

Extra Practice: Mastery Words

A. **1.** where **2.** dear **3.** were **4.** here
B. **5.** dear, here **6.** Example: The cats were asleep.

Extra Practice: Bonus Words

A. **1.** return **2.** early **3.** learn **4.** person
5. world **6.** circus
B. **7.** learn **8.** return **9.** person
C. **10.** world **11.** circus **12.** learn **13.** early

Spelling and Language

A. **1.** The following words should be circled: gril, neer. That girl lives near me. **2.** The following words should be circled: here, hir. I often hear her singing **3.** The following words should be circled: yer, berd. Last year she bought a bird.
B. **4.**

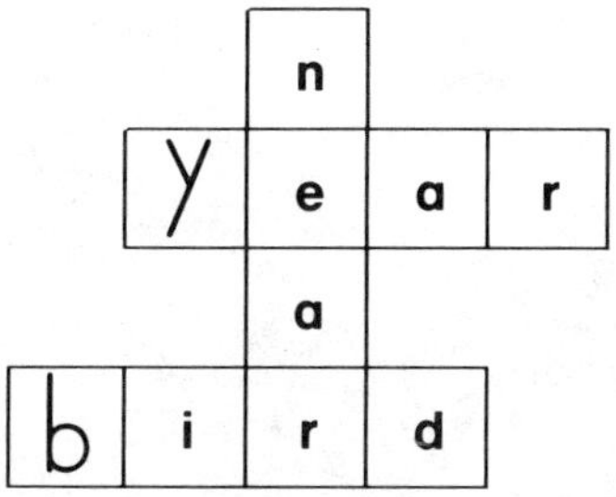

5.

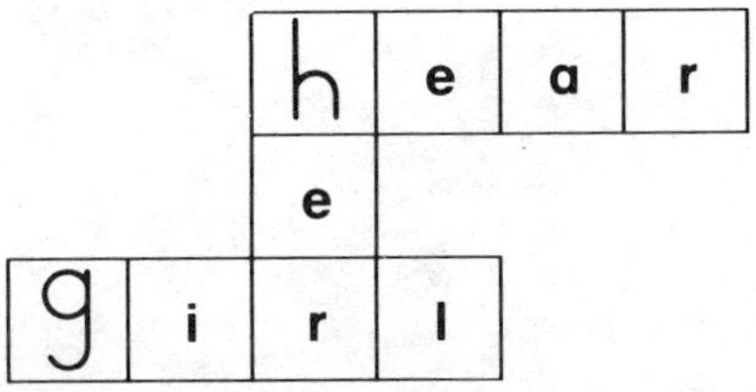

UNIT 35

Extra Practice: This Week's Words

1. other **2.** father **3.** sister, doctor **4.** ever
5. winter **6.** after **7.** color **8.** over
9. dollar

Extra Practice: Mastery Words

1. brother, Charles is Amy's brother. **2.** flower, A rose is a flower. **3.** mother, Kim's mother will drive the car. **4.** water, I am drinking water.

Extra Practice: Bonus Words

A. **1.** letter **2.** mirror **3.** another **4.** flavor
5. sugar **6.** sweater
B. **7.** sweater **8.** mirror **9.** letter

Spelling and Language

A. **1.** Each winter, we visit my grandmother.
2. My sister and father have the same color hair. **3.** I saw the other doctor last time I was here.
B. **4.** Are apples ever other colors? **5.** I have saved one dollar.

UNIT 36

Review A: Units: 31–32

A. **1.** water, tall **2.** because, caught **3.** draw
B. **4.** now **5.** about, house **6.** our **7.** how

Review B: Units 33–34

A. **1.** part, start **2.** before, door **3.** hard
B. **4.** girl, her, turn **5.** turn, work, year

Review C: Unit 35 and Test Exercise

A. **1.** after, color, dollar **2.** dollar, other, over
B. **3.** dollar **4.** other **5.** over **6.** color
C. **1.** w **2.** r **3.** w **4.** w **5.** w **6.** r

Language Study

A. **1.** tall **2.** work **3.** part **4.** start
5. water **6.** girl **7.** before **8.** hard
9. over **10.** now
B. **11.** draw **12.** house **13.** door **14.** year
15. dollar

Mastery Words Review: Units 31–35

1. saw, ball **2.** boy, toy **3.** cow, down **4.** jar, are **5.** for, or **6.** here, dear **7.** brother, mother

Bonus Words Review: Units 31–35

1. Possible answers: always, awful, talk, straw, walk, taught **2.** Possible answers: clown, owl, ground, round, mouse, sound **3.** farm, hardly, park **4.** order, short, corner **5.** Possible answers: early, person, circus, return, learn, world
6. Possible answers: another, mirror, flavor, sugar, letter, sweater

Reteaching Follow-up Masters and Answer Key

The following section provides black-line copying masters to be used in conjunction with the two reteaching strategies provided at the end of each instructional unit in the Teacher's Edition.

Reteaching Follow-up Master A offers an inductive approach to reinforce the spelling generalizations taught in the unit. **Reteaching Follow-up Master B** focuses on the configuration, or shape, of words to reinforce the spellings of words taught in the unit.

Each copying master also appears in reduced form within the teaching plan it accompanies.

The **Answer Key** for the activities follows these copying masters in this Teacher's Resource Book. Note that for activities with unnumbered items, the order of items is generally determined by reading across the page. Also note that for some activities the order of answers may vary.

Contents

Name

Reteaching Follow-up A

Discovering Spelling Ideas

UNIT 1

THIS WEEK'S WORDS

band	mad	neat	pan	real
bag	men	next	pat	rest

1. Write two words that begin with the same consonant sound as each picture name. Use This Week's Words.

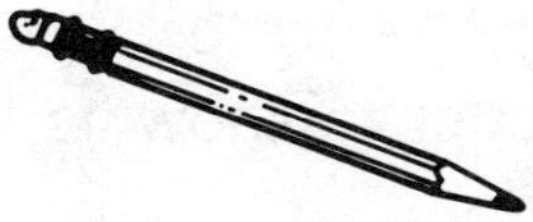

2. Circle the letter that spells the beginning consonant sound.

3. Read the sentences. Mark the box next to the one that is true.

☐ The letters n, r, b, p, and m spell consonant sounds.

☐ The letters n, r, b, p, and m do not spell consonant sounds.

Name

UNIT 1

Reteaching Follow-up B

Word Shapes

A. Write each of This Week's Words in its correct shape. The first one has been done for you.

THIS WEEK'S WORDS
band
bag
mad
men
neat
next
pan
pat
real
rest

1. b a g
2.
3.
4.
5.
6.
7.
8.
9.
10.

B. Add a consonant letter for the beginning sound /b/, /m/, /n/, /p/, or /r/ to make a new word. Write the word. Draw a box around each letter to show its shape. The first one has been done for you.

11. ___ ade m a d e

12. ___ aby

13. ___un

14. ___ o

15. ___ ot

Name

UNIT 2

Reteaching Follow-up A

Discovering Spelling Ideas

THIS WEEK'S WORDS

tell	dear	felt	very	woman
ten	does	fit	went	your

1. Write a word that begins with the same consonant sound as each picture name. Use This Week's Words.

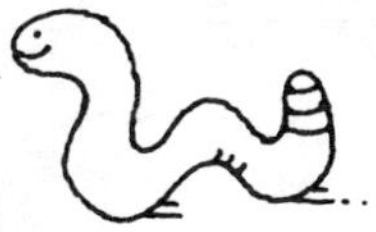

2. Circle the letter that spells the beginning consonant sound.

3. Read the sentences. Mark the box next to the one that is true.

☐ The letters d, f, w, y, t, and v spell consonant sounds.

☐ The letters d, f, w, y, t, and v do not spell consonant sounds.

Name

UNIT 2

Reteaching Follow-up B

Word Shapes

A. Write each of This Week's Words in its correct shape. The first one has been done for you.

THIS WEEK'S WORDS
tell
ten
dear
does
felt
fit
very
went
woman
your

1. d e a r
2.
3.
4.
5.
6.
7.
8.
9.
10.

B. Add a consonant letter for the beginning sound /t/, /d/, /w/, /f/, /v/, or /y/ to make a new word. Write the word. Draw a box around each letter to show its shape. The first one has been done for you.

11. ___ ip t i p
12. ___ ace
13. ___ ance
14. ___ ing

Name

UNIT 3

Reteaching Follow-up A

Discovering Spelling Ideas

THIS WEEK'S WORDS

gold	hall	jar	left	seed
gone	has	jet	live	soon

1. Write two words that begin with the same consonant sound as each picture name. Use This Week's Words.

2. Circle the letter that spells the beginning consonant sound.

3. Read the sentences. Mark the box next to the one that is true.

☐ The letters g, h, j, l, and s do not spell consonant sounds.

☐ The letters g, h, j, l, and s spell consonant sounds.

Name

Reteaching Follow-up B

Word Shapes

UNIT 3

A. Write each of This Week's Words in its correct shape. The first one has been done for you.

THIS WEEK'S WORDS
gold
gone
hall
has
jar
jet
left
live
seed
soon

1. jet
2.
3.
4.
5.
6.
7.
8.
9.
10.

B. Add a consonant letter for the beginning sound /g/, /h/, /j/, /l/, or /s/ to make a new word. Write the word. Draw boxes around each letter to show its shape. The first one has been done for you.

11. ___ ive — give

12. ___ is

13. ___ ump p

14. ___ un

15. ___ ast

Name ____________________

Reteaching Follow-up A

Discovering Spelling Ideas

UNIT 4

THIS WEEK'S WORDS

cat	duck	kite	cup	cake
keep	cow	sick	pick	cook

1. Write the missing letter or letters in each of This Week's Words. Write the word.

___ at ____________ ___ ite ____________

___ ow ____________ ___ up ____________

___ ake ____________ ___ eep ____________

___ ook ____________ du ___ ___ ____________

si ___ ___ ____________ pi ___ ___ ____________

2. Say the words. What sound is spelled by the letters you wrote? ______

3. Complete this sentence. The sound /k/ can be spelled with the letters ___, ___, and ___ ___.

Name

Reteaching Follow-up B

Word Shapes

UNIT 4

A. Write each of This Week's Words in its correct shape. The first one has been done for you.

THIS WEEK'S WORDS
cat
keep
duck
cow
kite
sick
cup
pick
cake
cook

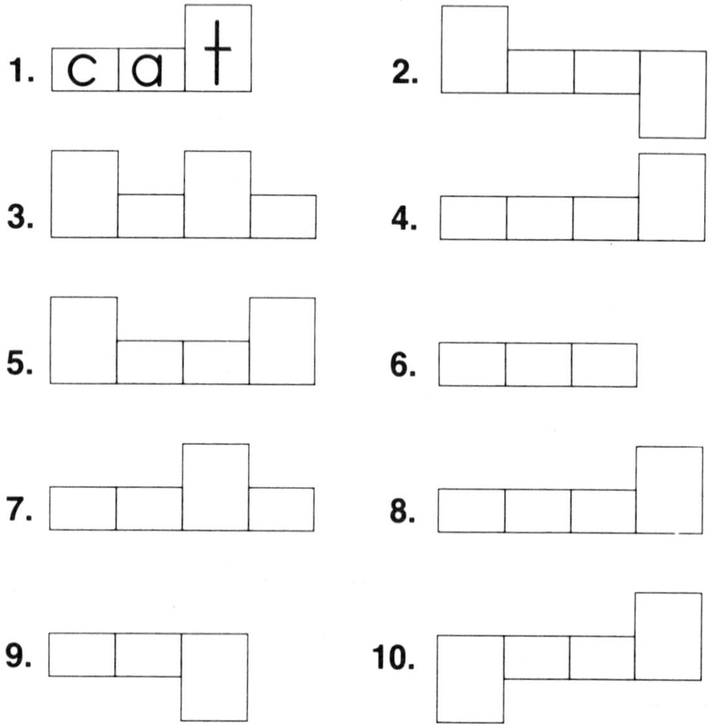

B. Add a letter or letters for the sound /k/ to make a new word. Write the word. Draw a box around each letter to show its shape. The first one has been done for you.

11. ___ ome come

12. ___ iss ____________

13. par ___ ____________

14. sti ___ ___ ____________

Name

UNIT 5

Reteaching Follow-up A

Discovering Spelling Ideas

THIS WEEK'S WORDS

ant	man	as	fast	hand
past	and	bad	fat	last

1. Write the missing letter in each of This Week's Words. Write the word.

___ s ____________

f ___ st ____________

___ nt ____________

m ___ n ____________

p ___ st ____________

b ___ d ____________

h ___ nd ____________

___ nd ____________

f ___ t ____________

l ___ st ____________

2. Say the words. What sound does the missing letter you wrote spell? ______

3. How many ways did you spell the short vowel sound /a/? ______

4. Complete this sentence.
The short vowel sound /a/ is spelled with the letter ______.

Name

Reteaching Follow-up B

Word Shapes

UNIT 5

A. Write each of This Week's Words in its correct shape. The first one has been done for you.

THIS WEEK'S WORDS
ant
past
man
and
as
bad
fast
fat
hand
last

1. past
2.
3.
4.
5.
6.
7.
8.
9.
10.

B. Write the letter that spells the short vowel sound /a/ to make a new word. Write the word. Draw a box around each letter to show its shape. The first one has been done for you.

11. p ___ nts pants
12. fl ___ t
13. cr ___ sh
14. tr ___ ck

Name

Reteaching Follow-up A

Discovering Spelling Ideas

UNIT 7

THIS WEEK'S WORDS

pet	dress	help	sent	well
best	end	leg	set	yet

1. Write the missing letter in each of This Week's Words. Write each word.

b ___ st ________

l ___ g ________

w ___ ll ________

y ___ t ________

p ___ t ________

dr ___ ss ________

s ___ nt ________

h ___ lp ________

___ nd ________

s ___ t ________

2. Say the words. What sound does each missing letter you wrote spell? ________

3. Complete this sentence.
The short vowel sound /e/ is spelled with the letter ________ .

Name

Reteaching Follow-up B

Word Shapes

UNIT 7

A. Write each of This Week's Words in its correct shape. The first one has been done for you.

THIS WEEK'S WORDS
pet
best
dress
end
help
leg
sent
set
well
yet

1. leg
2.
3.
4.
5.
6.
7.
8.
9.
10.

B. Write the letter for the short vowel sound /e/ to make a new word. Write the word. Draw a box around each letter to show its shape. The first one has been done for you.

11. m __ t met
12. f __ lt
13. ch __ ck
14. k __ pt

Name

Reteaching Follow-up A

Discovering Spelling Ideas

UNIT 8

THIS WEEK'S WORDS

fill	fix	his	if	mix
dig	him	hit	is	sit

1. Write the missing letter in each of This Week's Words. Write each word.

___ s ______________

h ___ m ______________

d ___ g ______________

s ___ t ______________

h ___ t ______________

h ___ s ______________

___ f ______________

f ___ ll ______________

m ___ x ______________

f ___ x ______________

2. Say the words. What sound does each missing letter you wrote spell? ______

3. Complete this sentence.
The short vowel sound /i/ is spelled with the letter ______.

Name

Reteaching Follow-up B

Word Shapes

UNIT 8

A. Write each of This Week's Words in its correct shape. The first one has been done for you.

THIS WEEK'S WORDS
fill
dig
fix
him
his
hit
if
is
mix
sit

1. d i g
2.
3.
4.
5.
6.
7.
8.
9.
10.

B. Write the letter that spells the short vowel sound /i/ to make a new word. Write the word. Draw a box around each letter to show the shape of the word. The first one has been done for you.

11. f ___ t   f i t
12. bl ___ mp
13. st ___ ck
14. d ___ p

Name

Reteaching Follow-up A

Discovering Spelling Ideas

THIS WEEK'S WORDS

jump	bug	truck	until	done
rub	just	luck	come	some

1. Add the missing letter to each of This Week's Words. Write the word.

tr ___ ck

___ ntil

j ___ mp

r ___ b

b ___ g

l ___ ck

j ___ st

2. Say the words. What short vowel sound does each missing letter you wrote spell?

3. Complete this sentence.

The sound /u/ is spelled with the letter ___.

4. Write the three words that spell the sound /u/ with the letters o-consonant-e.

Name

Reteaching Follow-up B

Word Shapes

UNIT 9

A. Write each of This Week's Words in its correct shape. The first one has been done for you.

THIS WEEK'S WORDS
jump
rub
bug
just
truck
luck
until
come
done
some

1. r u b
2.
3.
4.
5.
6.
7.
8.
9.
10.

B. Write the letter that spells the short vowel sound /u/ to make a new word. Write the word. Draw a box around each letter to show its shape. The first one has been done for you.

11. m __ d   mud
12. p __ mp
13. st __ ck
14. c __ ff

Name

Reteaching Follow-up A

Discovering Spelling Ideas

THIS WEEK'S WORDS

top	job	pond	shop	soft
dog	lot	pop	lost	song

1. Add the missing letter to each of This Week's Words. Write the word.

j ___ b ______________ s ___ ft ______________

t ___ p ______________ l ___ st ______________

p ___ p ______________ d ___ g ______________

sh ___ p ______________ l ___ t ______________

p ___ nd ______________ s ___ ng ______________

2. Say the words. What two sounds does the missing letter you wrote spell? ______ and ______

3. Complete this sentence.
The sounds /o/ and /ô/ are spelled with the letter ______.

Name

Reteaching Follow-up B

Word Shapes

UNIT 10

A. Write each of This Week's Words in its correct shape. The first one has been done for you.

THIS WEEK'S WORDS
top
dog
job
lot
pond
pop
shop
lost
soft
song

1. dog
2.
3.
4.
5.
6.
7.
8.
9.
10.

B. Write the letter that spells the sound /o/ or /ô/ to make a new word. Write the word. Draw a box around each letter to show its shape. The first one has been done for you.

11. st __ p stop

12. bl __ b

13. t __ ss

14. dr __ p

Name ______

Reteaching Follow-up A

Discovering Spelling Ideas

UNIT 11

THIS WEEK'S WORDS

buzz	ball	cross	grass	off
across	egg	fell	miss	pass

1. Add the double consonant letters to make each of This Week's Words. Write the word.

bu __ __ ______

mi __ __ ______

ba __ __ ______

cro __ __ ______

acro __ __ ______

o __ __ ______

fe __ __ ______

gra __ __ ______

pa __ __ ______

e __ __ ______

2. Say each word. How many sounds does each double consonant spell? ______

3. Complete this sentence. A double consonant is two alike letters that spell ______ sound.

Name

UNIT 11

Reteaching Follow-up B

Word Shapes

A. Write each of This Week's Words in its correct shape. The first one has been done for you.

THIS WEEK'S WORDS

- buzz
- across
- ball
- egg
- cross
- fell
- grass
- miss
- off
- pass

1. a c r o s s
2.
3.
4.
5.
6.
7.
8.
9.
10.

B. Write the missing consonant letter to make a new word. Write the word. Draw a box around each letter to show its shape. The first one has been done for you.

11. hal ___ hall
12. bos ___
13. mil ___
14. cuf ___

Name

Reteaching Follow-up A

Discovering Spelling Ideas

UNIT 13

THIS WEEK'S WORDS

stand	store	glass	plant	most
still	glad	place	please	must

1. Add the missing letters to make This Week's Words. Write each word.

__ __ and ______

__ __ ad ______

__ __ ace ______

__ __ ill ______

__ __ ant ______

__ __ ease ______

__ __ ass ______

__ __ ore ______

mo __ __ ______

mu __ __ ______

2. Say each word. How many sounds do you hear together for each consonant cluster? ______

3. Complete this sentence. A consonant cluster is ______ letters that spell ______ sounds you hear together.

Name

Reteaching Follow-up B

Word Shapes

UNIT 13

A. Write each of This Week's Words in its correct shape. The first one has been done for you.

THIS WEEK'S WORDS
stand
still
store
glad
glass
place
plant
please
most
must

1. stand
2.
3.
4.
5.
6.
7.
8.
9.
10.

B. Write in the consonant clusters gl, st, or pl to make a new word. Write the word. Draw a box around each letter to show its shape. The first one has been done for you.

11. ___ ow glow

12. ___ ay

13. ___ ep

14. ne ___

Name ____________________

Reteaching Follow-up A

Discovering Spelling Ideas

UNIT 14

THIS WEEK'S WORDS

small	swim	friend	front	pretty
spot	brother	from	great	true

1. Add the missing letters to make This Week's Words. Write each word.

__ __ all ____________

__ __ im ____________

__ __ iend ____________

__ __ ont ____________

__ __ ot ____________

__ __ other ____________

__ __ om ____________

__ __ eat ____________

__ __ ue ____________

__ __ etty ____________

2. Say each word. How many sounds do you hear together for each consonant cluster? ____________

3. Complete this sentence. A consonant cluster is ____________ letters that spell ____________ sounds you hear together.

Name

Reteaching Follow-up B

Word Shapes

UNIT 14

A. Write each of This Week's Words in its correct shape. The first one has been done for you.

THIS WEEK'S WORDS
small
spot
swim
brother
friend
from
front
great
pretty
true

1. s m a l l
2.
3.
4.
5.
6.
7.
8.
9.
10.

B. Write in the consonant clusters sm, gr, br, or fr to make a new word. Write the word. Draw a box around each letter to show its shape. The first one has been done for you.

11. ___ og f r o g

12. ___ ay

13. ___ ile

14. ___ own

Name

Reteaching Follow-up A

Discovering Spelling Ideas

UNIT 15

THIS WEEK'S WORDS

sheep	shut	finish	wish	thing
shoe	dish	push	thank	teeth

1. Write This Week's Words spelled with sh under the letters sh. Write the words spelled with th under the letters th.

sh	sh	th

2. Say the words spelled with sh. How many sounds do the letters sh spell?

3. Say the words spelled with th. How many sounds do the letters th spell?

4. Complete this sentence. When words are spelled with the letters ________ or ________ the letters sh and th each spell ________ sound.

Name

Reteaching Follow-up B

Word Shapes

UNIT 15

A. Write each of This Week's Words in its correct shape. The first one has been done for you.

THIS WEEK'S WORDS
sheep
shoe
shut
dish
finish
push
wish
thank
thing
teeth

1. s h e e p

2.

3.

4.

5.

6.

7.

8.

9.

10.

B. Write in the letters sh or th to make a new word. Write the word. Draw a box around each letter to show its shape. The first one has been done for you.

11. ___ ine s h i n e

12. ___ ink

13. wa ___

14. pa ___

Name

Reteaching Follow-up A

Discovering Spelling Ideas

UNIT **16**

THIS WEEK'S WORDS

their	than	then	each	much
chair	them	these	lunch	watch

1. Write This Week's Words spelled with th under the letters th. Write the words spelled with ch under the letters ch. Write the word spelled with tch under the letters tch.

th

ch

ch

tch

2. Say the words spelled with th. How many sounds do the letters th spell? ______

3. Say the words spelled with ch and tch. How many sounds do the letters ch and tch spell? ______

4. Complete this sentence. When words are spelled with the letters ______, ______, and ______ the letters th, ch, and tch each spell ______ sound.

Name

Reteaching Follow-up B

Word Shapes

UNIT 16

A. Write each of This Week's Words in its correct shape. The first one has been done for you.

THIS WEEK'S WORDS
their
chair
than
them
then
these
each
lunch
much
watch

1. their
2.
3.
4.
5.
6.
7.
8.
9.
10.

B. Write in the letters th and ch to make a new word. Write the word. Draw a box around each letter to show its shape. The first one has been done for you.

11. ___ ere there

12. ___ in

13. ___ at

14. pea ___

Name

UNIT 17

Reteaching Follow-up A

Discovering Spelling Ideas

THIS WEEK'S WORDS

there	were	when	want	been
here	what	where	again	use

1. Write two words that end like the word below but do not rhyme.

there ______ ______

2. Write a word that ends like each word below but does not rhyme.

seen ______ rain ______

3. Say the words what and want. Listen to the vowel sound in each word. Now circle the correct sentence about what and want.

The a in what and the a in want stand for the same sound.

The a in what and the a in want stand for different sounds.

4. Circle the correct sentence about This Week's Words.

In some words, the same letters don't stand for the same sound.

In all the words, the same letters stand for the same sound.

5. Complete this sentence about spelling This Week's Words.

I must ______ all the ______ that make up each ______ .

Name

Reteaching Follow-up B

Word Shapes

UNIT **17**

A. Write each of This Week's Words in its correct shape. The first one has been done for you.

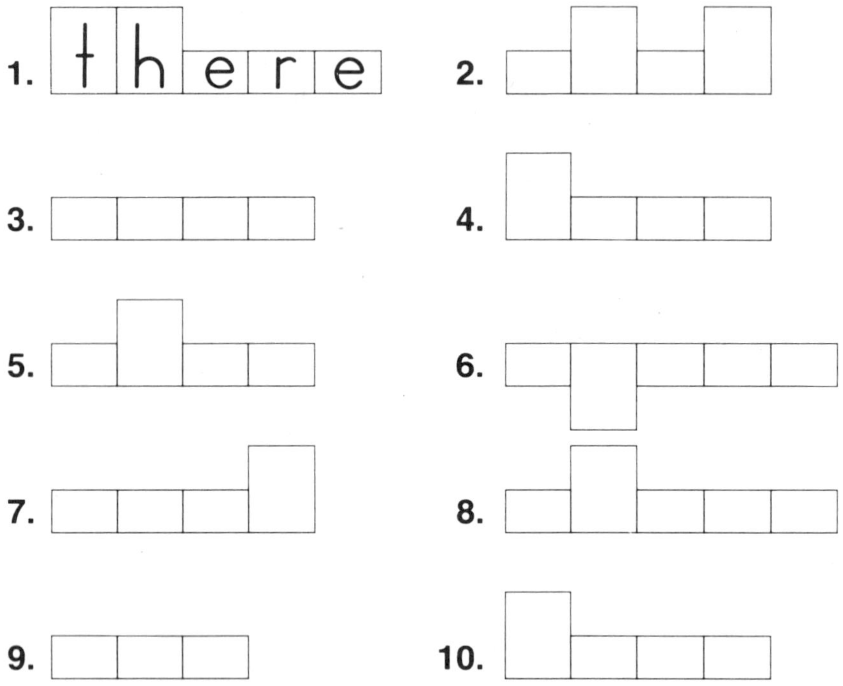

THIS WEEK'S WORDS

there
here
were
what
when
where
want
again
been
use

B. Follow the directions. Use This Week's Words. Write the word. Draw a box around each letter to show its shape.

11. Write the word that begins with two tall letters. Draw boxes around the tall letters. ____________

12. Write the word with a tail letter. Draw a box around the tail letter. ____________

13. Write the two words that have no tall letters or tail letters. ____________ ____________

Name

Reteaching Follow-up A

Discovering Spelling Ideas

UNIT 19

THIS WEEK'S WORDS

wave	bake	gave	race	save
ate	face	late	same	have

1. Say each of This Week's Words. Write all the words with the long vowel sound /ā/.

2. Which two vowels are in each word? ______ and ______

3. How many consonants come between the vowels? Circle the answer. one two

4. Complete this sentence.

Words spelled with ______ -consonant- ______ spell the ______________ vowel sound ______.

5. Write This Week's Word that is spelled with a-consonant-e but does not have the sound /ā/.

Name

Reteaching Follow-up B

Word Shapes

UNIT 19

A. Write each of This Week's Words in its correct shape. The first one has been done for you.

THIS WEEK'S WORDS
wave
ate
bake
face
gave
late
race
same
save
have

1. wave
2.
3.
4.
5.
6.
7.
8.
9.
10.

B. Write in the letters that spell the long vowel /ā/ to make a new word. Write the word. Draw a box around each letter to show its shape. The first one has been done for you.

11. l __ k __ lake

12. m __ d __

Name

Reteaching Follow-up A

Discovering Spelling Ideas

UNIT 20

THIS WEEK'S WORDS

train	paint	tail	may	stay
nail	plain	away	pay	they

1. Write This Week's Words that have the letters ai and ay. Circle the ai or ay in each word.

2. Say the words. What vowel sound do you hear in *all* the words?

3. Complete this sentence.

The sound ______ can be spelled ______ or ______.

4. Write the word that has the sound /ā/, but is not spelled with ai or ay.

Name

Reteaching Follow-up B

Word Shapes

UNIT 20

A. Write each of This Week's Words in its correct shape. The first one has been done for you.

THIS WEEK'S WORDS
train
nail
paint
plain
tail
away
may
pay
stay
they

1. train
2.
3.
4.
5.
6.
7.
8.
9.
10.

B. Write the letters that spell the sound /ā/ to make a new word. Write the word. Draw a box around each letter to show its shape. The first one has been done for you.

11. r ___ ___ n   rain

12. p ___ ___ n

Name

Reteaching Follow-up A

Discovering Spelling Ideas

UNIT 21

THIS WEEK'S WORDS

deep	free	three	leave	many
feel	street	mean	teach	easy

1. Write This Week's Words. Circle the letters ee, ea, or y in each word.

2. Say the words. What vowel sound do you hear in all the words?

3. Write the vowel letter or letters that spell the sound /ē/ in This Week's Words.

4. Complete this sentence.

The three ways to spell ______ are with the letters ______, ______, and ______.

Name

Reteaching Follow-up B

Word Shapes

UNIT 21

A. Write each of This Week's Words in its correct shape. The first one has been done for you.

THIS WEEK'S WORDS
deep
feel
free
street
three
mean
leave
teach
many
easy

1. deep
2.
3.
4.
5.
6.
7.
8.
9.
10.

B. Write the letters that spell the sound /ē/ to make a new word. Write the word. Draw a box around each letter to show its shape. The first one has been done for you.

11. f ___ ___ t feet

12. p ___ ___ ch

Name

Reteaching Follow-up A

Discovering Spelling Ideas

UNIT 22

THIS WEEK'S WORDS

write	fine	nice	time	wide
bike	fire	side	tire	give

1. Add the missing vowel letters to make some of This Week's Words. Write the words.

wr ___ t ___ f ___ n ___ n ___ c ___

b ___ k ___ t ___ m ___ w ___ d ___

f ___ r ___ s ___ d ___ t ___ r ___

2. Say each word. What vowel sound do you hear? ______

3. Complete this sentence.

Words spelled with ______ -consonant- ______ spell the long vowel sound ______.

4. Write the word that has the vowel spelled i-consonant-e but does not have the sound /ī/. ______

Name

Reteaching Follow-up B

Word Shapes

UNIT 22

A. Write each of This Week's Words in its correct shape. The first one has been done for you.

THIS WEEK'S WORDS
write
bike
fine
fire
nice
side
time
tire
wide
give

1. write
2.
3.
4.
5.
6.
7.
8.
9.
10.

B. Write the letters that spell the sound /ī/ to make a new word. Write the word. Draw a box around each letter to show its shape. The first one has been done for you.

11. h ___ d ___ hide

12. p ___ n ___

Name

Reteaching Follow-up A

Discovering Spelling Ideas

UNIT 23

THIS WEEK'S WORDS

sky	try	find	high	right
dry	why	kind	night	tie

1. Add the missing letters to spell some of This Week's Words. Write the words.

sk __ dr __ tr __

wh __ f __ __ __ k __ __ __

h __ __ __ r __ __ __ t n __ __ __ t

2. Say the words. What vowel sound do you hear in each word?

3. Write the three ways you spell the sound /ī/ in This Week's Words.

________, ________ before nd, and ________

4. Write the word that spells the sound /ī/ with the letters ie.

Name

Reteaching Follow-up B

Word Shapes

UNIT 23

A. Write each of This Week's Words in its correct shape. The first one has been done for you.

THIS WEEK'S WORDS
sky
dry
try
why
find
kind
high
night
right
tie

1. sky
2.
3.
4.
5.
6.
7.
8.
9.
10.

B. Write the letters that spell the sound /ī/ to make a new word. Write the word. Draw a box around each letter to show its shape. The first one has been done for you.

11. p __ __ pie

12. m __ n __

Harcourt Brace School Publishers

Name ___

Reteaching Follow-up A

Discovering Spelling Ideas

UNIT 25

THIS WEEK'S WORDS

row	note	those	know	slow
hope	stone	grow	low	own

1. Write the missing vowel letters to make each of This Week's Words. Write the word.

h ___ p ___ ____________

n ___ t ___ ____________

st ___ n ___ ____________

th ___ s ___ ____________

r ___ ___ ____________

gr ___ ___ ____________

kn ___ ___ ____________

l ___ ___ ____________

sl ___ ___ ____________

___ ___ n ____________

2. Say the words. What vowel sound do you hear in each word?

______

3. Write the two ways to spell the sound /ō/ in This Week's Words.

______-consonant-______ and ______

Name

Reteaching Follow-up B

Word Shapes

A. Write each of This Week's Words in its correct shape. The first one has been done for you.

THIS WEEK'S WORDS

row
hope
note
stone
those
grow
know
low
slow
own

1. r o w
2.
3.
4.
5.
6.
7.
8.
9.
10.

B. Write the letters that spell the sound /ō/ to make a new word. Write the word. Draw a box around each letter to show its shape. The first one has been done for you.

11. j ___ k ___   j o k e

12. bl ___ ___

Name

Reteaching Follow-up A

Discovering Spelling Ideas

UNIT 26

THIS WEEK'S WORDS

cold	told	also	oak	soap
toad	ago	goat	road	hold

1. Write the missing vowel letters to make each of This Week's Words. Write the word.

c __ ld ________ t __ ld ________

ag __ ________ als __ ________

h __ ld ________ t __ __ d ________

g __ __ t ________ __ __ k ________

r __ __ d ________ s __ __ p ________

2. Say the words. What vowel sound do you hear in each word?

____

3. Write the two ways to spell the sound /ō/ in This Week's Words.

________ and ________

Name ______________________________

Reteaching Follow-up B

Word Shapes

UNIT 26

A. Write each of This Week's Words in its correct shape. The first one has been done for you.

THIS WEEK'S WORDS
cold
toad
told
ago
also
goat
oak
road
soap
hold

1. c o l d
2.
3.
4.
5.
6.
7.
8.
9.
10.

B. Write the letters that spell the sound /ō/ to make a new word. Write the word. Draw a box around each letter to show its shape. The first one has been done for you.

11. f ___ ld   f o l d
12. g ___   ______________
13. b ___ t   ______________
14. sc ___ ld   ______________

Name

Reteaching Follow-up A

Discovering Spelling Ideas

UNIT 27

THIS WEEK'S WORDS

long	along	ring	young	drink
trunk	hang	sing	bank	think

1. Write the missing letters to make each of This Week's Words. Write the word.

lo ___ ___ ________

alo ___ ___ ________

ha ___ ___ ________

ri ___ ___ ________

si ___ ___ ________

you ___ ___ ________

tru ___ ___ ________

ba ___ ___ ________

dri ___ ___ ________

thi ___ ___ ________

2. Say the words in the first column. How many sounds do the letters ng spell? ________

3. Say the words in the second column. Then complete this sentence.

The letter ________ in trunk stands for the sound /ng/

as the letters ___ ___ do in young.

Name

Reteaching Follow-up B

Word Shapes

UNIT 27

A. Write each of This Week's Words in its correct shape. The first one has been done for you.

THIS WEEK'S WORDS
long
trunk
along
hang
ring
sing
young
bank
drink
think

1. 2. 3. 4. 5. 6. 7. 8. 9. 10.

B. Write in the letters ng or nk to make a new word. Write the word. Draw a box around each letter to show its shape. The first one has been done for you.

11. so ___ ___

12. ta ___ ___

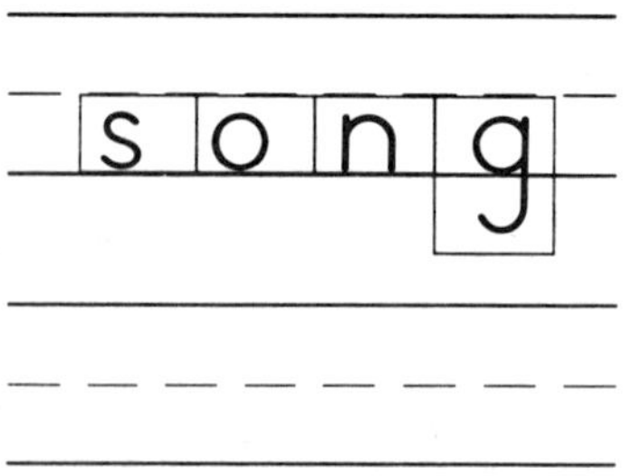

Name

Reteaching Follow-up A

Discovering Spelling Ideas

THIS WEEK'S WORDS

two	boot	do	too	school
new	to	who	room	blew

1. Write the words spelled with o in the first column. Write the words spelled with oo in the middle column. Write the words spelled with ew in the last column.

o	oo	ew
________	________	________
________	________	________
________	________	
________	________	

2. Say the words. What vowel sound do you hear in each word? ________

3. Write the ways you learned to spell the sound /o͞o/. ____, ____, and ____

4. Circle the word below that has the vowel sound /o͞o/. Write the word.

got grew grow ________

Name ____________________

Reteaching Follow-up B

Word Shapes

UNIT **28**

A. Write each of This Week's Words in its correct shape. The first one has been done for you.

THIS WEEK'S WORDS
two
new
boot
to
do
who
too
room
school
blew

1. two
2. ____
3. ____
4. ____
5. ____
6. ____
7. ____
8. ____
9. ____
10. ____

B. Write the letters that spell the sound /o͞o/ to make a new word. Write the word. Draw a box around each letter to show its shape. The first one has been done for you.

11. t ___ ___ l   tool

12. m ___ ___ n   ____

Name

Reteaching Follow-up A

Discovering Spelling Ideas

UNIT 29

THIS WEEK'S WORDS

pull	put	took	wool	should
full	foot	wood	could	would

1. Write the words spelled with u in the first column. Write the words spelled with oo in the middle column. Write the words spelled with ou in the last column.

u	oo	ou

2. Say the words. What vowel sound do you hear in each word?

3. Write the ways you learned to spell the sound /o͝o/. ____, ____, and ____

4. Circle the word below that has the vowel sound /o͝o/. Write the word.

book boat but

Name

Reteaching Follow-up B

Word Shapes

UNIT 29

A. Write each of This Week's Words in its correct shape. The first one has been done for you.

THIS WEEK'S WORDS
pull
full
put
foot
took
wood
wool
could
should
would

1. 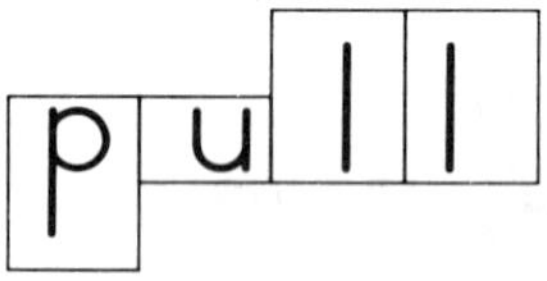

2. 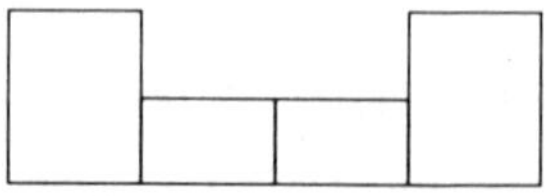

3. 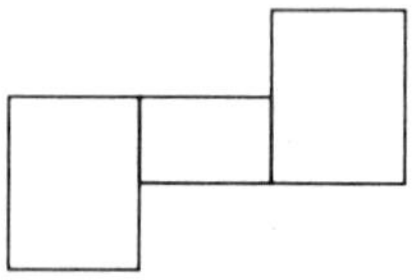

4. 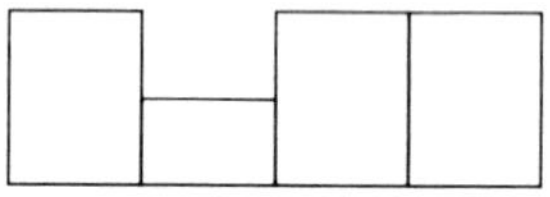

5. 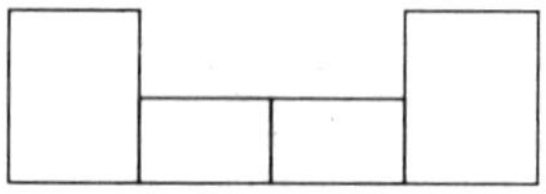

6. 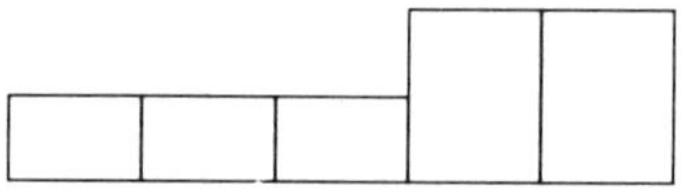

7. 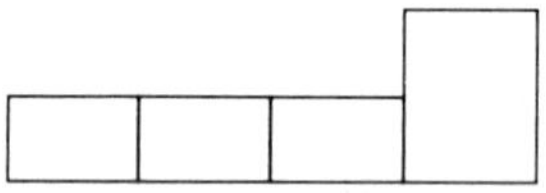

8. 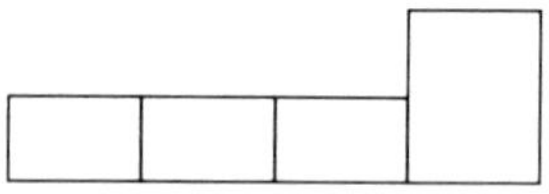

9. 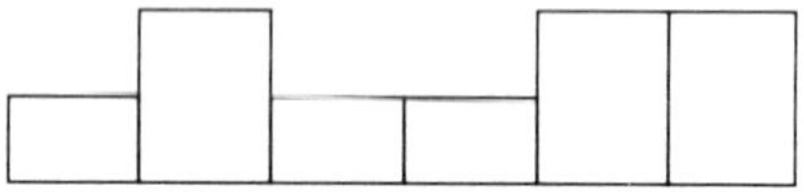

10. 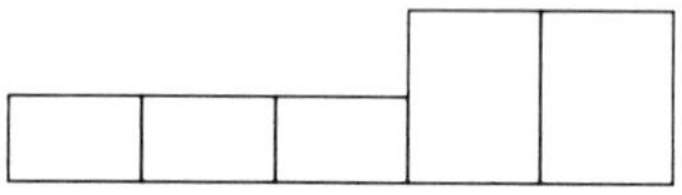

B. Write the letters that spell the sound /o͝o/ to make a new word. Write the word. Draw a box around each letter to show its shape. The first one has been done for you.

11. g __ __ d 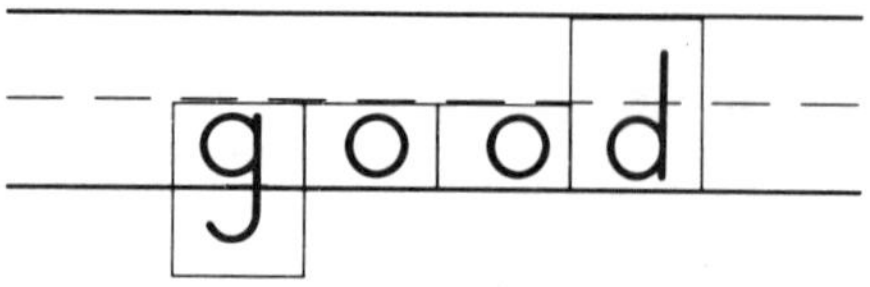

12. b __ ll

Name

Reteaching Follow-up A

Discovering Spelling Ideas

UNIT 31

THIS WEEK'S WORDS

tall	fall	water	draw	because
call	wall	paw	crawl	caught

1. Write the words spelled with a in the first column. Write the words spelled with aw in the middle column. Write the words spelled with au in the last column.

a	aw	au
______	______	______
______	______	______
______	______	
______		
______		

2. Say the words. What vowel sound do you hear in each word? ______

3. Write the ways you learned to spell the sound /ô/. ____, ____, and ____

Name

Reteaching Follow-up B

Word Shapes

UNIT 31

A. Write each of This Week's Words in its correct shape. The first one has been done for you.

THIS WEEK'S WORDS

tall
call
fall
wall
water
paw
draw
crawl
because
caught

1. t a l l

2.

3.

4.

5.

6.

7.

8.

9.

10.

B. Write the letters that spell the sound /ô/ to make a new word. Write the word. Draw a box around each letter to show its shape. The first one has been done for you.

11. c __ __ se   c a u s e

12. s __ __

Name

Reteaching Follow-up A

Discovering Spelling Ideas

UNIT 32

THIS WEEK'S WORDS

house	about	our	how	tower
flower	found	out	now	town

1. Write the words spelled with ou in one column. Write the words spelled with ow in the other column.

ou ow

2. Say the words. What vowel sound do you hear in each word?

3. Write the ways you learned to spell the sound /ou/. ______ and ______

4. Circle the word below that has the vowel sound /ou/. Write the word.

shot shout shoe

Name

Reteaching Follow-up B

Word Shapes

UNIT 32

A. Write each of This Week's Words in its correct shape. The first one has been done for you.

THIS WEEK'S WORDS
house
flower
about
found
our
out
how
now
tower
town

1. h o u s e
2.
3.
4.
5.
6.
7.
8.
9.
10.

B. Write the letters that spell the sound /ou/ to make a new word. Write the word. Draw a box around each letter to show its shape.The first one has been done for you.

11. p __ __ nd   p o u n d

12. sh __ __ er

Name

Reteaching Follow-up A

Discovering Spelling Ideas

UNIT 33

THIS WEEK'S WORDS

part	far	start	torn	more
arm	hard	morning	before	door

1. Add the missing letters. Write This Week's Words.

p __ __ t ________

st __ __ t ________

__ __ m ________

bef __ __ __ ________

f __ __ ________

m __ __ __ ________

h __ __ d ________

t __ __ n ________

m __ __ ning ________

2. Say the words. What letter follows the vowel in each word? ________

3. What letters did you use to spell the sounds /är/? ________

4. Write two ways to spell the sounds /ôr/. ________ and ________

5. Write a word in which /ôr/ is spelled oor. ________

Name

Reteaching Follow-up B

Word Shapes

UNIT 33

A. Write each of This Week's Words in its correct shape. The first one has been done for you.

THIS WEEK'S WORDS
part
arm
far
hard
start
morning
torn
before
more
door

1. part
2.
3.
4.
5.
6.
7.
8.
9.
10.

B. Write the letters that spell the sound /är/ or /ôr/ to make a new word. Write the word. Draw a box around each letter to show its shape. The first one has been done for you.

11. c ___ ___ t   cart

12. st ___ ___ e

Name ______

Reteaching Follow-up A

Discovering Spelling Ideas

UNIT 34

THIS WEEK'S WORDS

work	girl	hurt	word	near
bird	her	turn	hear	year

1. Add the missing letters. Write This Week's Words.

w ___ ___ k ______

t ___ ___ n ______

b ___ ___ d ______

w ___ ___ d ______

g ___ ___ l ______

h ___ ___ ___ ______

h ___ ___ ______

n ___ ___ ___ ______

h ___ ___ t ______

y ___ ___ ___ ______

2. Say the words. What letter follows the vowel sound in each word? ___

3. Write four ways to spell the sounds /ûr/.

______, ______, ______, and ______

4. Write the letters that spell the sounds /ir/ in This Week's Words. ______

Name

Reteaching Follow-up B

Word Shapes

UNIT 34

A. Write each of This Week's Words in its correct shape. The first one has been done for you.

THIS WEEK'S WORDS
work
bird
girl
her
hurt
turn
word
hear
near
year

1. w o r k
2.
3.
4.
5.
6.
7.
8.
9.
10.

B. Write the letters that spell the sounds /ûr/ or /ir/ to make a new word. Write the word. Draw a box around each letter to show its shape. The first one has been done for you.

11. sk ___ ___ t   s k i r t

12. w ___ ___ m

Name

Reteaching Follow-up A

Discovering Spelling Ideas

UNIT 35

THIS WEEK'S WORDS

winter	sister	ever	over	doctor
father	after	other	color	dollar

1. Add the missing letters. Write This Week's Words.

wint ___ ___ ________

fath ___ ___ ________

sist ___ ___ ________

aft ___ ___ ________

ev ___ ___ ________

oth ___ ___ ________

ov ___ ___ ________

col ___ ___ ________

doct ___ ___ ________

doll ___ ___ ________

2. Say the words. What letter follows the vowel sound in each word? ________

3. Write three ways to spell the sounds /ər/.

______, ______, and ______

4. Circle the word with the sounds /ər/. Write the word.

star dancer deer ________

Name

Reteaching Follow-up B

Word Shapes

UNIT 35

A. Write each of This Week's Words in its correct shape. The first one has been done for you.

1. winter
2.
3.
4.
5.
6.
7.
8.
9.
10.

THIS WEEK'S WORDS

winter
father
sister
after
ever
other
over
color
doctor
dollar

B. Write the letters that spell the sounds /ər/ to make a new word. Write the word. Draw a box around each letter to show its shape. The first one has been done for you.

11. pol ___ ___ polar

12. nev ___ ___

Answer Key for Reteaching Follow-up Masters

UNIT 1

Reteaching Follow-up A

1. neat, next; real, rest; band, bag; pan, pat; mad, men **2.** see above **3.** The first box should be marked.

Reteaching Follow-up B

A. 1. bag **2.** band **3.** neat/real/next/rest **4.** men **5.** mad **6.** neat/real/next/rest **7.** neat/real/next/rest **8.** pat **9.** pan **10.** neat/real/next/rest

B. 11. made **12.** baby **13.** run **14.** no **15.** pot

UNIT 2

Reteaching Follow-up A

1. dear, does; felt, fit; woman, went; your; ten, tell; very **2.** see above **3.** The first box should be marked.

Reteaching Follow-up B

A. 1. dear **2.** fit **3.** very **4.** ten **5.** tell/felt **6.** your **7.** tell/felt **8.** woman **9.** does **10.** went

B. 11. tip **12.** face **13.** dance **14.** wing

UNIT 3

Reteaching Follow-up A

1. seed, soon; left, live; hall, has; jar, jet; gold, gone **2.** see above **3.** The second box should be marked.

Reteaching Follow-up B

A. 1. jet **2.** gold **3.** left/hall **4.** gone **5.** has **6.** seed **7.** left/hall **8.** live **9.** soon **10.** jar

B. 11. give **12.** his **13.** jump **14.** sun **15.** last

UNIT 4

Reteaching Follow-up A

1. cat, kite, cow, cup, cake, keep, cook, duck, sick, pick **2.** /k/ **3.** c, k, and c k

Reteaching Follow-up B

A. 1. cat **2.** keep **3.** kite **4.** sick/cook **5.** duck **6.** cow **7.** cake **8.** sick/cook **9.** cup **10.** pick

B. 11. come **12.** kiss **13.** park **14.** stick

UNIT 5

Reteaching Follow-up A

1. as, fast, ant, man, past, bad, hand, and, fat, last **2.** /a/ **3.** one **4.** a

Reteaching Follow-up B

A. 1. past **2.** fat/bad **3.** ant/and **4.** fast/hand/last **5.** ant/and **6.** fat/bad **7.** man **8.** fast/hand/last **9.** fast/hand/last **10.** as

B. 11. pants **12.** flat **13.** crash **14.** track

UNIT 7

Reteaching Follow-up A

1. best, leg, well, yet, pet, dress, sent, help, end, set **2.** /e/ **3.** e

Reteaching Follow-up B

A. 1. leg **2.** pet/yet **3.** best **4.** sent **5.** dress **6.** well **7.** end/set **8.** end/set **9.** pet/yet **10.** help

B. 11. met **12.** felt **13.** check **14.** kept

UNIT 8

Reteaching Follow-up A

1. is, him, dig, sit, hit, his, if, fill, mix, fix **2.** /i/ **3.** i

Reteaching Follow-up B

A. 1. dig **2.** if **3.** fill **4.** hit **5.** fix/his/him **6.** mix **7.** fix/his/him **8.** is **9.** fix/his/him **10.** sit

B. 11. fit **12.** blimp **13.** stick **14.** dip

UNIT 9

Reteaching Follow-up A

1. truck, until, jump, rub, bug, luck, just **2.** /u/ **3.** u **4.** come, some, done

Reteaching Follow-up B

A. 1. rub **2.** jump **3.** truck **4.** luck **5.** bug **6.** just **7.** done **8.** come/some **9.** until **10.** come/some

B. 11. mud **12.** pump **13.** stuck **14.** cuff

UNIT 10

Reteaching Follow-up A
1. job, soft, top, lost, pop, dog, shop, lot, pond, song **2.** /o/, /ô/ **3.** o

Reteaching Follow-up B
A. 1. dog **2.** top **3.** pond **4.** pop **5.** job **6.** lot **7.** soft **8.** song **9.** shop **10.** lost
B. 11. stop **12.** blob **13.** toss **14.** drop

UNIT 11

Reteaching Follow-up A
1. buzz, miss, ball, cross, across, off, fell, grass, pass, egg **2.** one **3.** one

Reteaching Follow-up B
A. 1. across **2.** buzz **3.** cross **4.** fell/ball **5.** fell/ball **6.** egg **7.** off **8.** miss **9.** grass **10.** pass
B. 11. hall **12.** boss **13.** mill **14.** cuff

UNIT 13

Reteaching Follow-up A
1. stand, glad, place, still, plant, please, glass, store, most, must **2.** two **3.** two, two

Reteaching Follow-up B
A. 1. stand **2.** glad **3.** glass/place **4.** still **5.** store **6.** please **7.** most/must **8.** glass/place **9.** plant **10.** most/must
B. 11. glow **12.** play/stay **13.** step **14.** nest

UNIT 14

Reteaching Follow-up A
1. small, swim, friend, front, spot, brother, from, great, true, pretty **2.** two **3.** two, two

Reteaching Follow-up B
A. 1. small **2.** brother **3.** swim **4.** spot **5.** friend **6.** from/true **7.** front **8.** great **9.** from/true **10.** pretty
B. 11. frog **12.** gray **13.** smile **14.** grown/brown/frown

UNIT 15

Reteaching Follow-up A
1. sh: sheep, dish, shoe, finish, shut, push, wish; th: thank, thing, teeth **2.** one **3.** one
4. sh, th, one

Reteaching Follow-up B
A. 1. sheep **2.** dish **3.** finish **4.** shoe **5.** shut **6.** thank **7.** wish **8.** push **9.** thing **10.** teeth
B. 11. shine **12.** think **13.** wash **14.** path

UNIT 16

Reteaching Follow-up A
1. th: their, than, them, these, then; ch: chair, each, lunch, much; tch: watch **2.** one **3.** one
4. th, ch, tch; one

Reteaching Follow-up B
A. 1. their **2.** them/than/then **3.** them/than/then **4.** chair **5.** them/than/then **6.** watch **7.** lunch **8.** each/much **9.** each/much **10.** these
B. 11. there **12.** thin/chin **13.** that/chat **14.** peach

UNIT 17

Reteaching Follow-up A
1. here, were **2.** been, again **3.** The following sentence should be circled: The a in what and the a in want stand for different sounds. **4.** The following sentence should be circled: In some words, the same letters don't stand for the same sound. **5.** remember, letters, word

Reteaching Follow-up B
A. 1. there **2.** what **3.** were **4.** here/been **5.** when **6.** again **7.** want **8.** where **9.** use **10.** here/been
B. 11. there **12.** again **13.** were, use

UNIT 19

Reteaching Follow-up A
1. wave, face, race, ate, gave, same, bake, late, save **2.** a, e **3.** one **4.** a, e, long, /ā/
5. have

Reteaching Follow-up B
A. 1. wave **2.** face/have **3.** bake/late **4.** ate **5.** same/save/race **6.** bake/late **7.** gave **8.** face/have **9.** same/save/race **10.** same/save/race
B. 11. lake **12.** made

UNIT 20

Reteaching Follow-up A
1. tr(ai)n, m(ay), pl(ai)n, p(ai)nt, st(ay), aw(ay), t(ai)l, n(ai)l, p(ay) **2.** /ā/ **3.** /ā/, ai/ay **4.** they

Reteaching Follow-up B

A. **1.** train **2.** plain **3.** may **4.** nail **5.** tail **6.** they **7.** paint **8.** pay **9.** stay **10.** away

B. **11.** rain **12.** pain

UNIT 21

Reteaching Follow-up A

1. deep, street, teach, feel, three, many, free, mean, easy, leave **2.** /ē/ **3.** ee, ea, y **4.** /ē/, ee, ea, y

Reteaching Follow-up B

A. **1.** deep **2.** feel **3.** free **4.** street **5.** three **6.** mean **7.** leave **8.** teach **9.** many/easy **10.** many/easy

B. **11.** feet **12.** peach

UNIT 22

Reteaching Follow-up A

1. write, fine, nice, bike, time, wide, fire, side, tire **2.** /ī/ **3.** i, e, /ī/ **4.** give

Reteaching Follow-up B

A. **1.** write **2.** bike **3.** fine/fire/time/tire **4.** fine/fire/time/tire **5.** nice **6.** side/wide **7.** fine/fire/time/tire **8.** fine/fire/time/tire **9.** side/wide **10.** give

B. **11.** hide **12.** pine

UNIT 23

Reteaching Follow-up A

1. sky, dry, try, why, find, kind, high, right, night **2.** /ī/ **3.** y, i, igh **4.** tie

Reteaching Follow-up B

A. **1.** sky **2.** why **3.** try/dry **4.** try/dry **5.** find/kind **6.** find/kind **7.** high **8.** tie **9.** right/night **10.** right/night

B. **11.** pie **12.** mind

UNIT 25

Reteaching Follow-up A

1. hope, note, stone, those, row, grow, know, low, slow, own **2.** /ō/ **3.** o, e, ow

Reteaching Follow-up B

A. **1.** row **2.** stone **3.** those **4.** hope **5.** note **6.** grow **7.** slow **8.** own **9.** know **10.** low

B. **11.** joke **12.** blow

UNIT 26

Reteaching Follow-up A

1. cold, told, ago, also, hold, toad, goat, oak, road, soap **2.** /ō/ **3.** o, oa

Reteaching Follow-up B

A. **1.** cold **2.** ago **3.** told/hold **4.** toad **5.** also **6.** goat **7.** oak **8.** road **9.** soap **10.** told/hold

B. **11.** fold **12.** go **13.** boat **14.** scold

UNIT 27

Reteaching Follow-up A

1. long, young, along, trunk, hang, bank, ring, drink, sing, think **2.** one **3.** n, n g

Reteaching Follow-up B

A. **1.** long **2.** hang **3.** along **4.** trunk/drink **5.** ring/sing **6.** bank **7.** young **8.** ring/sing **9.** trunk/drink **10.** think

B. **11.** song **12.** tank

UNIT 28

Reteaching Follow-up A

1. o: two, to, do, who; oo: boot, too, room, school; ew: new, blew **2.** /o͞o/ **3.** o, oo, ew **4.** grew

Reteaching Follow-up B

A. **1.** two **2.** to/do **3.** to/do **4.** new **5.** boot **6.** who **7.** school **8.** blew **9.** too **10.** room

B. **11.** tool **12.** moon

UNIT 29

Reteaching Follow-up A

1. u: pull, full, put; oo: foot, took, wood, wool; ou: could, should, would **2.** /o͝o/ **3.** u, oo, ou **4.** book

Reteaching Follow-up B

A. **1.** pull **2.** foot/took **3.** put **4.** full **5.** foot/took **6.** could/would **7.** wool/wood **8.** wool/wood **9.** should **10.** could/would

B. **11.** good **12.** bull

UNIT 31

Reteaching Follow-up A

1. a: tall, call, fall, wall, water; aw: paw, draw, crawl; au: because, caught **2.** /ô/ **3.** a, aw, au

Reteaching Follow-up B

A. 1. tall **2.** wall/call **3.** fall **4.** wall/call **5.** water **6.** crawl **7.** draw **8.** paw **9.** because **10.** caught

B. 11. cause **12.** saw

UNIT 32

Reteaching Follow-up A

1. ou: house, about, found, our, out; ow: flower, how, now, tower, town **2.** /ou/ **3.** ou, ow **4.** shout

Reteaching Follow-up B

A. 1. house **2.** found **3.** about **4.** flower **5.** how **6.** now/our **7.** now/our **8.** out **9.** tower **10.** town

B. 11. pound **12.** shower

UNIT 33

Reteaching Follow-up A

1. part, start, arm, before, far, more, hard, torn, morning **2.** r **3.** ar **4.** or, ore **5.** door

Reteaching Follow-up B

A. 1. part **2.** hard **3.** far **4.** arm **5.** start **6.** before **7.** torn/door **8.** morning **9.** more **10.** torn/door

B. 11. cart **12.** store

UNIT 34

Reteaching Follow-up A

1. work, turn, bird, word, girl, hear, her, near, hurt, year **2.** r **3.** er, ir, ur, or **4.** ear

Reteaching Follow-up B

A. 1. work **2.** her **3.** girl **4.** bird/hurt **5.** bird/hurt **6.** hear/turn **7.** word **8.** hear/turn **9.** near **10.** year

B. 11. skirt **12.** worm

UNIT 35

Reteaching Follow-up A

1. winter, father, sister, after, ever, other, over, color, doctor, dollar **2.** r **3.** er, or, ar **4.** dancer

Reteaching Follow-up B

A. 1. winter **2.** after/other **3.** sister **4.** father/dollar **5.** ever/over **6.** color **7.** ever/over **8.** after/other **9.** doctor **10.** father/dollar

B. 11. polar **12.** never

Additional Testing Masters and Answer Keys

The following section provides additional testing materials for diagnosis and evaluation in black-line copying master format.

You will find two optional Diagnostic Pretests: **Diagnostic Pretest A** is in standardized-test format and consists of twenty items; **Diagnostic Pretest B** has children proofread a passage containing twenty-five spelling words. Directions for administering both tests and **Answer Keys** are provided.

For each review unit, you will find an optional **Mastery Words Test** and an optional **Bonus Words Test** in multiple-choice format. Words are drawn from the preceding units. Each copying master also appears in reduced form within the teaching plan it accompanies. An **Answer Key** for the test items appears at the end of this section of the Teacher's Resource Book.

A **Writing Sample Test** is also provided for each review unit. The child is asked to complete a writing assignment given a picture stimulus and motivational statement or question. The child's writing is then analyzed for spelling errors to determine common error patterns.

Contents

Name

Diagnostic Pretest

PRETEST **A**

Mark the circle for the correct spelling.

Sample A

A She liked to ___ in the lake.
a. swimn c. swimm
b. swam d. swim

Sample B

B We'll watch the ___ in the morning.
a. rece c. rase
b. race d. raice

1. The ___ drove to work together.
a. menn c. mann
b. man d. men

2. The ___ ate breakfast at the table.
a. womun c. wonam
b. woman d. womnan

3. He ran down the ___ to the bedroom.
a. hall c. hal
b. holl d. haul

4. The birthday ___ was for the boy.
a. cake c. cace
b. caek d. cak

5. Her ___ was very small.
a. hadn c. hand
b. hend d. haend

6. He ___ a letter to me.
a. sant c. satn
b. sent d. saent

7. I will ___ the TV show tonight.
a. miess c. mes
b. mess d. miss

8. He put the letter in the right ___.
a. plece c. plass
b. place d. plac

9. The boy looked for his ___ under the bed.
a. shoe c. shhoe
b. shoo d. show

10. I think ___ pictures are ready.
a. thease c. thesse
b. thees d. these

ANSWERS

A ⓐ ⓑ ⓒ ⓓ
B ⓐ ⓑ ⓒ ⓓ

1 ⓐ ⓑ ⓒ ⓓ
2 ⓐ ⓑ ⓒ ⓓ
3 ⓐ ⓑ ⓒ ⓓ
4 ⓐ ⓑ ⓒ ⓓ
5 ⓐ ⓑ ⓒ ⓓ
6 ⓐ ⓑ ⓒ ⓓ
7 ⓐ ⓑ ⓒ ⓓ
8 ⓐ ⓑ ⓒ ⓓ
9 ⓐ ⓑ ⓒ ⓓ
10 ⓐ ⓑ ⓒ ⓓ

Name

Diagnostic Pretest *(continued)*

PRETEST
A

11. ____ is my surprise?
a. Warre c. Where
b. Whare d. Whrre

12. Are you done with your ____?
a. wrok c. work
b. wurk d. worrk

13. He had to ____ the party before it was over.
a. leeve c. leafe
b. leave d. leavve

14. The teacher ____ a story to the children.
a. tolld c. todl
b. toold d. told

15. She began to ____ a beautiful song.
a. singe c. sign
b. seng d. sing

16. The little boy ____ not run up the hill.
a. could c. coudl
b. coold d. coud

17. His brother ____ the toy outside.
a. foond c. foudn
b. found d. fownd

18. The mayor went to work in the ____.
a. monring c. morning
b. murning d. mourning

19. Grandma put the ____ in the box.
a. dollar c. dolar
b. doller d. doallar

20. The ____ is not open.
a. schoul c. scholl
b. school d. showl

ANSWERS

11 (a) (b) (c) (d)
12 (a) (b) (c) (d)
13 (a) (b) (c) (d)
14 (a) (b) (c) (d)
15 (a) (b) (c) (d)
16 (a) (b) (c) (d)
17 (a) (b) (c) (d)
18 (a) (b) (c) (d)
19 (a) (b) (c) (d)
20 (a) (b) (c) (d)

DIAGNOSTIC PRETEST A

Administering the Test

1. Direct the children's attention to Sample A. Note that a word has been omitted. Have a volunteer read the sentence with the word included. Then have the children find the correct spelling from among the four spellings below the sentence. (swim) Have them identify the correct option by spelling the word and giving the correct letter. (d) Have the children note that the circle for this letter has been filled in.

2. Now proceed similarly with Sample B. Note the sentence and the omitted word. Then have the children find the correct spelling among the four options. (race) Have a volunteer identify the correct option by spelling the word and giving the letter in front of the word. (b) Have the children fill in the appropriate circle. After checking to see that the children have completed Sample B correctly, have the children proceed with the test.

3. Have the children complete the test. Collect the children's papers to check their answers.

Evaluating the Results

Use the following Answer Key to correct the children's tests. Review the test results to identify common error patterns and note them on the reproducible chart. Discuss errors with children.

ANSWER KEY

1	d
2	b
3	a
4	a
5	c
6	b
7	d
8	b
9	a
10	d
11	c
12	c
13	b
14	d
15	d
16	a
17	b
18	c
19	a
20	b

Name ______________________

PRETEST B

Diagnostic Pretest

Read the paragraph. Notice the underlined words.
Mark the circle for the correct spelling of the underlined word.

The little gurl found a verry big turtle in the grass. She asked her mother and fahter if she could kepp the turtle. She put the turtle in a box. She put a pan of watar in the box. He cuold swim in the water. She put some sand in the box. The turtle liked to dig in the sand. The little girl would wacth him every mornning. He could not walk fast. She wood give him a bug to eat. He ate the bug for lanch. One day the girl took the turtle to schoul. She tuld the children about herr turtle. Then thay played with the turtle.

1. a. girl c. gril
b. gurl d. girrl

2. a. vrey c. very
b. viry d. verry

3. a. graes c. grras
b. gress d. grass

4. a. and c. andd
b. end d. annd

5. a. fathir c. fahter
b. father d. fether

6. a. iff c. if
b. ef d. iif

7. a. keap c. kepp
b. keep d. keip

8. a. pan c. pann
b. pin d. pen

9. a. waiter c. waterr
b. watar d. water

10. a. cuold c. culdd
b. could d. coudd

11. a. some c. sune
b. sume d. soeme

12. a. wacth c. watch
b. wetch d. watsh

13. a. himm c. him
b. hem d. ham

14. a. mornnig c. monring
b. murning d. morning

15. a. wuold c. woudl
b. would d. wood

16. a. gife c. give
b. geve d. givve

17. a. aet c. atte
b. ete d. ate

18. a. bug c. bugg
b. big d. beg

ANSWERS

1 (a) (b) (c) (d)
2 (a) (b) (c) (d)
3 (a) (b) (c) (d)
4 (a) (b) (c) (d)
5 (a) (b) (c) (d)
6 (a) (b) (c) (d)
7 (a) (b) (c) (d)
8 (a) (b) (c) (d)
9 (a) (b) (c) (d)
10 (a) (b) (c) (d)
11 (a) (b) (c) (d)
12 (a) (b) (c) (d)
13 (a) (b) (c) (d)
14 (a) (b) (c) (d)
15 (a) (b) (c) (d)
16 (a) (b) (c) (d)
17 (a) (b) (c) (d)
18 (a) (b) (c) (d)

Name

PRETEST **B**

Diagnostic Pretest *(continued)*

19. a. lunch c. lucch
b. lanch d. lench

20. a. shcool c. school
b. schoul d. shoull

21. a. tuld c. tolld
b. tald d. told

22. a. abuot c. abbott
b. about d. aboat

23. a. hir c. herr
b. her d. hur

24. a. Thenn c. Tenn
b. Thin d. Then

25. a. they c. tayy
b. thay d. thaye

ANSWERS

19 (a) (b) (c) (d)
20 (a) (b) (c) (d)
21 (a) (b) (c) (d)
22 (a) (b) (c) (d)
23 (a) (b) (c) (d)
24 (a) (b) (c) (d)
25 (a) (b) (c) (d)

DIAGNOSTIC PRETEST B

Administering the Test

1. Direct the children to read the paragraph. Tell them to notice the underlined words.

2. Tell the children that for each underlined word in the paragraph they should find the correct spelling from among the four options. Have the children fill in the circle for the correct spelling.

3. Have the children complete the test. Collect the children's papers to check their answers.

Evaluating the Results

Use the following Answer Key to correct the children's tests. Review the test results to identify common error patterns and note them on the reproducible chart. Discuss errors with children.

ANSWER KEY

Item	Answer	Item	Answer
1	a	14	d
2	c	15	b
3	d	16	c
4	a	17	d
5	b	18	a
6	c	19	a
7	b	20	c
8	a	21	d
9	d	22	b
10	b	23	b
11	a	24	d
12	c	25	a
13	c		

Name

Test: Units 1–5

Mastery Words

UNIT 6

Mark the circle for the word that is spelled wrong.

Sample A

A	fast (a)	kup (b)	bag (c)

Sample B

B	jet (a)	has (b)	wint (c)

1	duck (a)	yes (b)	dadd (c)
2	rin (a)	came (b)	am (c)
3	hand (a)	cae (b)	say (c)
4	bag (a)	men (b)	seg (c)
5	bad (a)	noo (b)	soon (c)
6	cut (a)	let (b)	hee (c)
7	se (a)	be (b)	car (c)
8	came (a)	saye (b)	real (c)
9	let (a)	yess (b)	can (c)
10	went (a)	am (b)	fete (c)
11	weat (a)	very (b)	had (c)
12	gone (a)	ate (b)	cup (c)
13	cook (a)	kame (b)	see (c)
14	hadd (a)	last (b)	pick (c)
15	yes (a)	cae (b)	your (c)
16	dad (a)	pan (b)	satt (c)
17	kut (a)	pat (b)	woman (c)
18	has (a)	bea (b)	ran (c)
19	no (a)	he (b)	ame (c)
20	wet (a)	pig (b)	lat (c)

Name

Test: Units 1–5

Bonus Words

UNIT 6

Mark the circle for the word that is spelled wrong.

Sample A

	(a)	(b)	(c)
A	has	sed	cake

Sample B

	(a)	(b)	(c)
B	yur	hall	bag

	(a)	(b)	(c)
1	mail	gone	nek
2	kee	pick	cup
3	men	roben	dinner
4	visit	today	fergot
5	wash	sunny	godness
6	yard	cooky	happy
7	joke	lucky	larje
8	baer	pants	cave
9	candy	klap	kick
10	falt	left	rest
11	large	duck	nast
12	kitten	clap	candie
13	luky	bear	very
14	pan	yerd	jet
15	flat	terp	next
16	page	forgot	todae
17	bag	fast	wach
18	apple	dinnar	robin
19	mael	gold	band
20	goodness	kittin	woman
21	kik	real	nest
22	key	neck	kave
23	felt	vist	trap
24	keep	haerd	does

Name

Test: Units 7–11

Mastery Words

UNIT 12

Mark the circle for the word that is spelled wrong.

Sample A

A	lig (a)	fell (b)	top (c)

Sample B

B	pet (a)	some (b)	bal (c)

1	bug (a)	henn (b)	fill (c)
2	stop (a)	truck (b)	foks (c)
3	big (a)	git (b)	rub (c)
4	boks (a)	well (b)	shop (c)
5	across (a)	littel (b)	egg (c)
6	got (a)	bud (b)	mix (c)
7	tel (a)	jump (b)	run (c)
8	buzz (a)	upp (b)	end (c)
9	it (a)	fix (b)	hil (c)
10	did (a)	stip (b)	pond (c)
11	got (a)	done (b)	fune (c)
12	box (a)	tell (b)	runn (c)
13	in (a)	gote (b)	come (c)
14	up (a)	his (b)	weel (c)
15	uss (a)	hill (b)	soft (c)
16	until (a)	fil (b)	help (c)
17	bed (a)	get (b)	ine (c)
18	little (a)	itt (b)	miss (c)
19	reg (a)	fox (b)	us (c)
20	hen (a)	dog (b)	ded (c)

Name

Test: Units 7–11

Bonus Words

UNIT **12**

Mark the circle for the word that is spelled wrong.

Sample A

	a	b	c
A	job	best	acros

Sample B

	a	b	c
B	shop	halp	just

	a	b	c
1	step	spel	sent
2	laft	test	best
3	trick	milk	spind
4	son	wun	month
5	drop	some	forg
6	adde	come	butter
7	song	rabit	clock
8	desk	breng	soft
9	middle	better	sommer
10	stepp	grass	spell
11	his	lost	sity
12	shop	shel	stuff
13	truck	bring	wunder
14	funnie	jump	until
15	lift	trik	spend
16	shell	pinny	across
17	bug	cost	stuf
18	moss	fell	sonn
19	lock	melk	dog
20	funny	rabbit	middel
21	summer	munth	luck
22	tess	well	add
23	ball	nuss	won
24	bettar	penny	wonder

Name

Test: Units 13–17

Mastery Words

UNIT 18

Mark the circle for the word that is spelled right.

Sample A

A	hiz (a)	his (b)	hiss (c)	hes (d)

Sample B

B	tel (a)	tile (b)	tele (c)	tell (d)

1	fiss (a)	fich (b)	fish (c)	fesh (d)
2	wuz (a)	was (b)	waz (c)	wass (d)
3	pla (a)	paye (b)	pey (c)	play (d)
4	gras (a)	grass (b)	gress (c)	garss (d)
5	sleep (a)	slepe (b)	slep (c)	sleap (d)
6	thee (a)	tha (b)	the (c)	teh (d)
7	doez (a)	dos (b)	doz (c)	does (d)
8	of (a)	ov (b)	oft (c)	oof (d)
9	storie (a)	storey (b)	story (c)	sotry (d)
10	thes (a)	this (b)	thiz (c)	thise (d)
11	scop (a)	shop (b)	shope (c)	shep (d)
12	with (a)	vith (b)	wich (c)	wiht (d)
13	childen (a)	chilren (b)	childrin (c)	children (d)
14	tath (a)	that (b)	tatt (c)	dat (d)
15	dres (a)	drest (b)	dress (c)	driss (d)
16	tree (a)	trea (b)	tre (c)	trie (d)
17	saed (a)	said (b)	sade (c)	sed (d)
18	bes (a)	bast (b)	bess (c)	best (d)
19	cleen (a)	clean (b)	kleen (c)	klean (d)
20	she (a)	shea (b)	shay (c)	shee (d)

Name

Test: Units 13–17

Bonus Words

UNIT 18

Mark the circle for the word that is spelled right.

Sample A

A	shu (a)	shou (b)	shoe (c)	shue (d)

Sample B

B	thees (a)	these (b)	theze (c)	theez (d)

1	dost (a)	duss (b)	dest (c)	dust (d)
2	patf (a)	path (b)	ptaf (c)	pafh (d)
3	shaut (a)	shuat (b)	shout (c)	showt (d)
4	prize (a)	prise (b)	priez (c)	prieze (d)
5	wether (a)	waether (b)	weather (c)	wheater (d)
6	roung (a)	worng (b)	rong (c)	wrong (d)
7	listen (a)	listin (b)	lissen (c)	leson (d)
8	stepe (a)	steep (b)	steap (c)	steip (d)
9	thum (a)	thumb (b)	thoum (c)	thumm (d)
10	kitchin (a)	kichen (b)	kichin (c)	kitchen (d)
11	playground (a)	playgrond (b)	plaground (c)	playgrund (d)
12	trak (a)	trac (b)	track (c)	trakk (d)
13	familee (a)	familie (b)	famaly (c)	family (d)
14	shien (a)	chine (b)	shean (c)	shine (d)
15	laff (a)	lauft (b)	laugh (c)	laugf (d)
16	stare (a)	stari (b)	satre (c)	stear (d)
17	turst (a)	trust (b)	trist (c)	trast (d)
18	stick (a)	stik (b)	stic (c)	steck (d)
19	bred (a)	braed (b)	bread (c)	biard (d)
20	chersh (a)	church (b)	cherch (c)	chircht (d)
21	thaugt (a)	tought (b)	thougt (c)	thought (d)
22	catch (a)	ketch (b)	cetch (c)	katch (d)
23	bauther (a)	bother (b)	brither (c)	bothur (d)
24	batween (a)	betwene (b)	bitween (c)	between (d)

Name

Test: Units 19–23

Mastery Words

UNIT 24

Mark the circle for the word that is spelled right.

Sample A

A	ait (a)	af (b)	eit (c)	ate (d)

Sample B

B	bick (a)	byke (b)	bike (c)	baik (d)

1	daye (a)	daiy (b)	day (c)	dae (d)
2	ride (a)	reid (b)	ryde (c)	ried (d)
3	Aye (a)	I (b)	Ai (c)	Iye (d)
4	gaym (a)	gaim (b)	gam (c)	game (d)
5	flie (a)	fly (b)	fli (c)	fligh (d)
6	nede (a)	neid (b)	need (c)	nead (d)
7	maide (a)	made (b)	mayd (c)	maed (d)
8	five (a)	fiev (b)	fyv (c)	feiv (d)
9	eet (a)	ete (b)	ite (c)	eat (d)
10	rein (a)	rane (b)	rign (c)	rain (d)
11	maik (a)	maek (b)	make (c)	maec (d)
12	mee (a)	mei (b)	me (c)	migh (d)
13	kite (a)	kight (b)	kiet (c)	kyte (d)
14	wai (a)	way (b)	wae (c)	wey (d)
15	bie (a)	bi (b)	bey (c)	by (d)
16	kake (a)	cake (b)	caik (c)	cayk (d)
17	my (a)	mie (b)	mi (c)	mye (d)
18	like (a)	liek (b)	lyke (c)	leik (d)
19	wate (a)	weit (b)	wait (c)	wayt (d)
20	wee (a)	we (b)	wye (c)	wea (d)

Name

Test: Units 19–23

Bonus Words

UNIT **24**

Mark the circle for the word that is spelled right.

Sample A

A	trane (a)	train (b)	trayn (c)	tiran (d)

Sample B

B	sky (a)	skie (b)	ske (c)	skye (d)

1	sheck (a)	shaik (b)	shake (c)	sheak (d)
2	asleap (a)	aslepe (b)	asleep (c)	alseep (d)
3	slyde (a)	slide (b)	slied (c)	siled (d)
4	sight (a)	citte (b)	syght (c)	siate (d)
5	clai (a)	kleigh (b)	clay (c)	klay (d)
6	dreem (a)	draem (b)	dreme (c)	dream (d)
7	twyce (a)	twies (b)	twice (c)	twise (d)
8	laik (a)	lake (b)	laek (c)	layk (d)
9	maybee (a)	mayby (b)	maiby (c)	maybe (d)
10	hide (a)	hyde (b)	hied (c)	highed (d)
11	snaik (a)	snake (b)	snayk (c)	snaek (d)
12	trial (a)	trale (b)	trail (c)	trayl (d)
13	tyger (a)	tiegr (b)	tygre (c)	tiger (d)
14	eite (a)	eight (b)	ait (c)	eigh (d)
15	friten (a)	fryten (b)	fritan (c)	frighten (d)
16	buzy (a)	bisy (b)	busy (c)	bizy (d)
17	brave (a)	braiv (b)	barve (c)	braive (d)
18	miself (a)	mysefl (b)	myseff (c)	myself (d)
19	emtee (a)	empty (b)	emptie (c)	epmty (d)
20	afaid (a)	afrade (b)	afraid (c)	afraed (d)
21	liyf (a)	leif (b)	lief (c)	life (d)
22	shie (a)	shy (b)	shigh (c)	shye (d)
23	strait (a)	streight (b)	strate (c)	straight (d)
24	lieon (a)	lion (b)	lyon (c)	loiyn (d)
25	safe (a)	saif (b)	sayf (c)	saef (d)
26	outside (a)	owtside (b)	outsied (c)	owtsied (d)
27	trete (a)	traet (b)	treet (c)	treat (d)
28	skate (a)	skait (b)	skayt (c)	skaet (d)
29	cheak (a)	cheek (b)	cheke (c)	cheak (d)
30	wize (a)	wyse (b)	wise (c)	wyze (d)

Name

Test: Units 25–29

Mastery Words UNIT **30**

Mark the circle for the word that is spelled right.

Sample A

	(a)	(b)	(c)
A	roe	roo	row

Sample B

	(a)	(b)	(c)
B	pull	poal	pule

	(a)	(b)	(c)
1	hoam	hoom	home
2	bende	band	boad
3	bote	bowt	boat
4	shue	shoo	shoe
5	nose	noze	noas
6	wint	went	whent
7	gud	good	goud
8	most	muste	moast
9	min	men	mian
10	sewe	soe	so
11	buk	book	bouk
12	show	shoa	shoo
13	you	yoo	yu
14	couk	cuk	cook
15	go	goe	gow
16	trew	true	troo
17	sune	seun	soon
18	aun	on	onn
19	roap	rowp	rope
20	luk	louk	look

Name

Test: Units 25–29

Bonus Words

UNIT 30

Mark the circle for the word that is spelled right.

Sample A

	(a)	(b)	(c)
A	sope	soap	sowp

Sample B

	(a)	(b)	(c)
B	grow	groe	groa

	(a)	(b)	(c)
1	brume	broom	brome
2	both	bothe	boath
3	angre	angry	anry
4	woak	woke	woek
5	floo	flue	flew
6	windoe	wyndow	window
7	string	stirng	stinrg
8	bruck	brook	bruk
9	roast	roste	rowst
10	blanket	blankit	blenkit
11	shuk	shook	shouk
12	flote	float	flowt
13	storng	strang	strong
14	stove	stoav	stoov
15	spune	spoun	spoon
16	thro	throe	throw
17	blenk	blink	blick
18	stood	stoud	stude
19	hellow	hello	hullo
20	baloon	ballon	balloon
21	gruw	grew	grue
22	hungree	hungry	hungrey
23	spoke	spoek	spoak
24	buldog	bulldog	bulldug
25	bushs	bushez	bushes
26	futball	fotball	football
27	folloe	follow	fallow
28	oatmeal	otemeel	oatmele
29	raccoon	raccune	racoon
30	toest	towst	toast

Name

Test: Units 31–35

Mastery Words

UNIT 36

Decide if the underlined word is spelled right or wrong. Mark the correct circle.

Sample A

	Right	Wrong
A He is far away.	(r)	(w)

Sample B

	Right	Wrong
B She likes hur puppy.	(r)	(w)

	Right	Wrong
1 We all went out.	(r)	(w)
2 That boy runs fast.	(r)	(w)
3 My bother is asleep.	(r)	(w)
4 This is for you.	(r)	(w)
5 Put the chair hear.	(r)	(w)
6 I like yur hat.	(r)	(w)
7 I walked down the stairs.	(r)	(w)
8 This flowar is pretty.	(r)	(w)
9 I have a toye duck.	(r)	(w)
10 Throw the bal to me.	(r)	(w)

	Right	Wrong
11 He saw a tiger.	(r)	(w)
12 We were lucky.	(r)	(w)
13 A caw eats grass.	(r)	(w)
14 Is it a dog or a cat?	(r)	(w)
15 Please water the plant.	(r)	(w)
16 Follow the holl to my room.	(r)	(w)
17 I gave mother my tooth.	(r)	(w)
18 We aer sisters.	(r)	(w)
19 Were did you go?	(r)	(w)
20 She is a dear friend.	(r)	(w)

Name

Test: Units 31–35

Bonus Words

UNIT 36

Decide if the underlined word is spelled right or wrong. Mark the correct circle.

Sample A

		Right	Wrong
A	The rock is hard.	(r)	(w)

Sample B

		Right	Wrong
B	We must stert soon.	(r)	(w)

		Right	Wrong
1	He is allways busy.	(r)	(w)
2	She taut me everything.	(r)	(w)
3	Don't make a sound.	(r)	(w)
4	I can hardly wait.	(r)	(w)
5	It is a shourt ride.	(r)	(w)
6	The bus was early.	(r)	(w)
7	Let's retern home.	(r)	(w)
8	May I have another?	(r)	(w)
9	We will tawk about it.	(r)	(w)
10	A mouse ran in the room.	(r)	(w)
11	Mom will park the car.	(r)	(w)
12	I will write a letter.	(r)	(w)
13	The wirld has many people.	(r)	(w)
14	He will ordor the dog to stay.	(r)	(w)
15	Sugar is sweet.	(r)	(w)

		Right	Wrong
16	Let's take a walk.	(r)	(w)
17	It was an awfull day.	(r)	(w)
18	We grow food on the form.	(r)	(w)
19	The ball is rownd.	(r)	(w)
20	I am a person.	(r)	(w)
21	The circus is in town.	(r)	(w)
22	I see myself in the mirrer.	(r)	(w)
23	We lern to spell.	(r)	(w)
24	Use a straw to drink.	(r)	(w)
25	The clown was funny.	(r)	(w)
26	A sweter keeps me warm.	(r)	(w)
27	The owel is a bird.	(r)	(w)
28	I like the flavor of milk.	(r)	(w)
29	Turn left at the korner.	(r)	(w)
30	The ground was white with snow.	(r)	(w)

Introduction to the Writing Sample Tests

Spelling Error Analysis

The Writing Sample Tests that follow can be used in conjunction with an error-analysis approach to spelling instruction. This method allows you to address not only spelling principles but also spelling errors in a systematic way. When children participate by recognizing, correcting, and discussing their own misspellings, error analysis becomes a collaborative and highly effective part of the learning process.

Children's spelling errors are seldom random. Instead they represent inaccurate predictions that are based on a child's knowledge of our written language system. Error analysis examines the misspellings in a consistent way by grouping them into error types. Once the misspellings have been categorized, you and the child can work together to identify and correct faulty spelling strategies.

The Writing Samples

Writing provides a purposeful context for children to develop their spelling competence and for you to examine the spelling patterns they have formulated. The six **Writing Sample Tests** are designed to generate a variety of writing forms (for example, narrative, descriptive, how-to) through written and visual stimuli. The tests can be administered and evaluated at the end of each review unit, or whenever you consider them most appropriate and helpful.

Student-Teacher Conferences

Joint observation and discussion of errors develop children's awareness of correct spelling strategies as well as problem areas that require attention. After you have checked the writing passages and have recorded the spelling errors in the **Error Analysis** chart, you can arrange individual conferences to discuss the results with each child. During the conference, children can provide valuable information by explaining why they chose to spell a word in a particular way. You, in turn, can provide valuable guidance by pointing out the recurrence of certain types of errors and assigning review material and follow-up activities to suit each child's needs. The guidelines on page 19 suggest ways to organize the student-teacher conference.

Error Categories

Certain errors occur with great regularity and fit into identifiable patterns. These errors can be grouped into categories according to causal factors. The **Error Analysis** chart lists major error categories for this grade level. The chart that follows lists some specific examples for each type of error.

CAUSE	EXAMPLE OF ERROR
1. Phonetic substitution	
• Consonant sounds	*sity* for *city*; *kat* for *cat*
• Vowel sounds	*gloo* for *glue*; *wont* for *want*
2. Omission and insertion of silent letters	*nit* for *night* *no* for *know* *cak* for *cake*
3. Inaccurate pronunciation	*libery* for *library* *buder* for *butter* *ninedy* for *ninety*
4. Transposition of letters	*littel* for *little*
5. Double consonants	
• Doubling when not appropriate	*citty* for *city*
• Leaving out double letters	*litle* for *little*
• When adding endings	*runing* for *running*
6. Double vowel confusion	*streem* for *stream*
7. Homophones	
• Incorrect meaning	*reed* for *read*
8. Common spelling patterns applied to irregular words (overgeneralization)	*wuz* for *was* *munny* for *money*
9. Inflectional endings and suffixes • Incorrectly added	*skateing* for *skating* *cherryies* for *cherries* *judgement* for *judgment*

Directions for Using the Writing Sample Tests

Administering the Test

1. Encourage the children to examine the picture stimulus.
2. Read the written stimulus aloud while the children follow along on their own sheets.
3. Allow the children a few minutes for prewriting activities such as brainstorming, clustering, and charting. You may wish to encourage them to use spelling words from previous lessons where possible.
4. Allow twenty minutes for the children to complete the writing. If they seem to need additional time, you may wish to permit them to work beyond the twenty minutes.
5. Encourage the children to proofread their work for correct spelling and punctuation before handing it in.

Evaluating the Test

1. Read each writing sample and circle any misspelled words.
2. If a writing sample contains ten or more misspelled words, prepare an **Error Analysis** chart. First list the misspelled words in the *Misspelling* column. Then indicate where the error appears in each word by putting a check in the appropriate column. Next indicate the nature of the error by putting a check in the column for the type of letters or word involved and, where applicable, note the cause of the error (for example, substitution, omission, meaning confusion).
3. Return the writing samples, along with the Error Analysis chart, to the children. Have them use the **Spelling Dictionary** and a larger dictionary to find the correct spelling of each misspelled word. Then have them write the correct spelling in the column provided in the chart. (Note that it is not necessary to prepare an **Error Analysis** chart for children whose writing samples contain only a small number of misspelled words. Children who did not receive a chart can simply write the correct spellings above the misspelled words in their writing sample.)

Guidelines for Student-Teacher Conferences

Many factors influence the way in which you and the child analyze and discuss spelling errors. Class size, children's age and spelling abilities, and schedule demands all must be taken into account when planning conference time. The following guidelines are suggestions for organizing conferences.

1. Meet with one child at a time. Allow at least five to ten minutes for each conference.
2. Consult the completed **Error Analysis** chart to determine whether a significant pattern of errors exists. For example, the various spellings of a single vowel sound may be underused or used incorrectly. Letters may be reversed or omitted in consonant clusters. Some children may have difficulty with certain types of words—for example, those that contain silent letters or have irregular spellings.
3. Use discussion time to point out problem areas in the children's spelling strategies. (You may also wish to reinforce correct strategies by pointing out groups of words that were spelled correctly.) Encourage children to examine their errors and explain why they chose particular spellings. In this way, you may be able to determine whether the errors are due to problems with visual memory, auditory discrimination, or lack of familiarity with certain spelling principles.
4. Assign follow-up material that focuses on the problem area. You may refer to the reteaching strategies in the Teacher's Edition and the **Extra Practice** and **Reteaching** copying masters in the **Teacher's Resource Book.**

Name

Writing Sample Tests: Error Analysis

			Where in the word is the error?			Substitutions, Omissions, Insertions, Reversals				Other		
Unit	Correct Spelling	Misspelling	Beginning	Middle	End	Vowel	Consonant	Silent Letters	Double Letters	Homophones	Irregular Words	Inflectional Endings and Suffixes

Name

Writing Sample Test 1

UNIT
6

"Hi, my name is Mylex. I am from the planet Geldron. Will you be my friend? Take me to visit your school."

Write about your adventure with Mylex.

Name

Writing Sample Test 2

Jenny stopped to look in the window of the pet store each day. Her birthday was in three days. If only her parents would get her one of the puppies! What will happen? Write your story below.

Name

Writing Sample Test 3

UNIT 18

Karen has just lost her front tooth. She is writing her grandma to tell her when and how it came out. Pretend you are Karen and write the letter.

Harcourt Brace School Publishers

Name

Writing Sample Test 4

UNIT 24

You can have a dream adventure. Where will you go? What will you do? Complete the sentence below. Then write more about your adventure.

In my magic dream I am

Name

Writing Sample Test 5

UNIT
30

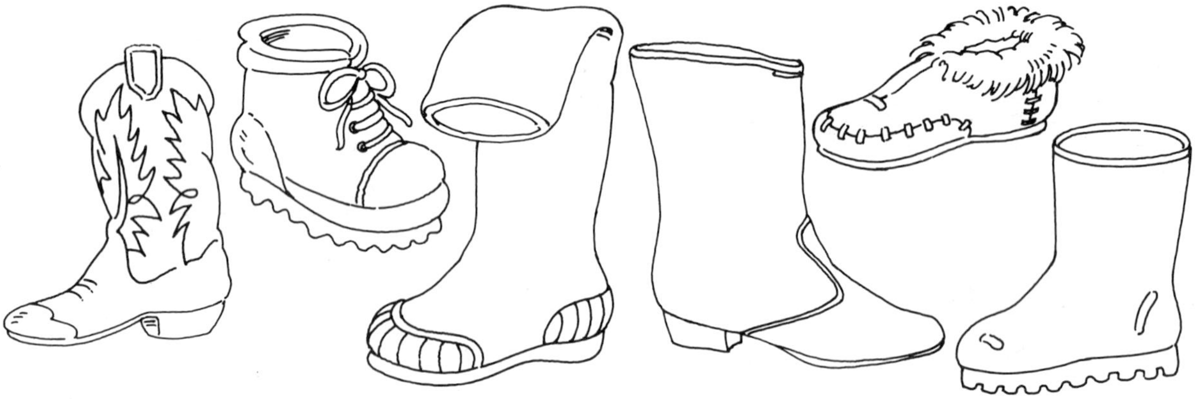

Choose the pair of boots you would like to wear. Where are you going in your new boots? Whom will you meet? What will you do? Write your story below.

Name

Writing Sample Test 6

UNIT **36**

You have just made a monster sandwich. What did you put in it? How big is it? What will you do with it now?

Answer Key for Additional Testing Masters

UNIT 6

Test: Units 1–5
Mastery Words

1. c
2. a
3. b
4. c
5. b
6. c
7. a
8. b
9. b
10. c
11. a
12. b
13. b
14. a
15. b
16. c
17. a
18. b
19. c
20. c

Test: Units 1–5
Bonus Words

1. c
2. a
3. b
4. c
5. c
6. b
7. c
8. a
9. b
10. a
11. c
12. c
13. a
14. b
15. b
16. c
17. c
18. b
19. a
20. b
21. a
22. c
23. b
24. b

UNIT 12

Test: Units 7–11
Mastery Words

1. b
2. c
3. b
4. a
5. b
6. b
7. a
8. b
9. c
10. b
11. c
12. c
13. b
14. c
15. a
16. b
17. c
18. b
19. a
20. c

Test: Units 7–11
Bonus Words

1. b
2. a
3. c
4. b
5. c
6. a
7. b
8. b
9. c
10. a
11. c
12. b
13. c
14. a
15. b
16. b
17. c
18. c
19. b
20. c
21. b
22. a
23. b
24. a

UNIT 18

Test: Units 13–17
Mastery Words

1. c
2. b
3. d
4. b
5. a
6. c
7. d
8. a
9. c
10. b
11. b
12. a
13. d
14. b
15. c
16. a
17. b
18. d
19. b
20. a

Test: Units 13–17
Bonus Words

1. d
2. b
3. c
4. a
5. c
6. d
7. a
8. b
9. b
10. d
11. a
12. c
13. d
14. d
15. c
16. a
17. b
18. a
19. c
20. b
21. d
22. a
23. b
24. d

UNIT 24

Test: Units 19–23
Mastery Words

1. c
2. a
3. b
4. d
5. b
6. c
7. b
8. a
9. d
10. d
11. c
12. c
13. a
14. b
15. d
16. b
17. a
18. a
19. c
20. b

Test: Units 19–23
Bonus Words

1. c
2. c
3. b
4. a
5. c
6. d
7. c
8. b
9. d
10. a
11. b
12. c
13. d
14. b
15. d
16. c
17. a
18. d
19. b
20. c
21. d
22. b
23. d
24. b

25. a
26. a
27. d
28. a
29. b
30. c

UNIT 30

Test: Units 25–29 Mastery Words

1. c
2. b
3. c
4. c
5. a
6. b
7. b
8. a
9. b
10. c
11. b
12. a
13. a
14. c
15. a
16. b
17. c
18. b
19. c
20. c

Test: Units 25–29 Bonus Words

1. b
2. a
3. b
4. b
5. c
6. c
7. a
8. b
9. a
10. a
11. b
12. b
13. c
14. a
15. c
16. c
17. b
18. a
19. b
20. c
21. b
22. b
23. a
24. b
25. c
26. c
27. b
28. a
29. a
30. c

UNIT 36

Test: Units 31–35 Mastery Words

1. r
2. r
3. w
4. r
5. w
6. w
7. r
8. w
9. w
10. w
11. r
12. r
13. w
14. r
15. r
16. w
17. r
18. w
19. w
20. r

Test: Units 31–35 Bonus Words

1. w
2. w
3. r
4. r
5. w
6. r
7. w
8. r
9. w
10. r
11. r
12. r
13. w
14. w
15. r
16. r
17. w
18. w
19. w
20. r
21. r
22. w
23. w
24. r
25. r
26. w
27. w
28. r
29. w
30. r

Teaching Aids

The following section provides black-line copying masters for graph paper, home letters, the Study Steps to Learn a Word form, the Your Own Spelling Words form, progress reports, answer sheets, writing lines, and composition evaluation forms.

Graph Paper: If you are using the hardcover Pupil's Edition, you may wish to duplicate this master for children when they are instructed to complete word puzzles.

Home Letters: Letters that inform parents of the spelling skills their children are being taught and spelling activities they can do at home with their children are provided in English and Spanish.

Study Steps to Learn a Word: This form is to be used by children throughout the school year to help them learn spelling words that are difficult for them.

Your Own Spelling Words: Children often encounter words that are difficult for them to spell in their content-area reading. This form provides a convenient way for them to record such words throughout the school year.

Progress Reports: The first of these forms will allow children to monitor their own progress on trial tests, unit tests, Form A and Form B tests, the Midyear test, and the End-of-Year test. The second form provides a convenient way for you to record each child's performance on the Skills Check Inventory, Form A tests, Form B tests, the Midyear test, and the End-of-Year test.

Answer Sheets: Answer forms for unit tests and review unit tests are included.

Writing Lines: A page of primary writing lines is provided. You may wish to duplicate it and supply children with these pages for various writing assignments.

Composition Evaluation Forms: Two forms for evaluating children's compositions are provided. You can use Composition Evaluation Form A for a quick, holistic appraisal of a child's writing. Composition Evaluation Form B can be used for analytical evaluation. It involves assessing a child's writing according to a set of detailed criteria. Columns are provided on this form for self appraisal, peer-group appraisal, and teacher appraisal of a child's writing. A guide for using these two forms appears on pages TE 60 and TE 61 of the Teacher's Edition for this level.

Contents

Dear ______________________________,

Your child will be working with *Harcourt Brace Spelling* in the year ahead. The goal of *Harcourt Brace Spelling* is to assist your child in becoming a better writer. This program views spelling as a tool of good communication.

You can help your child become a better communicator by encouraging him or her to develop good habits in reading, writing (including spelling), listening, and speaking. During the course of the year, you will be receiving six more letters, which will detail the spelling skills that your child has been learning and offer suggestions for spelling activities you can do with your child. In addition, you can help your child in the course of the year by assisting him or her in the following ways.

- Review your child's writing assignments and help him or her correct spelling errors.
- Look through *Harcourt Brace Spelling* and encourage your child to use the independent study features at the back of the book. These features are the **Writer's Guide,** the **Spelling Thesaurus,** and the **Spelling Dictionary.**

Listed below are some specific activities that you may want to try at home to help your child become a better speller.

Activities That Develop Spelling Skills

- Write some letters of the alphabet on index cards. Make three cards for each vowel, *a, e, i, o,* and *u,* and two or more cards for frequently used consonants. Then make up games to play with the cards. For example, you and your child might alternate drawing cards until someone can make a spelling word.
- Use the cards you made for another game. Select cards with the letters for one of your child's spelling words, and scramble the cards. Let your child rearrange the cards to spell the word correctly.
- On a magic or individual chalkboard, let your child create "doodle words." Have your child write a spelling word, then fill the space in and around the letters with designs.
- For an outdoor activity, have your child play "I spy" by spotting spelling words on billboards and on business, street, or traffic signs.

Please feel free to contact me with any questions regarding your child's progress.

Sincerely,

Estimado/a señor/a ________________________________:

Su niño/a trabajará este año con un nuevo programa de ortografía en inglés. El título del programa es *Harcourt Brace Spelling.* El propósito del programa es ayudar al alumno a expresarse mejor por escrito. La ortografía se considera un aspecto importante de la expresión escrita.

Durante el año escolar, usted recibirá por lo menos seis de estas cartas, en las cuales se le informará lo que su niño ha estado aprendiendo, y se le sugerirán actividades para practicar la ortografía en casa. A través del año escolar usted puede ayudar al niño de las siguientes maneras:

- Revise sus tareas escritas y ayúdelo a corregir sus errores de ortografía.

  Examine el texto del *Harcourt Brace Spelling* y anime al niño a que utilice los ejercicios de práctica independiente que aparecen al final del libro. Éstos incluyen **Writer's Guide** (la Guía del Escritor), **Spelling Thesaurus** (el Tesauro de Ortografía) y **Spelling Dictionary** (el Diccionario de Ortografía).

A continuación aparecen unas muestras de actividades que se pueden hacer en casa para ayudar al niño a mejorar su ortografía.

Actividades para mejorar la ortografía

- Haga tarjetas con las letras del alfabeto: tres con cada una de las vocales, *a, e, i, o* y *u,* y dos o tres tarjetas con cada una de las consonantes más comunes. Después, invente juegos para utilizar las tarjetas. Por ejemplo, baraje las tarjetas y túrnese con el niño para sacar tarjetas del montón a ver quién puede formar primero una palabra completa.
- Use las tarjetas en este otro juego: Forme una palabra completa, sin que el niño la vea, y mezcle las tarjetas. Déselas al niño para que vuelva a formar la palabra.
- Cuando vayan por la calle, juegue a "Veo, veo", haciendo que el niño deletree palabras que encuentre en anuncios, letreros, nombres de calles o avisos de tránsito.

Por favor, comuníquese conmigo si tiene cualquier pregunta acerca del programa o del progreso del niño.

Lo/a saluda atentamente,

Dear ______________________________,

Your child has just completed Units 1–6 of *Harcourt Brace Spelling.* As you know, spelling is an essential tool for effective communication through writing.

In these units of *Harcourt Brace Spelling,* your child learned to spell words with initial consonant sounds; words with the sound /k/ as in *cup*, *keep*, and *pick*; and words with the short vowel sound /a/ as in *man*.

You may wish to encourage your child to practice spelling the review words by completing the following activities.

Activities That Develop Spelling Skills

- Say each review word aloud. Have your child repeat the word and then write it on a piece of paper. Use the exercise to practice one set of review words each day.
- Write each review word on an individual index card or piece of paper. Have your child trace each word with crayon, pencil, or a colored marker. Encourage your child to use each word in a sentence or rhyming couplet.
- For an outdoor activity, have your child spell the review words while bouncing a ball. Toss or bounce the ball to your child as you say the word to be spelled. Have the child spell the word aloud while bouncing the ball—one bounce for each letter in the word. Then have the child repeat the word and bounce the ball back to you.

If you have any questions regarding your child's progress, please feel free to contact me.

Sincerely,

UNIT 1
bag
next
real
men
pan

UNIT 2
does
went
woman
your
very

UNIT 3
gone
left
has
soon
jet

UNIT 4
cook
keep
duck
cup
pick

UNIT 5
bad
last
hand
fast
man

Estimado/a señor/a ______________________________.

Su niño/a acaba de terminar las unidades 1–6 del programa de ortografía en inglés *Harcourt Brace Spelling*. Como usted ya sabe, la buena ortografía es un elemento esencial de la comunicación eficaz por escrito.

En estas unidades del *Harcourt Brace Spelling,* su niño aprendió a escribir palabras que empiezan con consonantes; palabras con el sonido /k/ como en *cup, keep* y *pick*; y palabras con el sonido corto de la vocal *a*, como en la palabra *man*.

Si desea practicar con el niño la ortografía de las palabras de repaso, puede utilizar las actividades que aparecen a continuación.

Actividades para mejorar la ortografía

- Pronuncie cada palabra de repaso. Haga que el niño la repita y la escriba en un papel. Cubra una lista de palabras cada día.
- Escriba cada palabra de repaso en una tarjeta o en un pedazo de papel. Haga que el niño siga con un lápiz de color o un marcador lo que usted escribió. Después, anímelo a que utilice la palabra en una oración, o a que encuentre una palabra que rime con ella.
- Fuera de la casa, haga que el niño deletree palabras a medida que hace rebotar una pelota. Al tirarle la pelota dígale la palabra que debe deletrear. Dígale que deletree la palabra diciendo una letra con cada rebote de la pelota. Cuando haya terminado, dígale que pronuncie la palabra completa y le devuelva la pelota.

Si tiene alguna pregunta acerca del progreso del niño, por favor comuníquese conmigo.

Lo/a saluda atentamente,

UNIDAD 1

bag
next
real
men
pan

UNIDAD 2

does
went
woman
your
very

UNIDAD 3

gone
left
has
soon
jet

UNIDAD 4

cook
keep
duck
cup
pick

UNIDAD 5

bad
last
hand
fast
man

Dear ______________________________,

Your child has just completed units 7–12 of *Harcourt Brace Spelling.* As your child progresses through *Harcourt Brace Spelling,* he or she will develop better communication skills and become a better writer.

In these units, your child learned to spell words with the following short vowel sounds: /e/ as in *pet*, /i/ as in *pin*, /u/ as in *luck*, and /o/ as in *top.* Your child also learned to spell words with double consonants, such as the word *off.*

You may wish to encourage your child to practice spelling the review words by completing the following activities.

Activities That Develop Spelling Skills

- Write a spelling word on a steamy mirror or window. Have your child say the word aloud. Then have your child close his or her eyes and spell the word. Let your child "erase" the word with a stroke of the finger if he or she spells it correctly.
- Cut out large, colorful letters from magazine headlines. Let your child arrange the letters into the review words. Then ask her or him to write a sentence using each of the words.
- For an outdoor activity, use chalk to draw three large circles on the pavement. Place one of the following letters inside each circle: *e, i, o.* Say a review word to your child and have her or him jump into the correct circle for the vowel sound in the word and then spell the word aloud. For example, you might say "lost." Your child would jump into the *o* circle and spell the word.

If you have any questions regarding your child's progress, please feel free to contact me.

Sincerely,

UNIT 7

best
help
well
sent
yet

UNIT 8

him
if
sit
his
is

UNIT 9

just
truck
some
until
done

UNIT 10

job
lost
song
dog
shop

UNIT 11

across
off
grass
ball
fell

Estimado/a señor/a ______________________________:

Su niño/a acaba de terminar las unidades 7–12 del programa de ortografía en inglés *Harcourt Brace Spelling.* A medida que progrese en este libro, el niño mejorará su capacidad para comunicarse y aprenderá a escribir mejor.

En estas unidades, el niño aprendió a escribir palabras que contienen los siguientes sonidos vocálicos: el sonido de la *e* en *pet,* de la *i* en *pin,* de la *u* en *luck,* y de la *o* en *top.* También aprendió palabras con consonantes dobles, tales como las de la palabra *off.*

Si desea practicar con el niño la ortografía de las palabras de repaso, puede utilizar las actividades que aparecen a continuación.

Actividades para mejorar la ortografía

- En un espejo o un vidrio empañado, trace con el dedo una de las palabras. Haga que el niño lea la palabra en voz alta. Después, dígale que cierre los ojos y que la deletree. Si lo hace correctamente, déjelo que la borre.
- Recorte de alguna revista letras grandes y de colores. Haga que el niño forme las palabras de repaso con ellas. Después, pídale que escriba una oración con cada palabra.
- Fuera de la casa, dibuje con tiza en el pavimento tres círculos grandes. Dentro de cada círculo, escriba una de estas tres vocales: *e, i, o.* Pronuncie una de las palabras de repaso y dígale al niño que salte al centro del círculo que tiene la vocal que oyó en la palabra, y que deletree la palabra en voz alta. Por ejemplo, si usted dice la palabra *lost,* el niño debe saltar al centro del círculo que continene la *o* y deletrear la palabra.

Si tiene alguna pregunta acerca del progreso de su niño, por favor comuníquese conmigo.

Lo/a saluda atentamente,

UNIDAD 7
best
help
well
sent
yet
UNIDAD 8
him
if
sit
his
is
UNIDAD 9
just
truck
some
until
done
UNIDAD 10
job
lost
song
dog
shop
UNIDAD 11
across
off
grass
ball
fell

Dear ______________________________,

Your child has just completed Units 13–18 of *Harcourt Brace Spelling*. The purpose of *Harcourt Brace Spelling* is to build children's communication skills through better spelling and writing.

In these units, your child learned to spell words with consonant clusters; words with consonant digraphs *sh, th,* and *ch*; and words with irregular spellings, such as *were*.

In order to encourage your child to practice spelling the review words, you may wish to try the following activities.

Activities That Develop Spelling Skills

- Have your child use pieces of yarn to form the letters of his or her spelling words. Reuse the yarn to spell each new word. Review one set of Unit words each day.
- Have your child write the letters of each review word on a piece of paper, leaving spaces between the letters. Then have your child use different colored crayons or markers to trace the letters of each word. Ask your child to say each letter aloud as he or she traces it. Then have your child write a sentence using each word.

Please contact me with any questions regarding your child's progress.

Sincerely,

UNIT 13
please stand must store glad

UNIT 14
brother friend swim great true

UNIT 15
shoe thing wish thank finish

UNIT 16
chair watch their these much

UNIT 17
again been were there here

Estimado/a señor/a ______________________________:

Su niño/a acaba de terminar las unidades 13–18 del programa de ortografía en inglés *Harcourt Brace Spelling*. El próposito de este programa es mejorar la capacidad del alumno para comunicarse, por medio de la buena ortografía y mejor redacción en lo que escribe.

En estas unidades, el niño aprendió a escribir palabras que contienen grupos de consonantes; palabras con las combinaciones *sh, th* y *ch;* y palabras con ortografía irregular, como *were.*

A fin de animar al niño a que practique la ortografía de las palabras de repaso, puede utilizar las actividades que aparecen a continuación.

Actividades para mejorar la ortografía

- Permítale al niño que use trozos de estambre para formar las letras de las palabras de repaso. El mismo estambre les puede servir para todas las palabras. Practique las palabras de repaso de una unidad cada día.
- Haga que el niño escriba las letras de cada palabra de repaso dejando espacios entre las letras. Después, haga que el niño coloree cada letra de un color distinto. A medida que marca la letra, dígale quelabra. A medida que coloree cada letra, pídale que la diga en voz alta. Luego, haga que escriba una oración completa con cada palabra.

Por favor, comuníquese conmigo si tiene alguna pregunta acerca del progreso del niño.

Lo/a saluda atentamente,

UNIDAD 13
please
stand
must
store
glad
UNIDAD 14
brother
friend
swim
great
true
UNIDAD 15
shoe
thing
wish
thank
finish
UNIDAD 16
chair
watch
their
these
much
UNIDAD 17
again
been
were
there
here

Dear ________________________________,

Your child has just completed Units 19–24 of *Harcourt Brace Spelling.* Spelling is a tool that will enable your child to write and communicate effectively. By learning spelling patterns, he or she will begin to be able to spell more words independently.

In these units, your child learned to spell words with the long vowel sound /ā/ spelled *a*-consonant-*e, ai, ay,* and *ey*; words with the long vowel sound /ē/ spelled *ee, ea,* and *y*; and words with the long vowel sound /ī/ spelled *i*-consonant-*e, y, i* before *nd, igh,* and *ie.*

You may wish to encourage your child to practice spelling the review words. Following are suggestions for activities you and your child can do together.

UNIT 19
ate
same
have
face
late

UNIT 20
train
away
they
tail
stay

UNIT 21
three
leave
many
street
easy

UNIT 22
time
write
give
fire
wide

UNIT 23
kind
right
why
sky
night

Activities That Develop Spelling Skills

- Play a simple guessing game with your child. Write blank lines on a piece of paper corresponding to the number of letters in one of your child's review words. Have your child guess letters that might be in the word. Fill them in as he or she guesses correctly. When your child has guessed the word, have him or her spell the word aloud. Repeat the activity until all the words in one or two units have been reviewed. (NOTE: If several words in the list have the same number of letters, provide a "clue" letter in its correct position among the blanks.)
- Play "Twenty Questions" with your child's spelling words. Choose a word and then give a clue for the word. For example, for the word *skate*, you might say, "I'm thinking of something you can do on ice." Allow your child to ask questions until he or she correctly identifies the spelling word. After your child guesses the word, have him or her spell the word aloud.
- Do this activity outdoors. Say a spelling word and have your child "paint" the word with water on the pavement or fence. The "brush" can be a stick, a large leaf, or a real brush. Continue until all the words have been spelled.

Please feel free to contact me with any questions regarding your child's progress.

Sincerely,

Estimado/a señor/a _______________________________:

Su niño/a acaba de terminar las unidades 19–24 del programa de ortografía en inglés *Harcourt Brace Spelling.* La buena ortografía ayuda al alumno a comunicarse con precisión por escrito. A medida que aprende modelos de ortografía, el alumno comienza a poder escribir más y más palabras independientemente.

En estas unidades, el niño aprendió a escribir palabras con el sonido vocálico /ei/ en las combinaciones *a-consonante-e, ai, ay* y *ey;* palabras que contienen el sonido /i/ en las combinaciones *ee, ea* y *y;* y palabras con el sonido vocálico /ai/, escrito *i-consonante-e, y, i* (antes de *nd*), *igh* o *ie.*

A continuación aparecen algunas actividades que usted puede hacer con el niño para practicar la ortografía de las palabras de repaso.

Actividades para mejorar la ortografía

- Juegue a las "Veinte preguntas" con las palabras de repaso. Seleccione una palabra y dele al niño una pista. Por ejemplo, para la palabra *skate* (patinar), puede decir: "Estoy pensando en algo que se puede hacer sobre el hielo". Permita que el niño le haga preguntas hasta que haya identificado la palabra. Una vez que la haya identificado, pídale que la pronuncie y que la deletree en voz alta.
- Esta actividad es para fuera de la casa. Diga una de las palabras de repaso y hagan que el niño la trace con agua en el pavimento. Puede usar el dedo, un palito, una hoja grande de un árbol o una brocha de verdad. Continúe el juego hasta que haya trazado todas las palabras de la unidad.

Por favor, no deje de comunicarse conmigo si tiene cualquier pregunta acerca del progreso del niño.

Lo/a saluda atentamente,

UNIDAD 19

ate
same
have
face
late

UNIDAD 20

train
away
they
tail
stay

UNIDAD 21

three
leave
many
street
easy

UNIDAD 22

time
write
give
fire
wide

UNIDAD 23

kind
right
why
sky
night

Dear ________________________________,

As you know, spelling is a basic building block of good writing, and good writing is a key to good communication.

Your child has just completed Units 25–30 of *Harcourt Brace Spelling*. In these units, your child learned to spell words with the long vowel sound /ō/ spelled *ow, o-e, o, oa*; words that end with *ng* or *nk*; words with the sound /o͞o/ as in *too*; and words with the sound /o͝o/ as in *took*.

You may wish to encourage your child to practice the review words for these units. Listed below are suggestions for activities you and your child can do together.

Activities That Develop Spelling Skills

- Cut letters out of magazines or newspapers for all the review words from one unit. Put the letters in a bowl and mix them up. Let your child draw letters, one at a time. Have your child form spelling words as he or she draws the letters. Continue until all the letters have been drawn and all the words have been formed.
- Using the letter blocks and a board from a commercial word game, help your child make simple crossword puzzles from review words. Have your child pick a different color crayon for each letter in a review word. Then have him or her write the word using the correct color for each letter.
- For an outdoor activity, play a game of Bounce and Spell with your child. Name a review word. Then say the first letter of the review word and bounce a ball to your child. He or she must add the second letter of the word, then bounce the ball back to you. Whoever finishes a word should hold the ball before beginning another word.

Please contact me with any questions regarding your child's progress.

Sincerely,

UNIT 25

grow
know
those
slow
note

UNIT 26

told
also
soap
cold
road

UNIT 27

along
think
young
sing
drink

UNIT 28

who
school
new
do
room

UNIT 29

took
pull
could
would
put

Estimado/a señor/a ______________________:

Como usted ya sabe, la buena ortografía es un aspecto muy importante de la expresión escrita, y la buena redacción al escribir es esencial para comunicar con precisión lo que uno quiere decir.

Su niño/a acaba de terminar las unidades 25–30 del programa de ortografía en inglés *Harcourt Brace Spelling*. En estas unidades, el niño aprendió a escribir palabras que contienen el sonido largo de la *o* que se escribe *ow*, *o-consonante-e* u *oa*; palabras que terminan en *ng* o *nk*; palabras con el sonido largo de la doble *o* en inglés, como en *too*; y palabras con el sonido corto de la doble *o*, como en *took*.

A continuación la sugiero algunas actividades que usted puede hacer con el niño para ayudarlo a practicar las palabras de repaso de estas unidades.

Actividades para mejorar la ortografía

- Usando fichas con letras de cualquier juego de tablero que las tenga, ayude al niño a formar crucigramas sencillos con las palabras de repaso.
- Deje que el niño escoja un color distinto para cada letra de una palabra de repaso. Después, dígale que escriba la palabra usando el color correspondiente para cada letra.
- Como actividad al aire libre, juegue a "Rebotar y deletrear" con el niño. Diga una de las palabras de repaso. Después, diga la primera letra y pásele la pelota al niño rebotándola contra el suelo. El niño entonces debe dar la segunda letra y devolverle la pelota. La persona que dé la última letra de la palabra se queda con las pelota para empezar la palabra que sigue.

Comuníquese conmigo con toda confianza si tiene preguntas acerca del progreso del niño.

Lo/a saluda atentamente,

UNIDAD 25
grow
know
those
slow
note
UNIDAD 26
told
also
soap
cold
road
UNIDAD 27
along
think
young
sing
drink
UNIDAD 28
who
school
new
do
room
UNIDAD 29
took
pull
could
would
put

Dear ______________________________,

As you know, your child is improving his or her communications skills through the *Harcourt Brace Spelling* program. Your child has just completed Units 31–36 of *Harcourt Brace Spelling*. These final units introduced your child to words with the sound /ô/ spelled *a, aw,* and *au*; words with the sound /ou/ spelled *ou* and *ow*; words with the sounds /är/ spelled *ar*; words with the sounds /ôr/ spelled *or, ore,* and *oor*; words with the sound /ûr/ spelled *er, ir, or,* and *ur*; words with the sounds /ir/ spelled *ear*; and words with the sounds /ər/ spelled *er, or,* and *ar*.

Over the summer, you may wish to encourage your child to practice the spelling words reviewed in Review Unit 36, as well as words reviewed in previous units. In this way, you can help your child maintain the skills he or she has acquired throughout the year. Listed below are suggestions for activities you and your child can do together.

Activities That Develop Spelling Skills

- Practice spelling /ô/ words while bouncing a ball. One letter of each word is spelled for each bounce of the ball.
- Have your child draw a house, and fill it with /ou/ words. Put words in which /ou/ is spelled *ou* inside the house. Then put words in which /ou/ is spelled *ow* on flowers in a flower garden outside of the house.
- Have your child make a rainbow, and fill it with words that have the sounds /ər/.
- Make opportunities over the summer for your child to write. Have him or her send notes to other family members. Encourage your child to write a story about a picture he or she draws, to write important events on the calendar, or to keep a diary of what he or she does over the summer. Let your child know how important words can be.

Please feel free to contact me with any questions regarding your child's progress.

Sincerely,

UNIT 31
water
because
caught
draw
tall

UNIT 32
our
about
how
house
now

UNIT 33
part
before
start
door
hard

UNIT 34
her
girl
year
work
turn

UNIT 35
after
other
color
dollar
over

Estimado/a señor/a ______________________________:

Como usted ya sabe, su niño/a está aprendiendo ortografía en inglés por medio del programa *Harcourt Brace Spelling.* Acabamos de terminar las unidades 31–36. Estas unidades finales le presentaron al niño palabras con el sonido /o/ escrito en inglés *a, aw* y *au*; palabras con el sonido /au/ escrito *ou* y *ow*; palabras con el sonido /ar/; palabras con el sonido /or/ escrito *or, ore* y *oor*; palabras con el sonido /er/ escrito *er, ir, or* y *ur*; palabras con el sonido /iar/ escrito *ear*; y palabras con el sonido especial que tienen las vocales *a, e* y *o* cuando van seguidas de *r* al final de una palabra.

Durante el verano, sería conveniente que usted ayudara al niño a practicar las palabras que se repasan en la Unidad de Repaso número 36, así como las que repasaron en las unidades anteriores. De esta manera, usted ayudará al niño a mantener las habilidades que adquirió durante el año escolar. A continuación le sugiero algunas actividades que usted puede hacer con el niño.

UNIDAD 31
- water
- because
- caught
- draw
- tall

UNIDAD 32
- our
- about
- how
- house
- now

UNIDAD 33
- part
- before
- start
- door
- hard

UNIDAD 34
- her
- girl
- year
- work
- turn

UNIDAD 35
- after
- other
- color
- dollar
- over

Actividades para mejorar la ortografía

- Practique las palabras que contienen el sonido /o/ haciendo que el niño deletree la palabra con una pelota, diciendo una letra cada vez que rebola la pelota.
- Haga que el niño dibuje una casa y que la llene con palabras que tienen el sonido /au/ escrito *ou.* Después dígale que dibuje un jardín con flores grandes, y que ponga en las flores palabras con el sonido /au/ escrito *ow.*
- Dígale al niño que dibuje un arco iris, y que lo llene después con palabras que contengan el sonido especial que tienen la *y,* la *e* y la *o* cuando van seguidas de *r* al final de una palabra.

Por favor, no deje de comunicarse conmigo si tiene alguna pregunta acerca del progreso del niño.

Lo/a saluda atentamente,

Name

Study Steps to Learn a Word

- **Say** the word. Listen to each sound. Think about what the word means.
- **Look** at the word. See how the letters are made. Try to see the word in your mind.
- **Spell** the word to yourself. Think about the way each sound is spelled.
- **Write** the word. Copy it from your book. Check the way you made your letters. Write the word again.
- **Check** your learning. Cover the word and write it. Did you spell it correctly? If not, do these steps until you know how to spell the word.

Do the Study Steps to learn your words.

Write the word. Copy it from your book. Check your spelling. Check the way you made your letters.	If the word is not clear or spelled right, write it again.	Cover the word. Write it again.	If the word is spelled wrong, follow the steps again. Write the word.	Check the word. If it is spelled wrong, write it again.

Name ______________________ Date ______________________

Your Own Spelling Words

Independent Study

Reading/ Language Arts	Mathematics	Social Studies	Science/ Health	Other

Name ______________________ Class ______________________

Progress Report

Spelling

	Number Right		Check Your Score	
	Trial Test	Unit Test	Improved	Perfect
Unit 1			○	○
Unit 2			○	○
Unit 3			○	○
Unit 4			○	○
Unit 5			○	○
Unit 6 **Review**			○	○
Form A • Test 1				○
Unit 7			○	○
Unit 8			○	○
Unit 9			○	○
Form B • Test 1				○
Unit 10			○	○
Unit 11			○	○
Unit 12 **Review**			○	○
Form A • Test 2				○
Unit 13			○	○
Unit 14			○	○
Unit 15			○	○
Unit 16			○	○
Unit 17			○	○
Unit 18 **Review**			○	○
Form A • Test 3				○
Form B • Test 2				○
Midyear Test				○
Unit 19			○	○
Unit 20			○	○
Unit 21			○	○
Unit 22			○	○
Unit 23			○	○
Unit 24 **Review**			○	○
Form A • Test 4				○
Unit 25			○	○
Unit 26			○	○
Unit 27			○	○
Form B • Test 3				○
Unit 28			○	○
Unit 29			○	○
Unit 30 **Review**			○	○
Form A • Test 5				○
Unit 31			○	○
Unit 32			○	○
Unit 33			○	○
Unit 34			○	○
Unit 35			○	○
Unit 36 **Review**			○	○
Form A • Test 6				○
Form B • Test 4				○
End-of-Year Test				○

Class

Class Progress Report

Spelling

Record the number of correct answers or percentage of correct answers for each test.

Names	Skills Check Inventory	Form A Test 1	Form B Test 1	Form A Test 2	Form A Test 3	Form B Test 2	Midyear Test	Form A Test 4	Form B Test 3	Form A Test 5	Form A Test 6	Form B Test 4	End-of-Year Test	Final Grade
1.														
2.														
3.														
4.														
5.														
6.														
7.														
8.														
9.														
10.														
11.														
12.														
13.														
14.														
15.														
16.														
17.														
18.														
19.														
20.														
21.														
22.														
23.														
24.														
25.														
26.														
27.														
28.														
29.														
30.														
31.														
32.														
33.														
34.														
35.														

Name Date

UNIT

Answer Sheet A

1.

2.

3.

4.

5.

6.

7.

8.

9.

10.

11.

12.

Name Date UNIT

Answer Sheet B

1.

2.

3.

4.

5.

6.

7.

8.

9.

10.

11.

12.

13.

14.

15.

16.

17.

18.

19.

20.

21.

22.

Name Date

UNIT

Answer Sheet B *(continued)*

23.

24.

25.

Harcourt Brace School Publishers

Composition Evaluation Form A

Writer ______________________________ Date __________

Teacher/Evaluator ______________________________

Writing Assignment ______________________________

General Areas	Rating
Content and Ideas	1 2 3 4 5
Organization and Structure	1 2 3 4 5
Grammar, Usage, Mechanics, Spelling	1 2 3 4 5

Strong Points: ______________________________

____

____

____

Weak Points: ______________________________

____

____

____

Comments: ______________________________

____

____

Rating Key
1. Weak
2. Fair
3. Satisfactory
4. Good
5. Outstanding

Composition Evaluation Form B

Writer ______________________________ Date __________

Writing Assignment ______________________________

Teacher Rating Key
1. Weak
2. Fair
3. Satisfactory
4. Good
5. Outstanding

Content	Self-Evaluation Yes No	Peer Group Evaluation Yes No	Teacher Evaluation 1 2 3 4 5	Teacher's Comments
1. Is each word group a sentence?				
2. Are the words strong and clear?				
3. Do the words fit the topic?				
4. Are the words right for the readers?				
5. Is the main idea clear?				
6. Are all the sentences about the main idea?				
7. Are more sentences needed to tell about the main idea?				

Mechanics	Teacher Evaluation 1 2 3 4 5	Teacher's Comments
1. Are capital letters used correctly?		
2. Are punctuation marks used correctly?		
3. Is each word spelled correctly?		
4. Is each word used correctly?		
5. Is the grammar correct?		
6. Is the handwriting neat and readable?		

Writer's Word Bank

The **Writer's Word Bank** consists of a list of words designed to help children become better writers. The words are divided into categories and listed in alphabetical order on black-line copying masters. The word lists include words taken from **Harcourt Brace Spelling,** Level 2, as well as other words that children may find useful in their writing.

Children may use the **Writer's Word Bank** in three ways: before they write, to get ideas; while they are writing, to find the words they need; and after they write, to replace words they have used with ones that are more precise or more colorful.

Each child in your class should have his or her own **Writer's Word Bank.** Reproduce enough copies to distribute to the class. Children may add words of their own to the lists; they may also add new categories as they come to mind. Suggestions to students on how they may use the **Writer's Word Bank** appear on the first copying master. Encourage children to use the **Writer's Word Bank** whenever they write.

Writer's Word Bank

Your **Writer's Word Bank** can help you to be a better writer. It may help you to get ideas for your writing. While you are writing, you can use it to find a word that you need. After you have read what you have written, you may want to change some words. Your **Writer's Word Bank** may help you find better ones.

The **Writer's Word Bank** is easy to use. The words are divided into groups and given in ABC order. Here are some ways you may use the **Writer's Word Bank.**

1. **Getting Ideas**
   Suppose you want to write a story. You need an idea. Look at the words under the headings People and Animals. What words might give you an idea for a story? You might decide to write about a juggler or even an owl.

2. **Finding Words**
   Sometimes you know what you want to say, but you cannot think of a word that is exactly right. You might want to describe what your grandmother looks like. Look under the heading Words That Describe. What word might you use? You might use the word happy or tired.

3. **Finding Better Words**
   After you write, you should read over what you have written. Sometimes changing a word can make your writing better. Read the sentence below.

   I chewed the apple loudly.

   Changing the word chewed would make the sentence better. Look under the heading Action Words. Which word might be better than chewed? You might use crunched.

As you write, you may think of words of your own that you would like to add. Fill them in under the heading Your Own Words. You may also think of word groups you would like to add. Write them in under Other Word Groups. Then add words under the new headings you have written.

Your **Writer's Word Bank** will help you to get ideas and use better words. Use it every time you write.

People

Your Spelling Words

clown
doctor

More Words

artist
astronaut
barber
carpenter
conductor
cowhand
explorer
juggler
king
mayor
miner
police officer
president
prince
queen
sailor
sheriff
soldier
star
zookeeper

Your Own Words

Animals

Your Spelling Words

bear
bee
cow
fox
frog
goat
hen
pig
rabbit
raccoon
sheep
snake

More Words

ant
bat
boar
bulldog
calf
camel
clam
collie
crab
crow
deer
donkey
duck
flounder
giraffe
gorilla
grasshopper
hawk
hound
horse
owl
peacock
mosquito
moth
otter
poodle
seagull
sheepdog
skunk
spaniel
starfish
swan
tuna
turtle
whale
zebra

Your Own Words

Story Characters

More Words

elf
dragon
fairy
giant
Martian
pirate

Your Own Words

Places

Your Spelling Words

Earth	hill	planet	pond

More Words

airport	drugstore	lake	stream
apartment	factory	library	sun
cabin	farm	mountain	swamp
cave	forest	museum	town
castle	fort	pond	tree house
city	hill	river	valley
clubhouse	hut	skyscraper	village
cottage	igloo	star	windmill

Your Own Words

Things

Your Spelling Words

balloon	football	paint	straw
bike	glass	paw	string
boat	grass	rope	tail
bush	jet	shell	thumb
car	moss	soap	wood
clay	nail	stone	wool

More Words

airplane
ambulance
ankle
baseball
basket
beak
beets
bingo
blender
brush
buggy
bugle
camera
camping
canoe
carton
cheek
chin
chop suey
claw
coach
coconut
covered wagon
daisy
dandelion
dominoes
drill
dump truck
egg beater
elbow
eyelash
feather
ferry

fife
fin
fire engine
flashlight
flipper
flute
forest
funny bone
fur
garbage truck
golf
grapefruit
hammer
harmonica
harp
heel
helicopter
hoe
horn
horse
hose
hunting
ice skates
jar
kickball
ladle
lawn mower
lily
mane
measuring cup
melon
mop
motorcycle

needle
oak
pail
palm
pan
pitchfork
pizza
plane
poppy
pumpkin
raft
rake
range
rocket
roller skates
rolling pin
rose
ruler
sail
sandpaper
sax
scale
screwdriver
shovel
skateboard
skis
sled
soccer
space shuttle
spaghetti
spatula
spoon
squash

stagecoach
station wagon
steam shovel
stove
strainer
submarine
subway
sundae
sweet potato
taco
taxi
thumbtack
toaster
toothbrush
tractor
train
tree house
trombone
trumpet
tugboat
underwater
vacuum
valley
village
violet
violin
wheelbarrow
whisker
windmill
wing
woods
yarn

Your Own Words

Words That Describe

Your Spelling Words

angry	dry	kind	shy
brave	flat	lucky	sly
busy	glad	neat	wide
cold	grand	new	wise
cross	happy	plain	young

More Words

bubbly	flowery	quiet	spicy
bumpy	free	scared	spooky
careful	fresh	selfish	spotted
cheerful	funny	sharp	sweet
crisp	hopeful	slippery	tasty
deep	icy	smooth	tired
dotted	jolly	soggy	wet
excited	plaid	sour	worn
fancy			

Your Own Words

Action Words

Your Spelling Words

bake
blink
buzz
catch
cook
cry
dream
fall
fish
fix
free
frighten
hide
jump
kick
mix
push
ring
roast
rub
shake
shout
sing
stuff
toast
trap
wave
wish

More Words

bark
chatter
chime
click
crunch
dance
giggle
growl
hoot
hum
juggle
laugh
pull
rattle
roar
scream
snap
sob
swing
thump
toss
trip
whisper
wink
wrestle

More Words

angrily
bravely
brightly
carefully
cleverly
freshly
happily
orderly
proudly
softly
wrongly

Your Own Words

Other Word Groups

Your Own Words

Words That Describe Action